The first high-level Red Army defector to tell us—

—How many fighting men the Soviet Union can actually mobilize into its army within days— rather than the official published figures.

—The ways in which Soviet weaponry is decisively superior to the West, despite the Free World's vaunted technological superiority.

—Why the concept of "defense" is forbidden in Red Army ruling circles, and how this affects the possibility of a Soviet nuclear first strike.

—The one great weakness of the Soviet armed forces the West has so far failed to exploit.

———————

"Authentic and of great significance. One hopes that the book is being studied by the Pentagon and NATO."
                                        —*John Barkham Reviews*

INSIDE THE SOVIET ARMY

VIKTOR SUVOROV

BERKLEY BOOKS, NEW YORK

To Andrei Andreevich Vlasov

This Berkley book contains the complete
text of the original hardcover edition.
It has been completely reset in a typeface
designed for easy reading, and was printed
from new film.

INSIDE THE SOVIET ARMY

A Berkley Book / published by arrangement with
Macmillan Publishng Company, Inc.

PRINTING HISTORY
Macmillan edition published 1983
Berkley edition / August 1984
Second printing / September 1984

ISBN: 0-425-07110-3

A BERKLEY BOOK ® TM 757,375
Berkley Books are published by The Berkley Publishing Group,
200 Madison Avenue, New York, New York 10016.
The name "BERKLEY" and the stylized "B" with design
are trademarks belonging to Berkley Publishing Corporation.
PRINTED IN THE UNITED STATES OF AMERICA

Contents

Foreword

The book, *Inside the Soviet Army,* is written under the name of "Viktor Suvorov." As a defector, under sentence of death in the USSR, the author does not use his own name and has chosen instead that of one of the most famous of Russian generals. This is a book that should command wide attention, not only in the armed forces of the free world, but among the general public as well. It is an account of the structure, composition, operational method, and general outlook of the Soviet military in the context of the Communist regime in the USSR and the party's total dominion, not only over the Soviet Union, but over the client states of the Warsaw Pact as well.

The book starts with a survey of the higher military leadership and an analysis of the types of armed services, and of the organization of Soviet Army formation. An examination of the Red Army's mobilization system that follows is of particular interest. The chapters that follow on strategy and tactics and on equipment are also of high interest. The first, on operational method, emphasizes the supreme importance attached in Soviet military thinking to the offensive and the swift exploitation of success. Defensive action is hardly studied at all except as an aspect of attack. The second, on equipment, examines Soviet insistence on simplicity in design and shows how equipment of high technical complexity (the T-72 tank, for instance) is also developed in another form, radically simplified in what the author calls "the monkey model," for swift wartime production. The last two chapters, on "The Soldier's Lot" and "The Officer's Path," will be found by many to be the most valuable and revealing of the whole book. We have here not so much a description of what the Red Army *looks* like from the outside, but what it *feels* like inside.

This book is based on the author's fifteen years of regular service in the Soviet Army, in troop command and on the staff, which included command of a motor rifle company in the invasion of Czechoslovakia in 1968. About this he has written another book, *The Liberators,* which is a spirited account of life in the Red Army, highly informative in a painless sort of way and often very funny. There is rather less to laugh at in this book than in that one: Viktor Suvorov writes here in deadly earnest.

There is no doubt at all of the author's right to claim unquestioned authority on matters which he, as a junior officer, could be expected to know about at firsthand and in great detail. Nevertheless, not everyone would agree with everything he has to say. Though I know him personally rather well, Viktor Suvorov is aware that I cannot myself go all the way with him in some of his arguments and I am sometimes bound to wonder whether he is always interpreting the evidence correctly.

Having said this, however, I hasten to add something that seems to be of overriding importance. The value of this book, which in my view is high, derives as much from its apparent weaknesses as from its clearly evident strengths—and perhaps even more. The author is a young, highly trained professional officer with very considerable troop service behind him as well as staff training. He went through the Frunze Military Academy (to which almost all the Red Army's elite officers are sent) and was thereafter employed as a staff officer. He tells the reader how he, being what he is—that is to say, a product of the Soviet Army and the society it serves—judges the military machine created in the Soviet Union under Marxism-Leninism, and how he responded to it. He found that he could take no more of the inefficiency, corruption, and blatant dishonesty of a regime which claimed to represent its people but had slaughtered millions of them to sustain its own absolute supremacy.

It would be unwise to suppose that what is found in this book is peculiar only to the visions and opinions of one young officer who might not necessarily be typical of the group as a whole. It might be sensible to suppose that if this is the way the scene has been observed, analyzed, and reported on by one Red Army officer of his generation, there is a high probability that others, and probably very many others, would see things in much the same way. Where he may seem to some readers to get it wrong, both in his conclusion about his own army and his opinions on military matters in the Western world, he is almost certainly representing views very widely held in his own service. Thus, it is just as important to take note of points upon which the reader may think the author is mistaken as it is to profit from his observation on those parts of the scene which he is almost uniquely fitted to judge.

This book should not, therefore, be regarded as no more than an argument deployed in a debate, to be judged on whether the argument is thought to be wrong or right. Its high importance lies far more in the disclosure of what Soviet officers are taught and how they think. This window opened into the armed forces of the Soviet Union is, up to the present time, unique of its kind, as far as I am aware. Every serving officer in the Western world should read it, whether he agrees with what he reads or not, and particularly if he does not. All politicians should read it, and so should any member of the public who takes seriously the threat of a third world war and wonders about the makeup and outlook of the armed forces in the free world's main adversary.

—GENERAL SIR JOHN HACKETT

PART ONE

THE HIGHER
MILITARY LEADERSHIP

Why did the Soviet Tanks
not threaten Romania?

1

It looked as though the soldiers had laid a very large, very heavy carpet at the bottom of the wooded ravine. A group of us, infantry and tank officers, looked at their work from a slope high above them with astonishment, exchanging wild ideas about the function of the dappled, greyish-green carpet, which gleamed dully in the sun.

"It's a container for diesel fuel," said the commander of a reconnaissance party confidently, putting an end to the argument.

He was right. When the heavy sheeting, as large as the hull of an airship, was finally unfolded, a number of grubby-looking soldiers laid a network of field pipelines through our battalion position.

All night long they poured liquid fuel into the container. Lazily and unwillingly it became fatter, crushing bushes and young fir trees under its tremendous weight. Towards morning the container began to look like a very long, flat, broad hot water bottle, made for some giant child. The resilient surface was carefully draped with camouflage nets. Sappers hung spirals of barbed wire around the ravine and a headquarters company set up field picquets to cover the approaches.

In a neighbouring ravine the filling of another equally large fuel container was in progress. Beyond a stream, in a depression, worn-out reservists were slowly spreading out a second huge canopy. Struggling through bogs and clearings, covered from head to foot in mud, the soldiers pulled and heaved at an endless web of field pipelines. Their faces were black, like photographic negatives, and this made their teeth seem unnaturally white when they showed them, in their enjoyment of

3

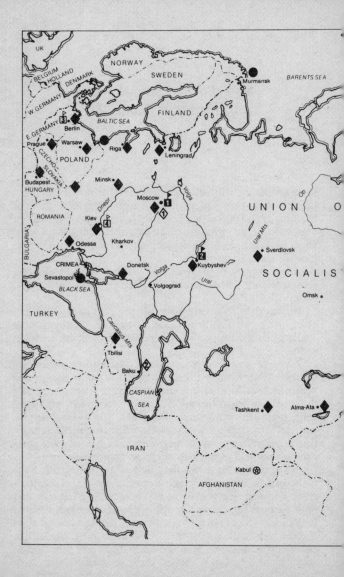

ARCTIC
OCEAN

Lena

SEA OF OKHOTSK

SOVIET

REPUBLICS

Novosibirsk

Lena

Khabarovsk

Chita

Ob

Ulan Bator

Vladivostok

MONGOLIA

CHINA

Soviet Russia

Supreme Command Post
1 Moscow 2 Volga

Command Post of Strategic Direction
3 Western 4 South-Western 5 Far Eastern

Military District and Group of Forces
(see separate maps)

Fleets

District of National Air Defence
1 Moscow 2 Baku

Soviet Forces in Afghanistan and Mongolia
(no status as Group of Forces)

obscenities so monstrous that they made their young reserve officer blush.

This whole affair was described, briefly, as "Rear Units Exercise." But we could see what was going on with our own eyes and we realised that this was more than an exercise. It was all too serious. On too large a scale. Too unusual. Too risky. Was it likely that they would amass such enormous stocks of tank fuel and ammunition, or build thousands of underground command posts, communications centres, depots and stores on the very borders of the country just for an exercise?

The stifling summer of 1968 had begun. Everyone realised quite clearly that the sultriness and tension in the air could suddenly turn into a summer storm. We could only guess when and where this would happen. It was quite clear that our forces would invade Romania but whether they would also go into Czechoslovakia was a matter for speculation.

The liberation of Romania would be a joy-ride. Her maize fields suited our tanks admirably. Czechoslovakia was another matter. Forests and mountain passes are not good terrain for tanks.

The Romanian army had always been the weakest in Eastern Europe and had the oldest equipment. But in Czechoslovakia things would be more complicated. In 1968 her army was the strongest in Eastern Europe. Romania had not even a theoretical hope of help from the West, for it had no common frontier with the countries of NATO. But in Czechoslovakia, in addition to Czech tank divisions, we risked meeting American, West German, British, Belgian, Dutch and possibly French divisions. A world war might break out in Czechoslovakia but there was no such risk in Romania.

So, although preparations were being made for the liberation of Romania, we clearly would not go into Czechoslovakia. The risk was too great . . .

2

For some reason, though, despite all our calculations and in the face of all common sense, they did send us into Czechoslovakia. Never mind, we reassured ourselves—we'll deal with Dubcek and then we'll get around to Ceaucescu. First of all we'll make the Czech people happy and then it'll be the turn of the Romanians.

But for some reason it never was. . . .

Elementary logic suggested that it was essential to liberate Romania and to do so immediately. The reasons for acting with lightning speed were entirely convincing. Ceaucescu had denounced our valiant performance in Czechoslovakia as aggression. Then Romania announced that henceforth no exercises by Warsaw Pact countries might be held on her territory. Next she declared that she was a neutral country and that in the event of a war in Europe she would decide for herself whether to enter the war or not and if so on which side. After this she vetoed a proposal for the construction of a railway line which was to have crossed her territory in order to link the Soviet Union and Bulgaria. Each year, too, Romania would reject suggestions by the Soviet Union that she should increase her involvement in the activities of the Warsaw Treaty Organisation.

Then there was a truly scandalous occurrence. Soviet military intelligence reported that Israel was in great need of spare parts for Soviet-built tanks, which had been captured in Sinai, and that Romania was secretly supplying these spare parts. Hearing of this, the commander of our regiment, without waiting for instructions, ordered that a start should be made with bringing equipment out of mothballing. He assumed that the last hour had struck for the stubborn Romanians. It turned out to be his last hour that had come. He was rapidly relieved of his command, the equipment was put back in storage and the regiment fell back into a deep sleep.

Things became even worse. The Romanians bought some military helicopters from France. These were of great interest to Soviet military intelligence, but our Romanian allies would not allow our experts to examine them, even from a distance. Some of the more hawkish generals and their juniors still believed that the Soviet leadership would change their mind and that Romania would be liberated or at least given a good fright by troop movements of a scale befitting a super-power along her borders. But the majority of officers had already given Romania up as a bad job. We had got used to the idea that Romania was allowed to do anything that she liked, that she could take any liberties she pleased. The Romanians could exchange embraces with our arch-enemies the Chinese, they

could hold their own opinions and they could make open criticisms of our own beloved leadership.

We began to wonder why the slightest piece of disobedience
or evidence of free thinking was crushed with tanks in East
Germany, in Czechoslovakia, in Hungary or inside the Soviet
Union itself, but not in Romania. Why was the Soviet Union
ready to risk annihilation in a nuclear holocaust in order to
save far-off Cuba but not prepared to try to keep Romania
under control? Why, although they had given assurances of
their loyalty to the Warsaw Treaty, were the Czech leaders
immediately dismissed, while the rulers of Romania were allowed to shed their yoke without complications of any sort?
What made Romania an exception? Why was she forgiven for
everything?

3

Many explanations are put forward for the behaviour of Soviet
Communists in the international arena. The most popular is
that the Soviet Union is, essentially, the old Russian Empire—
and an empire must grow. A good theory. Simple and easy to
understand. But it has one defect—it cannot explain the case
of Romania. In fact, none of the popular theories can explain
why the Soviet rulers took such radically differing approaches
to the problems of independence in Czechoslovakia and in
Romania. No single theory can explain both the intolerance
which the Soviet leadership showed towards the gentle criticism
which came from Czechoslovakia and their astonishing im-
perviousness to the furious abuse with which Romania show-
ered them.

If the Soviet Union is to be regarded as an empire, it is
impossible to understand why it does not try to expand south-
eastwards, towards the fertile fields and vineyards of Romania.
For a thousand years, possession of the Black Sea straits has
been the dream of Russian princes, tsars and emperors. The
road to the straits lies through Romania. Why does the Soviet
Union leap into wars for Vietnam and Cambodia, risking col-
lision with the greatest powers in the world and yet forget about
Romania, which lies right under its nose?

In fact the explanation is very simple. The USSR is not

Russia or the Russian Empire; it is not an empire at all. To
believe that the Soviet Union conforms to established historical
standards is a very dangerous simplification. Every empire has
expanded in its quest for new territories, subjects and wealth.
The motivating force of the Soviet Union is quite different.
The Soviet Union does not need new territory. Soviet Communists have slaughtered scores of millions of their own peasants and have nationalised their land, which they are unable to
develop, even if they wished to. The Soviet Union has no need
of new slaves. Soviet Communists have shot sixty million of
their own subjects, thus demonstrating their complete inability
to rule them. They cannot rule or even effectively control those
who remain alive. Soviet Communists have no need of greater
wealth. They squander their own limitless resources easily and
freely. They are ready to build huge dams in the deserts of
Africa for next to nothing, to give away their oil at the expense
of Soviet industry, to pay lavishly, in gold, for any adventurous
scheme, and to support all sorts of free-booters and anarchists,
no matter what the cost, even if this brings ruination to their
own people and to the national exchequer.

Different stimuli and other driving forces are at work upon
the Soviet Union in the international arena. Herein lies the
fundamental difference which distinguishes it from all empires,
including the old Russian version, and here too lies the main
danger.

The Soviet Communist dictatorship, like any other system,
seeks to preserve its own existence. To do this it is forced to
stamp out any spark of dissidence which appears, either on its
own territory or beyond its borders. A communist regime cannot feel secure so long as an example of another kind of life
exists anywhere near it, with which its subjects can draw com-
parisons. It is for this reason that any form of Communism,
not only the Soviet variety, is always at pains to shut itself off
from the rest of the world, with a curtain, whether this is made
of iron, bamboo or some other material.

The frontiers of a state which has nationalised its heavy
industry and collectivised its agriculture—which has, in other
words, carried out a 'socialist transformation'—are always
reminiscent of a concentration camp, with their barbed wire,
watch-towers with searchlights and guard-dogs. No Communist
state can allow its slaves free movement across its frontiers.

In the world today there are millions of refugees. All of

them are in flight from Communism. If the Communists were to open their frontiers, all their slaves would flee. It is for this reason that the Democratic Republic of Kampuchea has set up millions of traps along its borders—solely to prevent anyone from attempting to leave this Communist paradise. The East German Communists are enemies of the Kampuchean regime but they, too, have installed the same sort of traps along their own borders. But neither Asian cunning nor German orderliness can prevent people from fleeing from Communism and the Communist leaders are therefore faced with the immense problem of destroying the societies which might capture the imagination of their people and beckon to them.

Marx was right: the two systems cannot co-exist. And no matter how peace-loving Communists may be, they come unfailingly to the conclusion that world revolution is inescapable. They must either annihilate capitalism or be put to death by their own people.

There are some Communist countries which are considered peace-loving—Albania, Democratic Kampuchea, Yugoslavia. But the love of peace which these countries affect is simply the product of their weakness. They are not yet strong enough to speak of world revolution, because of their internal or external problems. But regimes which can hardly be much more self-confident than these, such as Cuba, Vietnam and North Korea, quickly plunge into the heroic struggle to liberate other countries, of which they know nothing, from the yoke of capitalism.

Communist China has her own very clear belief in the inevitability of world revolution. She has shown her hand in Korea, in Vietnam, in Cambodia and in Africa. She is still weak and therefore peace-loving, as the Soviet Union was during its period of industrialisation. But China, too, faces the fundamental problem of how to keep her billion-strong population from the temptation to flee from the country. Traps along the borders, the jamming of radio broadcasts, almost complete isolation—none of these produces the desired result and when China becomes an industrial and military superpower she, too, will be forced to use more radical measures. She has never ceased to speak of world revolution.

The fact that Communists of different countries fight between themselves for the leading role in the world revolution is unimportant. What is significant is that all have the same goal: if they cease to pursue it they are, in effect, committing suicide.

"Our only salvation lies in world revolution: either we achieve it whatever the sacrifices, or we will be crushed by the petty bourgeoisie," said Nikolay Bukharin, the most liberal and peace-loving member of Lenin's Politburo. The more radical members of the Communist forum advocated an immediate revolutionary war against bourgeois Europe. One of them, Lev Trotsky, founded the Red Army—the army of World Revolution. In 1920 this army tried to force its way across Poland to revolutionary Germany. This attempt collapsed. The world revolution has not taken place: it has been disastrously delayed but sooner or later the Communists must either bring it about or perish.

4

To the Soviet Union Romania is an opponent. An enemy. An obstinate and unruly neighbour. To all intents and purposes an ally of China and of Israel. Yet not a single Soviet subject dreams of escaping to Romania or aspires to exchange Soviet life for the Romanian version. Therefore Romania is not a dangerous enemy. Her existence does not threaten the foundations of Soviet Communism, and this is why drastic measures have never been taken against her. However, the first stirrings of democracy in Czechoslovakia represented a potentially dangerous contagion for the peoples of the Soviet Union, just as the change of regime in Hungary represented a very dangerous example for them. The Soviet leaders understood quite clearly that what happened in East Germany might also happen in Esthonia, that what happened in Czechoslovakia might happen in the Ukraine, and it was for this reason that Soviet tanks crushed Hungarian students so pitilessly beneath their tracks.

The existence of Romania, which, while it may be unruly, is nevertheless a typical Communist regime, with its cult of a supreme and infallible leader, with psychiatric prisons, with watch towers along its frontiers, presents no threat to the Soviet Union. By contrast, the existence of Turkey, where peasants cultivate their own land, is like a dangerous plague, an infection which might spread into Soviet territory. This is why the Soviet

Union does so much to destabilise the Turkish regime, while doing nothing to unseat the unruly government in Romania.

For the Communists any sort of freedom is dangerous, no matter where it exists—in Sweden or in El Salvador, in Canada or in Taiwan. For Communists any degree of freedom is dangerous—whether it is complete or partial, whether it is economic, political or religious freedom. "We will not spare our forces in fighting for the victory of Communism": these are the words of Leonid Brezhnev. "To achieve victory for Communism throughout the world, we are prepared for any sacrifice": these are the words of Mao Tse-Tung. They also sound like the words of fellow-thinkers.... For that is what they are. Their philosophies are identical, although they belong to different branches of the same Mafia. Their philosophies must be identical, for neither can sleep soundly so long as there is, anywhere in the world, a small gleam of freedom which could serve as a guiding light for those who have been enslaved by the Communists.

5

In the past every empire has been guided by the interests of the State, of its economy, of its people or at least of its ruling class. Empires came to a halt when they saw insuperable obstacles or invincible opposition in their paths. Empires came to a halt when further growth became dangerous or economically undesirable. The Russian Empire, for example, sold Alaska for a million dollars and its colonies in California at a similarly cheap price because there was no justification for retaining these territories. Today the Soviet Communists are squandering millions of dollars each day in order to hang on to Cuba. They cannot give it up, no matter what the cost may be, no matter what economic catastrophe may threaten them.

Cuba is the outpost of the world revolution in the western hemisphere. To give up Cuba would be to give up world revolution and that would be the equivalent of suicide for Communism. The fangs of Communism turn inwards, like those of a python. If the Communists were to set about swallowing the world, they would have to swallow it whole. The tragedy is that, if they should want to stop, this would be impossible because of their physiology. If the world should prove to be too big for it, the python would die, with gaping jaws, having buried its sharp fangs in the soft surface, but lacking the strength to withdraw them. It is not only the Soviet python which is attempting to swallow the world but the other breeds of Communism, for all are tied inescapably to pure Marxism, and thus to the theory of world revolution. The pythons may hiss and bite one another but they are all of one species.

The Soviet Army, or more accurately the Red Army, the Army of World Revolution, represents the teeth of the most dangerous but also the oldest of the pythons, which began to swallow the world by sinking its fangs into the surface and then realised just how big the world is and how dangerous for its stomach. But the python has not the strength to withdraw its fangs.

Why was the Warsaw Treaty Organisation set up later than NATO?

1

The countries of the West set up NATO in 1949 but the Warsaw Treaty Organisation was created only in 1955. For the Communists, comparison of these two dates makes excellent propaganda for consumption by hundreds of millions of gullible souls. Facts are facts—the West put together a military bloc while the Communists simply took counter-measures—and there was a long delay before they even did that. Not only that, but the Soviet Union and its allies have come forward repeatedly and persistently with proposals for breaking up military blocs both in Europe and throughout the world. The countries of the West have rejected these peace-loving proposals almost unanimously.

Let us take the sincerity of the Communists at face value. Let us assume that they do not want war. But, if that is so, the delay in establishing a military alliance of Communist states contradicts a fundamental tenet of Marxism: "Workers of the World Unite!" is the chief rallying cry of Marxism. Why did the workers of the countries of Eastern Europe not hasten to unite in an alliance against the bourgeoisie? Whence such disrespect for Marx? How did it happen that the Warsaw Treaty Organisation was set up, not in accordance with the Communist Manifesto but solely as a reaction to steps taken by the bourgeois countries—and then so belatedly?

Strange though it may seem, there is no contradiction with pure Marxism in this case. But, in trying to understand the aims and structures of the Warsaw Treaty Organisation, the interrelationships within it and the delay in its establishment (which at first sight is inexplicable), we shall not immerse ourselves in theory nor attempt to follow the intricate workings

The Warsaw Treaty Organisation

Supreme Command Post
Front
Group of Tank Armies
Fleet
Airborne Attack Area

0   400 miles

600 km

of this unwieldy bureaucratic organisation. If we study the fate
of Marshal K. K. Rokossovskiy we shall come to understand,
if not everything, at least the essentials.

2

Konstantin Konstantinovich Rokossovskiy was born in 1896 in
the old Russian town of Velikiye Luki. At eighteen he was
called up by the Russian army. He spent the whole of the war
at the front, first as a private, then as an NCO. In the very
first days of the Revolution he went over to the Communists
and joined the Red Army. He distinguished himself fighting
against both the Russian and Polish armies. He moved rapidly
upwards, ending the war in command of a regiment. After the
war he commanded a brigade, then a division and then a corps.

At the time of the Great Purge the Communists tortured or
shot those people who had miraculously survived until then
despite past connections with the Russian government, army,
police, diplomatic service, church or culture. Red Army Corps
Commander Rokossovskiy found himself among the millions
of victims because of his service with the Russian army.

During the investigations he underwent appalling tortures.
Nine of his teeth were knocked out, three of his ribs were
broken, his toes were hammered flat. He was sentenced to
death and spent more than three months in the condemned cell.
There is testimony, including his own, that twice, at least, he
was subjected to mock shootings, being led to the place of
execution at night, and made to stand at the edge of a grave
as generals on his right and left were shot, while he was "executed" with a blank cartridge fired at the nape of his neck.

On the eve of the war between Germany and the Soviet
Union Rokossovskiy was let out of gaol and given the rank of
Major-General of Tank Forces and command of a mechanised
corps. However, the charge resulting from his service with the
Russian army was not dropped and the death sentence was not
annulled. "Take command of this mechanised corps, prisoner,
and we'll see about your death sentence later. . . ."

On the second day of the war, Rokossovskiy's 9th Mechanised Corps struck an unexpected and powerful blow against
German tanks, which were breaking through in the area of

Rovno and Lutsk, at a moment when the rest of the Soviet forces were retreating in panic. In a situation of confusion and disorganisation, Rokossovskiy showed calmness and courage in his defence of the Soviet regime. He managed to maintain the fighting efficiency of his corps and to make several successful counter-attacks. On the twentieth day of the war he was promoted, becoming Commander of the 16th Army, which distinguished itself both in the battle of Smolensk and, especially, in the battle for Moscow, when, for the first time in the course of the war, the German army was heavily defeated. During the battle of Stalingrad Rokossovskiy commanded the Don front, which played a decisive role in the encirclement and complete destruction of the strongest German battle group, consisting of twenty-two divisions.

During the battle for Kursk, when weather conditions put the contestants on equal terms, Rokossovskiy commanded the Central Front, which played a major part in smashing Hitler's last attempt to achieve a decisive success. Thereafter Rokossovskiy successfully commanded forces in operations in Byelorussia, East Prussia, Eastern Pomerania and, finally, in Berlin.

Stars rained upon Rokossovskiy. They fell on to his shoulder boards, on to his chest and around his neck. In 1944 he was awarded the diamond Marshal's Star and a gold star to pin on his chest. In 1945 he was awarded both the Victory order, on which sparkle no less than one hundred diamonds, and a second gold star. Stalin conferred the highest honour on Rokossovskiy by giving him command of the Victory Parade on Red Square.

But what has all this to do with the Warsaw Treaty Organisation? The fact is that, immediately after the war, Stalin sent his favourite, Rokossovskiy, to Warsaw and gave him the title of Marshal of Poland to add to his existing rank as Marshal of the Soviet Union. In Warsaw Rokossovskiy held the posts of Minister of Defence, Deputy President of the Council of Ministers and Member of the Politburo of the Polish Communist Party. Think for a moment about the full significance of this —a Marshal of the Soviet Union as deputy to the head of the Polish government!

In practice Rokossovskiy acted as military governor of Poland, senior watchdog over the Polish government and supervisor of the Polish Politburo. As all-powerful ruler of Poland, Rokossovskiy remained a favourite of Stalin's, but a favourite who was under sentence of death, a sentence which was lifted only after the death of Stalin in 1953. A favourite of this sort could have been shot at any moment. But, even if the death sentence had been lifted, would it have taken long to impose a new one?

Now let us see the situation from the point of view of the Generalissimo of the Soviet Union, J. V. Stalin. His subordinate in Warsaw is Marshal of the Soviet Union Rokossovskiy. This subordinate carries out all orders unquestioningly, accurately and speedily. Why should Stalin conclude a military alliance with him? Even to contemplate such a step would show a flagrant disregard for the principles of subordination and would be an offence in itself. A sergeant has no right to make an agreement of any kind with the soldiers under him or a general with his officers. In the same way, a Generalissimo is not entitled to conclude alliances with his own Marshal. It is the right and duty of a commander to give orders and a subordinate is bound to obey these orders. Any other kind of relationship between commanders and their subordinates is entirely forbidden. The relationship between Stalin and Rokossovskiy was based upon the fact that Stalin gave the orders and that Rokossovskiy carried them out without question.

3

The fact that he knew no Polish did not disturb Rokossovskiy in the slightest. In those glorious days not a single general in the Polish army spoke Polish, relying instead on interpreters who were constantly in attendance.

In Russia in 1917 a Polish nobleman, Felix Dzerzhinskiy, established a blood-stained organisation; this was the Cheka, the forerunner of the GPU, NKVD, MGB, and KGB. Between 1939 and 1940 this organisation destroyed the flower of the Polish officer corps. During the war a new Polish army was formed in the Soviet Union. The soldiers and junior officers of this army were Poles, the senior officers and generals were Soviets. When they were transferred to the Polish army the Soviets received joint Polish-Soviet nationality and Polish military ranks, while remaining on the strength of the Soviet military hierarchy. Here is one case history from many thousands:

Fyodor Petrovich Polynin was born in 1906 in the province

of Saratov. He joined the Red Army in 1928 and became a pilot. In 1938–39 he fought in China with the forces of Chiang Kai-Shek. He used a Chinese name and was given Chinese nationality. Although thus a Chinese subject, he was nevertheless made a "Hero of the Soviet Union." He returned to the Soviet Union and reverted to Soviet nationality. During the war he commanded the 13th Bomber Division and then the 6th Air Army. He became a Lieutenant-General in the Soviet Air Force. In 1944 he became a Polish general. He never learned Polish. He was made Commander of the Air Force of sovereign, independent Poland.

In 1946, while still holding this high position in Poland, he received the rank of "Colonel-General of the Air Force." The Air Force concerned was, of course, the Soviet one, for Polynin was also a Soviet General. The announcement that this rank had been awarded to the officer commanding the Polish Air Force was signed by the President of the Council of Ministers of the USSR, Generalissimo of the Soviet Union, J. V. Stalin.

After a further short period in Poland, as if this was an entirely normal development, Fedya Polynin resumed his Soviet rank and was given the post of Deputy to the Commander-in-Chief of the Soviet Air Forces. During his years in command of the Polish Air Force, he learned not a single word of Polish. Why should he bother to do so? His orders reached him from Moscow in Russian and when he reported that they had been carried out he did so in Russian, too. None of his subordinates at the headquarters of the Polish Air Force spoke Polish either, so that there was no point in learning the language.

Once again, why should Stalin conclude a military alliance with Fedya Polynin, if the latter was no more than a subordinate of Rokossovskiy, who was himself subordinated to Stalin? Why set up a military alliance if a more reliable and simpler line of direct command was already in existence?

4

The Polish Army, which was set up in 1943 on Soviet territory, was simply a part of the Red Army, headed by Soviet commanders, and it did not, of course, recognise the Polish government-in-exile in London. In 1944 the Communists established a new "people's" government, a large part of which consisted of investigators from the NKVD and from Soviet military counter-intelligence (SMERSH). However, even after the "people's" government had been established, the Polish army did not come under its command, remaining a part of the Soviet Army. After the war, the "people's" government of Poland was quite simply not empowered to appoint the generals in the "Polish" army or to promote or demote them. This was understandable, since the generals were also Soviet generals and posting them would amount to interference in the internal affairs of the USSR.

There was no reason why the Soviet government should have had the slightest intention of setting up any kind of Warsaw Treaty, Consultative Committee or other similarly non-functional superstructure. No one needed a treaty, since the Polish army was nothing more than a part of the Soviet army, and the Polish government, brought up to strength with Soviet cut-throats and bully boys, was not allowed to intervene in the affairs of the Polish army.

Nevertheless, after the death of Stalin, the Soviet government, headed by Marshal of the Soviet Union Bulganin, decided to conclude an official military agreement with the countries it was occupying. Communist propaganda proclaimed, at the top of its voice, as it continues to do, that this was a voluntary agreement, made between free countries. But a single example from the time when the official document was signed is an indication of the truth. The signatory for the Soviet Union was Marshal of the Soviet Union G. K. Zhukov, and for free, independent, popular, socialist Poland Marshal of the Soviet Union Rokossovskiy, assisted by Colonel-General S. G. Poplavskiy—Rokossovskiy's deputy. Marshal of the Soviet Union Bulganin, who was present at the ceremony, took the opportunity to award Colonel-General Poplavskiy the rank of General of the Army. You have, of course, guessed that Poplavskiy, who signed for Poland, was also a Soviet general and the subordinate of Marshals Bulganin, Zhukov and Rokossovskiy. Within two years Poplavskiy had returned to the USSR and become deputy to the Inspector General of the Soviet Army. These were the sort of miracles which took place in Warsaw, irrespective of the existence of the Warsaw Treaty. Rokossovskiy, Poplavskiy, Polynin and the others were compelled by Soviet legislation to carry out the orders which reached them from Moscow. The Treaty neither increased nor lessened Po-land's dependence upon the USSR.

However, Poland is a special case. With other East European countries it was much easier. In Czechoslovakia there were reliable people like Ludwig Svoboda, who neutralised the Czech army in 1948 and did so again in 1968. He carried out the orders of the USSR promptly and to the letter and it was therefore not necessary to keep a Soviet Marshal in Prague holding a ministerial post in the Czech government. With the other East European countries, too, everything went well. During the war all of them had been enemies of the USSR and it was therefore possible to execute any political figure, general, officer or private soldier, at any given moment and to replace him with someone more cooperative. The system worked perfectly; the Soviet ambassadors to the countries of Eastern Europe kept a close eye on its operation. What sort of ambassadors these were you can judge from the fact that when the Warsaw Treaty was signed the Soviet Ambassador to Hungary, for instance, was Yuriy Andropov, who subsequently became head of the KGB. It was therefore understandable that Hungary should welcome the treaty warmly and sign it with deep pleasure.

Under Stalin, Poland and the other countries of Eastern Europe were governed by a system of open dictatorship, un-camouflaged in any way. The Warsaw Treaty did not exist for one simple reason—it was not needed. All decisions were taken in the Kremlin and monitored by the Kremlin. The Defence Ministers of the East European countries were regarded as equal in status to the Commanders of Soviet Military Districts and they came under the direct command of the Soviet Minister of Defence. All appointments and postings were decided upon by the Kremlin. The Defence Ministers of the "sovereign" states of Eastern Europe were either appointed from the ranks of Soviet generals or were "assisted" by Soviet military advisers. In Romania and Bulgaria, for instance, one such "adviser" was Marshal of the Soviet Union Tolbukhin. In East Germany there was Marshal Zhukov himself, in Hungary Marshal of the Soviet Union Konev. Each adviser had at his disposal at least one tank army, several all-arms armies and special SMERSH punitive detachments. To disregard his "advice" would be very risky business.

After Stalin's death the Soviet leadership embarked on the process of "liberalisation." In Eastern Europe everything stayed as it was, for all that happened was that the Soviet government had decided to conceal its wolf's jaws behind the mask of a "voluntary" agreement, after the NATO model.

To some people in Eastern Europe it really seemed as though dictatorship had come to an end and that the time for a voluntary military agreement had arrived. But they were quite wrong. Just one year after the signing of this "voluntary" alliance the actions of Soviet tanks in Poland and Hungary gave clear proof that everything was still as it had been under Stalin, except for some small, cosmetic alterations.

Communist propaganda quite deliberately blends two concepts: that of the military organisation in force in the Communist states of Eastern Europe and that of the Warsaw Treaty Organisation. The military organisation of the East European countries was set up immediately the Red Army arrived on their territories, in 1944 and 1945. In some cases, for example Poland and Czechoslovakia, military pro-Communist formations had been established even before the arrival of the Red Army.

The armies of East European countries which were set up by Soviet "military advisers" were fully supervised and controlled from Moscow. The military system which took shape was neither a multilateral organisation nor a series of bilateral defensive treaties, but was imposed, forcibly, on a unilateral basis in the form in which it still exists.

The Warsaw Treaty Organisation is a chimera, called into being to camouflage the tyranny of Soviet Communism in the countries under its occupation in order to create an illusion of free will and corporate spirit. Communist propaganda claims that it was as a result of the establishment of NATO that the countries of Eastern Europe came together in a military alliance. The truth is that, at the end of the Second World War, the Soviet Union took full control of the armies of the countries which it had overrun, long before NATO came into existence. It was many years later that the Communists decided to conceal their mailed fist and attempt to present the creation of NATO as the moment when the military framework of Eastern Europe was set up.

But the Communists lacked the imagination to establish this purely ornamental organisation, which exists solely to conceal grim reality, tactfully and with taste. During the Organisation's first thirteen years the Ministers of Defence of the sovereign

states, whether they were pro-Soviet puppets or actual Soviet
generals and Marshals, were subordinated to the Commander-
in-Chief, who was appointed by the Soviet government and
who was himself Deputy Minister of Defence of the USSR.
Thus, even in a legal sense, the Ministers of these theoretically
sovereign states were directly subordinated to a Soviet Minister's deputy. After the Czechoslovak affair the similarly spu-
rious Consultative Committee was set up. In this committee
Ministers of Defence and Heads of State gather supposedly to
talk as equals and allies. But this is pure play-acting. Everything
remains as it was several decades ago. Decisions are still made
in the Kremlin. The Consultative Committee takes no decisions
for itself.

Any attempt to understand the complex and fanciful structure of committees and staffs which make up the Warsaw Treaty
Organisation is a complete waste of time. It is rather like trying
to understand how the Supreme Soviet arrives at its decisions
or how the President of the Soviet Union governs the country
—the nature of his authority and the extent of his responsibilities. You know before you start that, despite its great complexity, the organisation has absolutely no reality. The Supreme
Soviet neither formulates policy nor takes decisions. It is purely
decorative, like the Warsaw Treaty Organisation, there for show
and nothing more. In the same way, the President of the Soviet
Union himself does nothing, takes no decisions, and has neither
responsibilities nor authority. His post was devised solely to
camouflage the absolute power of the General Secretary of the
Communist Party of the Soviet Union.

The Warsaw Treaty Organisation, then, is a body of the
same type as the Supreme Soviet. It is a showpiece whose only
function is to conceal the Kremlin's dictatorship. Its Consultative Committee was set up solely to hide the fact that all
decisions are taken at the Headquarters of the Soviet Army,
on Gogol Boulevard in Moscow. The function of the Commander-in-Chief of the Warsaw Treaty Organisation is purely
decorative. Like the President of the Soviet Union he is without
authority. Although he is still listed among the first deputies
of the Soviet Minister of Defence, this is a legacy of the past,
and is no more than an honour, for he is remote from real
power.

During a war, or any such undertaking as "Operation Dan-
ube," the "allied" divisions of the Warsaw Treaty Organisation

are integrated in the Soviet Armies. None of the East European countries has the right to set up its own Corps, Armies or Fronts. They have only divisions commanded by Soviet generals. In the event of war, their Ministers of Defence would be concerned only with the reinforcement, build-up and technical servicing of their own divisions, which would operate as part of the United (that is the Soviet) Armed Forces.

Lastly, a few words on the ultimate goal of the Warsaw Treaty Organisation: the disbandment of all military blocs, in Europe and throughout the world. This is the real aspiration of our Soviet "doves." It is based on a very simple calculation. If NATO is disbanded, the West will have been neutralised, once and for all. The system of collective self-defence of the free countries will have ceased to exist. If the Warsaw Treaty Organisation is disbanded at the same time, the USSR loses nothing except a cumbersome publicity machine. It will remain in complete control of the armies of its "allies." The military organisation will survive, untouched. All that will be lost is the title itself and the organisation's bureaucratic ramifications, which are needed by nobody.

Let us suppose, for example, that France should suddenly return to NATO. Would this be a change? Certainly—one of almost global significance. Next, let us suppose that Cuba drops its "non-alignment" and joins the Warsaw Treaty Organisation. What would this change? Absolutely nothing. Cuba would remain as aggressive a pilot fish of the great shark as she is today.

6

There are millions of people who regard NATO and the Warsaw Treaty Organisation as identical groupings. But to equate these two is absurd, because the Warsaw Treaty Organisation has no real existence. What does exist is Soviet dictatorship and this has no need to consult its allies. If it is able to do so, it seizes them by the throat; if not it bides its time—Communists do not acknowledge any other type of relationship with their associates.

This is a truism, something which is known to everyone, and yet, every year, hundreds of books are published in which the Soviet Army is described as one of the forces making up the Warsaw Treaty Organisation. This is nonsense. The forces of the Warsaw Treaty Organisation are a part of the Soviet Army. The East European countries are equipped with Soviet weapons, instructed in Soviet methods at Soviet military academies and controlled by Soviet "advisers." It is true that some of the East European divisions would be glad to turn round and use their bayonets on the Moscow leadership. But there are Soviet divisions who would be prepared to do this, too. Mutinies on Soviet ships and in Soviet divisions are far from rare.

A situation in which Soviet propaganda stands the truth on its head and yet is believed by the whole world is by no means a new one. Before the Second World War the Soviet Communists established an international union of communist parties —the Comintern. In theory, the Soviet Communist Party was simply one of the members of this organisation. In practice, its leader, Stalin, was able to cause the leader of the Comintern, Zinoviev, theoretically his superior, to be removed and shot. . . . Later, during the Great Purge, he had the leaders of fraternal communist parties executed without trial and without consequences to himself. Officially the Soviet Communist Party was a member of the Comintern, but in fact the Comintern itself was a subsidiary organisation of the Soviet Party. The standing of the Warsaw Treaty Organisation is exactly similar. Officially the Soviet Army is a member of this organisation but in practice the organisation is itself a part of the Soviet Army. And the fact that the Commander-in-Chief of the Warsaw Treaty Organisation is an official deputy of the Soviet Minister of Defence is no coincidence.

In the 1950s it was decided that a building should be erected in Moscow to house the staff of the Warsaw Treaty Organisation. But it was never put up because nobody needed it— any more than they need the whole organisation. The Soviet General Staff exists and this is all that is required to direct both the Soviet Army and all its "younger brothers."

The Bermuda Triangle

1

A triangle is the strongest and most rigid geometric figure. If the planks of a door which you have knocked together begin to warp, nail another plank diagonally across them. This will divide your rectangular construction into two triangles and the door will then have the necessary stability.

The triangle has been used in engineering for a very long time. Look at the Eiffel tower, at the metal framework of the airship *Hindenburg*, or just at any railway bridge, and you will see that each of these is an amalgamation of thousands of triangles, which give the structure rigidity and stability.

The triangle is strong and stable, not only in engineering but in politics, too. Political systems based on division of power and on the interplay of three balancing forces have been the most stable throughout history. These are the principles upon which the Union of Soviet Socialist Republics is built.

Enormous problems and difficulties are said to lie before the Soviet Union. But Soviet leaders have always been confronted by problems of considerable magnitude, from the very beginnings of Soviet power. Then, too, the collapse of the regime was thought to be inevitable. But it survived four years of bloody struggle against the Russian army; it survived the mutiny of the Baltic fleet, which had itself helped to bring about the Revolution; it survived the mass flight of the intelligentsia, the opposition of the peasants, the massive bloodletting of the revolutionary period, the Civil War, the unprecedented slaughter of millions during collectivisation, and endless bloody purges. It also withstood diplomatic isolation and political blockade, the starvation of scores of millions of those it enslaves and an unexpected onslaught by 190 German divisions, despite the unwillingness of many of its own soldiers to fight for its interests.

So one should not be in a hurry to bury the Soviet regime. It is still, fairly firmly, on its feet. There are several reasons for its stability—the scores of millions of corpses within its foundations, disinterested Western help, the reluctance of the free world to defend its own freedom. But there is one other most important factor which gives the Soviet regime its internal stability—the triangular structure of the state.

Only three forces are active in the Soviet political arena— the Party, the Army and the KGB. Each of these possesses enormous power, but this is exceeded by the combined strength of the other two. Each has its own secret organisation, which is capable of reaching into hostile countries and monitoring developments there. The Party has its Control Commission— a secret organisation which has almost as much influence inside the country as the KGB. The KGB is a grouping of many different secret departments, some of which keep an eye on the Party. The Army has its own secret service—the GRU— the most effective military intelligence service in the world.

Each of these three forces is hostile to the others and has certain, not unreasonable pretensions to absolute power but its initiatives will always fail in the face of the combined opposition of the other two.

Of the three, the Party has the smallest resources for self-defence in open conflict. But it has a strong lever at its disposal —the appointment and posting of all officials. Every general in the Army and every colonel in the KGB takes up his post and is promoted or demoted only with the approval of the Administrative Department of the Central Committee of the Party. In addition, the Party controls all propaganda and ideological work and it is always the Party which decides what constitutes true Marxism and what represents a deviation from its general line. Marxism can be used as an additional weapon when it becomes necessary to dismiss an unwanted official from the KGB, the Army or even the Party. The Party's right to nominate and promote individuals is supported by both the Army and the KGB. If the Party were to lose this privilege to the KGB, the Army would be in mortal danger. If the Army took it over, the KGB would be in an equally dangerous situation. For this reason, neither of them objects to the Party's privilege—and it is this privilege which makes the Party the most influential member of the triumvirate.

The KGB is the craftiest member of this troika. It is able, whenever it wishes, to recruit a party or a military leader as its agent: if the official refuses he can be destroyed by a compromise operation devised by the KGB. The Party remembers, only too clearly, how the KGB's predecessor was able to destroy the entire Central Committee during the course of a single year. The Army, for its part, remembers how, within the space of two months, the same organisation was able to annihilate all its generals. However, the secret power of the KGB and its cunning are its weakness as well as its strength. Both the Party and the Army have a deep fear of the KGB and for this reason they keep a very close eye on the behaviour of its leaders, changing them quickly and decisively, if this becomes necessary.

The Army is potentially the most powerful of the three and therefore it has the fewest rights. The Party and the KGB know very well that, if Communism should collapse, they will be shot by their own countrymen, but that this will not happen to the Army. The Party and the KGB acknowledge the might of the Army. Without it their policies could not be carried out, either at home or abroad. The Party and the KGB keep the Army at a careful distance, rather as two hunters might control a captured leopard with chains, from two different sides. The tautness of this chain is felt even at regimental and battalion level. The Party has a political Commissar in every detachment and the KGB a Special Department.

2

This triangle of power represents a Bermuda Triangle for those who live within it. The trio have long ago adopted the rule that none of the legs of this tripod may extend too far. If this should happen, the other two immediately intervene, and chop off the excess.

Let us look at an example of the way this triangle of power functions. Stalin died in 1953. Observers concluded unanimously that Beriya would take command—Beriya the chief inquisitor and head policeman. Who else was there? Beriya, his gang of ruffians, and the whole of his organisation realised that their chance to lead had arrived. The power in their hands was unbelievable. There was a special file on every senior party functionary and every general and there would be no difficulty in putting any one of them before a firing squad. It was this very power which destroyed Beriya. Both the Army and the Party understood their predicament. This brought them together and together they cut off the head of the chief executioner. The most powerful members of the security apparatus came to unpleasant ends and their whole machine of oppression was held up to public ridicule. The propaganda organisation of the Party worked overtime to explain to the country the crimes of Stalin and of his whole security apparatus.

However, having toppled Beriya from his pedestal, the Party began to feel uncomfortable; here it was, face to face with the captive leopard. The NKVD had released the chain it held around the animal's neck and it sensed freedom. The inevitable outcome was that the Army would gobble up its master. Marshal Zhukov acquired extraordinary power, at home and abroad. He demanded a fourth Gold Star of a Hero of the Soviet Union (Stalin had had only two and Beriya one). Perhaps such outward show was unimportant, but Zhukov also demanded the removal from the Army of all political commissars—he was trying to shake off the remaining chain. The Party realised that this could only end in disaster and that, without help, it was quite unable to resist the Army's pressure. An urgent request for assistance went to the KGB and, with the latter's help, Zhukov was dismissed. The wartime Marshals followed him into the wilderness, and then the ranks of the generals and of military intelligence were methodically thinned. The military budget was drastically reduced and purges and cuts followed thick and fast. These cost the Soviet Army 1,200,000 men, many of them front-line officers during the war.

The KGB was still unable to recover the stature it had lost after the fall of Beriya, and the Party began a new campaign of purges and of ridicule against it. 1962 marked the Party's triumph over both the KGB, defeated at the hands of the Army, and the Army, humiliated with the help of the KGB; with, finally, a second victory over the KGB won by the Party alone. The leg of the tripod represented by the Party began to extend to a dangerous degree.

But the triumph was short-lived. The theoretically impossible happened. The two mortal enemies, the Army and the KGB, each deeply aggrieved, united against the Party. Their great strength brought down the head of the Party, Khrushchev, who fell almost without a sound. How could he have withstood such a combination?

The era which followed his fall provided ample evidence of the remarkable inner stability of the triangular structure even in the most critical situations—Czechoslovakia, internal crises, economic collapse, Vietnam, Africa, Afghanistan. The regime has survived all these.

The Army has not thrown itself upon the KGB, nor has the KGB savaged the Army. Both tolerate the presence of the Party, which they acknowledge as an arbitrator or perhaps rather as a second in a duel, whose help each side tries to secure for itself.

In the centre of the triangle, or more accurately, above the centre, sits the Politburo. This organisation should not be seen as the summit of the Party, for it represents neutral territory, on which the three forces gather to grapple with one another.

Both the Army and the KGB are equally represented in the Politburo. With their agreement, the Party takes the leading role; the Party bosses restrain the others and act as peacemakers in the constant squabbles.

The Politburo plays a decisive part in Soviet society. In effect it has become a substitute for God. Portraits of its members are on display in every street and square. It has the last word in the resolution of any problem, at home or abroad. It has complete power in every field—legislative, executive, judicial, military, political, administrative, even religious.

Representing, as it does, a fusion of three powers, the Politburo is fully aware that it draws its own stability from each of these sources. It can be compared to the seat of a three-legged stool. If one of the legs is longer than the others, the stool will fall over. The same will happen if one of the legs is shorter than the others. For their own safety, therefore, the members of the Politburo, whether they come from the Party, the KGB or the Army, do everything they can to maintain equilibrium. The secret of Brezhnev's survival lay in his skill in keeping the balance between the trio, restraining any two from combining against the third.

Why does the system of higher military control appear complicated?

When Western specialists talk about the organisation of Soviet regiments and divisions, their explanations are simple and comprehensive. The diagrams they draw, too, are simple. At a single glance one can see who is subordinated to whom. But, once the specialists begin talking about the organisational system of control at higher levels, the picture becomes so complicated that no one can understand it. The diagrams explaining the system of higher military control published in the West resemble those showing the defences of a sizeable bank in Zurich or Basle: square boxes, lines, circles, intersections. The uninitiated might gain the impression that there is dual control at the top—or, even worse, that there is no firm hand and therefore complete anarchy.

In fact, the control structure from top to bottom is simple to the point of primitiveness. Why, then, does it seem complicated to foreign observers? Simply because they study the Soviet Union as they would any other foreign country; they try to explain everything which happens there in language their readers can understand, in generally accepted categories—in other words, in the language of common sense. However, the Soviet Union is a unique phenomenon, which cannot be understood by applying a frame of reference based on experience elsewhere. Only 3% of arable land in the Soviet Union is in the hands of private owners, and not a single tractor or a kilogram of fertiliser. This 3% feeds practically the whole country. If the private owners were given another 1/2% there would be no problem with food production. But the Communists prefer to waste 400 tons of gold each year buying wheat abroad. Just try to explain this in normal common sense language.

Thus, when examining the system of higher military control,

the reader must not attempt to draw parallels with human society in other parts of the world. Remember that Communists have their own logic, their own brand of common sense.

2

Let us take a diagram explaining the system of higher military control, drawn by some Western specialist on Soviet affairs, and try to simplify it. Among the maze of criss-crossing lines we will try to pick out the outlines of a pyramid of granite.

Our specialist has, of course, shown the President at the very top, with the Praesidium of the Supreme Soviet next and then the two chambers of the Supreme Soviet. But the Party must not be forgotten. So there, together with the President, are the General Secretary of the Party, the Politburo, and the Central Committee. Here there is disagreement among the experts about who should be shown higher up the page and who lower—the General Secretary or the President.

Let us clarify the picture. Here are the names of past General Secretaries: Stalin, Khrushchev, Brezhnev. Try to remember the names of the Presidents of the Soviet Union during the periods when those three were in power. Even the experts cannot remember. I have put other questions to these experts. Why, when Stalin went to meet the President of the United States, did he not take the Soviet President with him? When the Cuban rocket crisis was at its height and Khrushchev discussed the fate of the world on the hot line with the American President, why was it he who did this rather than the Soviet President? Surely it was the two Presidents who should have talked the matter over? And why, when Brezhnev talks about missiles with the American President, does he not give the Soviet President a seat at the conference table?

In order to decide which of the two—President or General Secretary—should be shown at the top, it is worth recalling the relationship between Stalin and his President, Kalinin. Stalin gave orders that Kalinin's wife and his closest friends should be shot but that it should appear that the President himself had issued the order. One Soviet historian tells us that, as he signed the death sentence on his own wife, the President "wept from grief and powerlessness."

In order to simplify our diagram, take a red pencil and cross out the Presidency. It is nothing but an unnecessary ornament which leads to confusion. If war breaks out, no future historian will remember that standing by the side of the General Secretary was some President or other now totally forgotten who was weeping from grief and powerlessness.

As well as the Presidency, cross out the Praesidium of the Supreme Soviet and both of its chambers. They are not involved in any way with either the government of the country or the control of its armed forces. Judge for yourself—this Soviet "parliament" meets twice a year for four or five days and discusses thirty to forty questions each day. Bearing in mind that the Deputies do not overwork themselves, one can calculate the number of minutes they spend on each question. The Soviet parliament has fifteen or so permanent committees dealing with such questions as the supply of consumer goods (where to buy lavatory paper) or the provision of services (how to get taps mended). But none of these committees concerns itself with the affairs of the armed forces, with the KGB, with military industry (which provides employment for twelve separate ministries), or with prisons. The Soviet parliament has never discussed the reasons why Soviet forces are in Hungary, Czechoslovakia, Cuba or Afghanistan. During the Second World War it did not meet once. Why should such an organisation be included among those concerned with questions of higher military control?

But this is not the most important point. The Soviet parliament is nothing but a parasite. All its decisions are reached unanimously. The nomination of a new President—unanimous. The removal and ignominious dismissal of his predecessor—also unanimous. In reality, these nominations and dismissals took place many months earlier. Parliament simply ratifies them subsequently—and unanimously. When Parliament does not meet for several years, nobody knows the reason and nothing changes as a result. If all its members were tried as parasites and sent to prison under Soviet law nothing would change: Soviet Presidents would continue to be appointed with great ceremony and chased from office in disgrace. According to Soviet law, the rank of Marshal must be conferred—and removed—by Parliament. But several Marshals have been shot without any reference to Parliament. Just try and work out how many Marshals have been appointed and how many shot with-

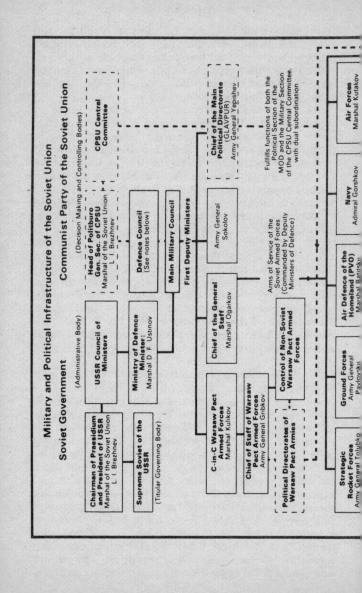

Military and Political Infrastructure of the Soviet Union

Soviet Government	Communist Party of the Soviet Union
(Administrative Body)	(Decision Making and Controlling Bodies)

Chairman of Praesidium and President of USSR
Marshal of the Soviet Union
L. I. Brezhnev

Supreme Soviet of the USSR
(Titular Governing Body)

USSR Council of Ministers

Head of Politburo
Gen. Sec. of CPSU
Marshal of the Soviet Union
L. I. Brezhnev

CPSU Central Committee

Ministry of Defence
Minister:
Marshal D. F. Ustinov

Defence Council
(See notes below)

Main Military Council

First Deputy Ministers

Chief of the Main Political Directorate (GLAVPUR)
Army General Yepishev

Fulfills functions of both the Political Section of the MOD and the Military Section of the CPSU Central Committee, with dual subordination

C-in-C Warsaw Pact Armed Forces
Marshal Kulikov

Chief of the General Staff
Marshal Ogarkov

Army General Sokolov

Chief of Staff of Warsaw Pact Armed Forces
Army General Gribkov

Control of Non-Soviet Warsaw Pact Armed Forces

Arms of Service of the Soviet Armed Forces
(Commanded by Deputy Ministers of Defence)

Political Directorates of Warsaw Pact Armies

Strategic Rocket Forces	Ground Forces	Air Defence of the Homeland (PVO)	Air Forces	Navy	Air Forces
Army General Tolubko	Army General Pavlovskii	Marshal Batitsky		Admiral Gorshkov	Marshal Kutakov

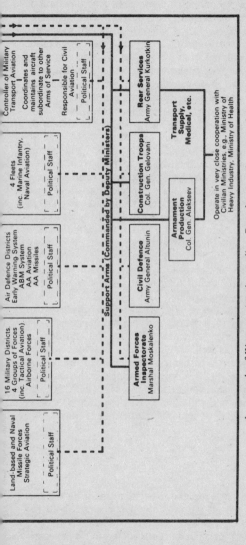

Land-based and Naval Missile Forces Strategic Aviation	16 Military Districts. 4 Groups of Forces (inc. Tactical Aviation). Airborne Forces	Air Defence Districts Early Warning System ABM System AA Aviation AA Missiles	4 Fleets (inc. Marine Infantry. Naval Aviation)	Controller of Military Transport Aviation Coordinates and maintains aircraft subordinate to other Arms of Service
Political Staff	Political Staff	Political Staff	Political Staff	Responsible for Civil Aviation Political Staff

Support Arms (Commanded by Deputy Ministers)

Armed Forces Inspectorate Marshal Moskalenko	Civil Defence Army General Altunin	Construction Troops Col. Gen. Gelovani	Rear Services Army General Kurkotkin

Armament Production Col. Gen. Alekseev

Transport Supply, Medical, etc.

Operate in very close cooperation with Civilian Ministries, e.g. Ministry of Heavy Industry, Ministry of Health

An example of Western misunderstanding. But who runs the country?

out the knowledge or consent of Parliament. And this did not only happen during the Stalinist Terror. It was under Khrushchev that Marshal of the Soviet Union Beriya was shot, that Marshal Bulganin was struck off the pay-roll, that eleven other Marshals were dismissed from their posts. All this was done without the knowledge or consent of the Soviet Parliament.

But, you will say, if neither the President nor Parliament does anything or is responsible for anything and is there only to approve any—absolutely any—decision unanimously, why were their positions in the system ever created? The answer is, as camouflage.

If all power were seen to rest entirely in the hands of the Politburo, this might offend both the Soviet people and the rest of the world. To avoid this, Soviet propaganda compiles extremely complicated diagrams, as complicated as those for a perpetual motion machine, which its inventor purposely makes more and more intricate, so that no one will realise that hidden inside his brainchild there is a dwarf who is turning the wheels.

It is a great pity that many Western specialists, who know that during the war the Soviet President was not allowed to attend the meetings of the military leadership, nevertheless show him at the very top of their diagrams just where he is said to be by Soviet propaganda.

There is one situation in which the Soviet President can become a person of importance, and this has happened only once in Soviet history. A General Secretary decided that he should be President as well. Naturally, this was done without an election of any sort. The name of this President was—and is—Brezhnev. However, it is only abroad that he is honoured as President. Everyone at home knows that "President" is completely meaningless and calls him by his real title—General Secretary—which has, of course, the true ring of power.

3

We have removed these useless embellishments from the diagram but that is not all we must do. Do not cross out the Council of Ministers, but move them to one side. Why? you may ask. Is the Minister of Defence not subject to the decisions of the Council of Ministers? That is correct. He is not. The

Council of Ministers only has control over industry, which in the USSR is almost entirely military. The Soviet Union uses more cloth, of much better quality, for the production of parachutes than for the manufacture of clothes for 260 million people. However, of these 260 million, very many receive military uniforms, of good quality; all that is left, for the remainder, is material of appalling quality, and there is not enough even of that.

In the Soviet Union the number of cars in private ownership is lower, per thousand head of the population, than the total owned by the black inhabitants of South Africa, for whose freedom the United Nations is fighting so fervently. But, against this, the number of tanks in the Soviet Union is greater than in the rest of the whole world put together.

Twelve of the Ministries which the Council controls produce nothing but military equipment. All the remainder (coal, steel production, energy, etc.) work in the interests of those which produce arms.

Thus, the Council of Ministers is, essentially, a single gigantic economic organisation, supporting the Army. It is, therefore, with all its military and auxiliary industry, a sort of subsidiary rear organisation of the Army. It possesses colossal power over those who produce military equipment but, against this, it has not even the authority to send a new doorman to one of the Soviet embassies abroad. This can be done only by the Party or, more accurately, by the Party's Central Committee.

Why is the make-up of
the Defence Council kept secret?

1

By now much of our diagram has been simplified. The summit of power has become visible—the Politburo, in which sit representatives of the Party, the KGB, and the Army. Decisions taken in the Politburo by the most senior representatives of these organisations are also implemented by them. For instance, when Afghanistan was suddenly invaded by the Army on the orders of the Politburo, the KGB removed unsuitable senior personnel, while the Party arranged diversionary operations and worked up propaganda campaigns at home and abroad.

The role of the Council of Ministers is important but not decisive. The Council is responsible for increasing military productivity, for the prompt delivery to the forces of military equipment, ammunition and fuel, for the uninterrupted functioning of the military industries and of the national economy, which works only in support of the military industries and therefore in the interests of the Army. The Chairman of the Council will certainly be present when decisions on these subjects are taken but as one of the members of the Politburo, working for the interests of the Army, rather than as the head of the Council.

What does the highly secret organisation known as the Defence Council do at a time like this? Officially, all that is known about this organisation is that it is headed by Brezhnev. The identities of the other members of the Council are kept secret. What sort of organisation is it? Why is its make-up given no publicity? Soviet propaganda publishes the names of the head of the KGB and of his deputies, those of the heads of ministries, of the heads of all military research institutions, of the Defence Minister and of all his deputies. The names of those responsible

for the production of atomic warheads and for missile programmes are officially known; so are those of the head of the
GRU and of the head of the disinformation service. Why are
the names of those who are responsible for overall decisions,
at the highest level of all, kept secret?

Let us examine the Defence Council from two different
points of view. Firstly, who sits on such a council? Some
observers believe that it is made up of the most prominent
members of the Politburo and the leading Marshals. They are
mistaken. These officials attend the Chief Military Council,
which is subordinate to the Defence Council. The Defence
Council is something more than a mixture of Marshals and
Politburo members. What could be superior to such a group?
The answer is—members of the Politburo without any out-
siders. Not all the members: only the most influential.

Secondly, what is the position of the Defence Council vis-
à-vis the Politburo—higher, the same or lower? If the Defence
Council had more power than the Politburo its first act would
be to split up this group of geriatrics, so that they would not
interfere. If the Defence Council were equal in power to the
Politburo we should witness a dramatic battle between these
two giants, for there is only room for one such organisation at
the top. A dictatorship cannot exist for long when power is
shared between two groups. Two dictators cannot co-exist.
Perhaps, then, the Defence Council is of slightly lower status
than the Politburo? But there would be no place for it in this
case, either. Directly below the Politburo is the Chief Military
Council, which links the Politburo with the Army, serving to
bond the two together. Thus the Defence Council cannot be
either inferior or superior to the Politburo; nor can it hold an
equal position. The Defence Council exists, in fact, within the
Politburo itself. Its membership is kept secret only because it
contains no one but members of the Politburo and it is considered undesirable to give unnecessary emphasis to the absolute
power enjoyed by this organisation.

Neither the Soviet Union nor its many vassal states contain
any power higher than or independent of the Politburo. The
Politburo possesses all legislative, executive, judicial, administrative, religious, political, economic and every other power.
It is unthinkable that such an organisation should be prepared
to allow any other to take decisions on the momentous problems
produced by Soviet usurpations and "adventures" throughout

the world, problems of war and peace, of life and death. The day when the Politburo releases its hold will be its last. That day has not yet come...

2

Many Western specialists believe the Defence Council to be something new, created by Brezhnev. But nothing changes in the Soviet Union, especially in the system by which it is governed. The system stabilised itself long ago and it is almost impossible to change it in any way. New, decorative organisations can be devised and added but changes to the basic structure of the Soviet Union are out of the question. Khrushchev tried to introduce some and the system destroyed him. Brezhnev is wiser and he makes no attempts at change. He rules with the help of a system which was established in the early days of Stalin and which has remained unchanged ever since.

Only the labels change in the USSR. The security organisation has been known successively as the VChK, GPU, OGPU, NKVD, NKGB, MGB, and KGB. Some think that these services differed from one another in some way but it was only their labels which did so. The Party has been called the RKP(B), the VKP(B), the KPSS. The Army began as the Red Army, then became the Soviet Army and its highest overall council has been successively labelled KVMD, SNKMVD, NKMVD, NKO, NKVS, MVS, and MO, while remaining one and the same organisation.

Exactly the same has happened with the Defence Council. It changes its name as a snake sheds its skin, painlessly. But it is still the same snake. In Lenin's day it was called the Workers' and Peasants' Defence Council or simply the Defence Council, then the Council for Labour and Defence. Subsequently, since its members all belonged to the Politburo, it became the Military Commission of the Politburo.

Immediately after the outbreak of war with Germany, the State Committee for Defence was established, which, entirely legally and officially, acquired the full powers of the President, the Supreme Soviet, the Government, the Supreme Court, the Central Committee of the Party and of all other authorities and organisations. The decisions of the State Committee for Defence had the force of martial law and were mandatory for all individuals and organisations including the Supreme Commander, and the President.

The State Committee for Defence had five members:

Stalin — its President

Molotov — his first deputy

Malenkov — the head of the Party's bureaucracy

Beriya — the head of the security organisation

Voroshilov — the senior officer of the Army

These five were the most influential members of the Politburo, so that the State Committee for Defence consisted not of the whole Politburo, but of its most influential component parts. Take another look at its composition and you will recognise our triangle. There are the Supreme Being, his Right Hand and, below them, the triangle—Party, KGB, Army. Note the absence of the President of the Soviet Union, Kalinin. He is a member of the Politburo, but a purely nominal one. He possesses no power and there is therefore no place for him in an organisation which is omnipotent.

Before the war the same powerful quintet existed inside the Politburo but at that time they called themselves simply the Military Commission of the Politburo. Then, too, these five were all-powerful but they worked discreetly behind the scenes, while the stage was occupied by the President, the Supreme Soviet, the Government, the Central Committee and other decorative but superfluous organisations and individuals. When war began nothing changed, except that the quintet took over the stage and were seen in their true roles, deciding the fate of tens of millions of people.

Naturally, this group did not allow power to slip from their grasp when the war ended; they disappeared back into the shadows, calling themselves the Military Commission of the Politburo once again and pushing to the front of the stage a series of pitiable clowns and cowards who "wept from grief and powerlessness" while this group slaughtered their nearest and dearest.

The Second World War threw up a group of brilliant military leaders—Zhukov, Rokossovskiy, Vasilevskiy, Konev, Yeremenko—but not one of them was allowed by the "big five" to enter the sacred precincts of the State Committee for Defence. The Committee's members knew quite well that in order to retain power they must safeguard their privileges with great care. For this reason, throughout the war, no single individual, however distinguished, who was not a member of the Politburo, was admitted to the Committee. All questions were decided by the Politburo members who belonged to the Committee and they were then discussed with Army representatives at a lower level, in the Stavka, to which both Politburo members and leading Marshals belonged.

Precisely the same organisation exists today. The Defence Council is yesterday's State Committee for Defence under another name. Its membership is drawn exclusively from the Politburo, and then only from those with the greatest power. It is they who take all decisions, which are then discussed at the Chief Military Council (otherwise known as the Stavka) which is attended by members of the Politburo and by the leading Marshals.

Brezhnev is the old wolf of the Politburo. His long period in power has made him the equal of Stalin. One can see why he is disinclined to experiment with the system by which power over the Army is exercised. He follows the road which Stalin built, carefully adhering to the rules laid down by that experienced old tyrant. These are simple: essentially, before you sit down at a table with the Marshals at the Chief Military Council decide everything with the Politburo at the Defence Council. Brezhnev knows that any modification of these rules would mean that he must share his present unlimited powers with the Marshals—and that this is equivalent to suicide. This is why the Defence Council—the highest institution within the Soviet dictatorship—consists of the most influential members of the Politburo and of no one else.

The Organisation of the Soviet Armed Forces

1

The system by which the Soviet Armed Forces are controlled is simplified to the greatest possible extent. It is deliberately kept simple in design, just like every Soviet tank, fighter aircraft, missile or military plan. Soviet marshals and generals believe, not unreasonably, that, in a war, other things being equal, it is the simpler weapon, plan or organisation which is more likely to succeed.

Western specialists make a careful study of the obscure and intricate lay-out of Soviet military organisation, for they see the Soviet Army as being similar to any other national army. However, to any other army peace represents normality and war an abnormal, temporary situation. The Soviet Army (more accurately the Red Army) is the striking force of world revolution. It was brought into being to serve the world revolution and, although that revolution has not yet come, the Soviet Army is poised and waiting for it, ready to fan into life any spark or ember which appears anywhere in the world, no matter what the consequences might be. Normality, for the Soviet Army, is a revolutionary war; peace is an abnormal and temporary situation.

In order to understand the structure of the military leadership of the Soviet Union, we must examine it as it exists in wartime. The same structure is preserved in peacetime, although a variety of decorative features, which completely distort the true picture, are added as camouflage. Unfortunately, most researchers do not attempt to distinguish the really important parts of the organisation from those which are completely unnecessary and there purely for show.

We already know that in wartime the Soviet Union and the countries which it dominates would be ruled by the Defence Council, an organisation first known as the Workers' and Peasants' Defence Council, next as the Labour and Defence Council and then as the State Committee for Defence.

On this Council are one representative each from the Party, the Army, and the KGB and two others who preside over these organisations—the General Secretary and his closest associate. Until his recent death the latter post was held by Mikhail Suslov.

The Defence Council possesses unrestricted powers. It functioned in wartime and has been preserved in peacetime with the difference that, whereas during wartime it worked openly and in full view, in peacetime it functions from behind the cover offered by the President of the Soviet Union, the Supreme Soviet, elections, deputies, public prosecutors and similar irrelevancies. Their only function is to conceal what is going on behind the scenes.

Directly subordinate to the Defence Council is the Headquarters (Stavka) of the Supreme Commander, which is known in peacetime as the Chief Military Council. To it belong the Supreme Commander and his closest deputies, together with certain members of the Politburo. The Supreme Commander is appointed by the Defence Council. He may be either the Minister of Defence, as was the case with Marshal Timoshenko, or the General Secretary of the Party, as with Stalin, who also headed both the Stavka and the civil administration. If the Minister of Defence is not appointed Supreme Commander he becomes First Deputy to the latter. The organisation working for the Stavka is the General Staff, which prepares proposals, works out the details of the Supreme Commander's instructions and supervises their execution.

2

In wartime, the armed forces of the USSR and of the countries under its rule are directed by the Stavka along two clearly differentiated lines of control: the operational (fighting) and administrative (rear).

The line of operational subordination:
Directly subordinate to the Supreme Commander are five Commanders-in-Chief and eight Commanders.

The Commanders-in-Chief are responsible for: —
> The Western Strategic Direction
> The South-Western Strategic Direction
> The Far Eastern Strategic Direction
> The Strategic Rocket Forces
> The National Air Defence Forces

The Commanders are responsible for: —
> The Long-Range Air Force
> The Airborne Forces
> Military Transport Aviation
> The Northern Fleet
> Individual Front — Northern, Baltic, Trans-Caucasian and Turkestan.

The Commander-in-Chief of the Western Strategic Direction has under his command four Fronts, one Group of Tank Armies and the Baltic Fleet.

The Commander-in-Chief of the South-Western Strategic Direction also commands four Fronts, one Group of Tank Armies and the Black Sea Fleet.

The Commander-in-Chief of the Far Eastern Strategic Direction is responsible for four Fronts and the Pacific Fleet.

The Fronts subordinated to the Strategic Directions and individual Fronts, subordinated directly to the Stavka, consist of All-Arms, Tank and Air Armies. The Armies are made up of Divisions. East European Divisions are included in Armies, which can be commanded only by Soviet generals. The commanders of East European divisions are thus subordinated directly to Soviet command—to Army Commanders, then to Fronts, Strategic Directions and ultimately to the Defence Council—in other words to the Soviet Politburo. East European governments can therefore exert absolutely no influence over the progress of military operations.

The line of administrative subordination:
The First Deputy of the Minister of Defence is subordinated to the Supreme Commander. At present the post is held by Marshal S. L. Sokolov, under whom come four Commanders-in-Chief (Air Forces, Land Forces, Naval Forces, Warsaw Treaty

Organisation) and sixteen Commanders of Military Districts.

The Commanders-in-Chief are responsible for the establishment of reserves, for bringing forces up to strength, re-equipment, supply of forces engaged in combat operations, development of new military equipment, study of combat experience, training of personnel, etc. The Commander-in-Chief of the Warsaw Treaty Organisation has precisely these responsibilities but only on behalf of the East European divisions operating as part of the United (i.e. Soviet) forces. He has full control over all the East European Ministries of Defence. His task is to ensure that these Ministries bring their divisions up to strength, and to re-equip and supply them according to schedule. In wartime he has only a modest role. It is now clear why the function of the Commander-in-Chief of the Warsaw Treaty Organisation is seen in the USSR as being a purely honorific legacy from the past, remote from real power.

Each of the sixteen Commanders of Military Districts is a territorial functionary, a sort of military governor. In questions concerning the stability of Soviet authority in the territories entrusted to them, they are responsible directly to the Politburo (Defence Council), while on subjects concerning the administration of military industries, transport and mobilisation they are subordinated to the First Deputy of the Minister of Defence, through him to the Stavka and ultimately to the Defence Council.

Troops acting as reserve forces, to be used to bring units up to strength, for re-equipment, etc., may be stationed in the territories of Military Districts. These troops are subordinate, not to operational commanders but to the Military District Commanders, through them to the Commander-in-Chief, to the First Deputy and then to the Stavka. For instance, during war, on the territory of the Urals Military District there would be one Air Division (to replace losses), one Tank Army (Stavka reserve), one Polish tank division (for re-equipment) and three battalions of marine infantry (a new formation). These units will be subordinate to the Commander of the Urals Military District and through him, as regards the Air Division, to the Commander-in-Chief of the Air Forces, while the Tank Army comes under the Commander-in-Chief of Land Forces, the Polish division to the Commander-in-Chief of the Warsaw Treaty Organisation and the battalions of marine infantry to the Commander-in-Chief of Naval Forces. Each Commander-in-Chief has the right to give orders to the Commander of a Military District, but only in matters concerning sub-units subordinate to him. Because the complement of each Military District always consists mainly of sub-units of the Land Forces some Western observers have the impression that Military Districts are subordinated to the Commanders-in-Chief of Land Forces. But this is not so. The Commander of a Military District has very wide powers, which are not in any way subject to the control of the Commander-in-Chief of Land Forces. As soon as the Stavka decides to transfer one or other sub-unit to an operational army, the sub-unit ceases to be controlled by the line of administrative subordination and comes under the instructions of the operational commander.

3

In wartime the system for controlling the Soviet Union, the countries which it has occupied and the entire united armed forces is stripped of the whole of its unnecessary decorative superstructure. The division between the operational and administrative lines of subordination then becomes apparent.

In peacetime the operational and administrative structures are blended with one another; this produces a misleading appearance of complexity, duplication and muddle. Despite this, the system which one can see clearly in wartime continues to function in peacetime. One simply needs to look at it carefully, to distinguish one structure from another and to ignore useless embellishments.

But is it possible to spot the summit of the edifice in peacetime—the Defence Council and the Stavka? This is quite simple. Each year on 7 November a military parade takes place on Red Square in Moscow. The whole military and political leadership gathers in the stands on top of Lenin's mausoleum. The position of each person is clearly discernible. For such a position, for each place in the stands, there is a constant, savage but silent struggle, like that which goes on in a pack of wolves for a place closer to the leader, and then for the leader's place itself. This jostling for position has already continued for many decades and each place has cost too much blood for it to be surrendered without a battle.

As is to be expected, the General Secretary and the Minister of Defence stand shoulder to shoulder in the centre of the tribune. To the left of the General Secretary are the members of the Politburo, to the right of the Minister of Defence are the Marshals. The stands on the mausoleum are the only place where the members of the political and military leadership parade, each in the position where he belongs. This is the only place where each individual shows his retinue, his rivals and his enemies, the whole country and the whole world how close he is to the centre of power. You can be sure that if the head of the KGB could take his place by the side of the General Secretary he would do so immediately, but this place is always occupied by a more influential individual—the Chief Ideologist. You can be certain that if the Commander-in-Chief of the Warsaw Treaty Organisation could move closer to the centre he would immediately do so, but the place he is after is already occupied by the almighty Chief of the General Staff.

On the day after the parade you can buy a copy of *Pravda* for three kopeks and on the front page, immediately beneath the masthead, you can see a photograph of the entire political and military leadership.

Take a red pencil and mark the General Secretary and the four other members of the Politburo standing closest to him. These are the members of the Defence Council. They run the country. It is to them that hundreds of millions are enslaved, from Havana to Ulan Bator. It is they who will control the fate of the hundreds of millions in their power when the time comes to "liberate" new peoples and new countries.

Now, mark the General Secretary, the member of the Politburo closest to him and the five Marshals nearest to him. This is the Stavka.

High Commands in the Strategic Directions

A platoon commander has three or four, sometimes five, sections under his command. It is pointless to give him more than this. He would be quite unable to exercise effective control over so large a platoon. If you have another, sixth, section it would be better to form two platoons of three sections each.

A company commander has three, four, or sometimes five platoons under his command. There is no point in giving him more—he just could not control them.

This system, under which each successive commander controls between three and five detachments, is used universally and at all levels. A Front Commander, for instance, directs three or four and sometimes five Armies. And it is at just this level that the system breaks down. The Soviet Army has sixteen Military Districts and four Army Groups. In the event of all-out war each District and each Army Group is able to form one Front from its own resources. How, though, can the Stavka control twenty Fronts simultaneously? Would it not be simpler to interpose a new intermediate link in the chain of command, which would control the operations of three or four and sometimes five Fronts? In this way the Stavka could be in immediate control not of twenty Fronts but of between three and five of the new intermediate units. Such an innovation would complete the whole balanced system of control, in a logical fashion.

In fact, intermediate control links between the Stavka and the Fronts do exist, but they are given no publicity. They are designated as High Commands in the Strategic Directions. The first mention of these command links occurred in the Soviet military press in 1929. They were set up two years later, but their existence was kept secret and was not referred to officially.

Immediately after the outbreak of the Second World War they were officially brought into existence.

During the first two weeks of the war, official announcements were made about the formation of North-Western, and Western and South-Western Strategic Directions. Each Direction consisted of between three and five Fronts. At the head of each Direction was a Commander-in-Chief, who was subordinated to the Stavka.

Just how important each of these High Commands were can be judged by looking at the composition of the Western Strategic Direction. The Commander-in-Chief was Marshal of the Soviet Union S. K. Timoshenko, who held the post of Minister of Defence at the outbreak of war. The Political Commissar was Politburo member N. A. Bulganin, one of those closest to Stalin, who later became a Marshal of the Soviet Union and President of the Council of Ministers. The Chief of Staff was Marshal B. M. Shaposhnikov, the pre-war Chief of the General Staff. The other Strategic Directions also had command personnel of approximately the same calibre—all the posts were occupied by Marshals or members of the Politburo.

In 1942 a further High Command, the North Caucasus Strategic Direction, was established, incorporating two Fronts and the Black Sea Fleet. Its Commander-in-Chief was Marshal S. M. Budenniy.

However, it was subsequently decided that no further steps in this direction should be taken for the time being. The High Commands of the Strategic Directions were abolished and the Stavka took over direct control of the Fronts, which totalled fifteen. However, the idea of an intermediate link was not abandoned. Frequently throughout the war representatives of the Stavka, usually Marshals Zhukov or Vasilyevskiy, were detached to work with those who were preparing large-scale operations and coordinating the work of several Fronts. Among the most brilliant of many examples of such coordinated efforts are the battles for Stalingrad and Kursk and the advance into Byelorussia. What amounted to a temporary grouping of Fronts, under a single command, was set up for each of these operations. A system of this sort provided greater flexibility and justified itself completely in conditions in which operations were being carried out against a single opponent. As soon as the decision had been taken to go to war with Japan, in 1945, the Far Eastern Strategic Direction was set up, consisting of three Fronts, one Fleet and the armed forces of Mongolia. The Commander-in-Chief of the Direction was Marshal A. M. Vasilyevskiy.

It is interesting to note that the very existence of a Far Eastern Strategic Direction with its own High Command was kept secret. As camouflage, Marshal Vasilyevskiy's headquarters were referred to as "Colonel-General Vasilyev's Group." Many officers, including some generals, among them all the division and corps commanders, had no idea of Vasilyevskiy's function, supposing that all the Far Eastern Fronts were directed from Moscow, by the Stavka. The fact that he had acted as Commander-in-Chief was only revealed by Vasilyevskiy after the advance into Manchuria at the end of the war.

The High Command of the Far Eastern Strategic Direction was not abolished at the end of the war and no official instructions for its disbandment were ever issued. All that happened was that from 1953 onwards all official mention of it ceased. Does it exist today? Do High Commands exist for other Strategic Directions or would they be set up only in the event of war?

They exist—and they are in operation. They are not mentioned officially, but no particular efforts are made to conceal their existence. Let us identify them. This is quite simple. In the Soviet Army there are sixteen Military Districts and four Army Groups. The senior officer in each District and each Army Group has the designation "Commander." Only in one case, that of the Group of Soviet Forces in Germany, is he given the title of "Commander-in-Chief." In the event of war most Districts would be made into Fronts. But Fronts, too, are headed only by "Commanders." The title "Commander-in-Chief" is considerably senior to "Commander of a Front." In a war the number of troops available would increase many times over. Platoon commanders would take over companies, battalion commanders would head regiments and regimental commanders would become divisional commanders. In this situation every officer might receive a higher rank; he would certainly retain the one he already holds. A general who in peacetime commands enough troops to be entitled to the designation "Commander-in-Chief" can hardly have his responsibilities reduced to those of a Front Commander at a time when many more troops are being placed under his command.

If during peacetime the importance of his post is so great, how can it diminish when war breaks out? Of course it cannot. And a general whose peacetime title is "Commander-in-Chief of the GSFG" will retain this rank, which is considerably higher than that of Front Commander.

There can be no doubt that the organisation known as the "Headquarters of the GSFG" in peacetime would become, not a Front Headquarters, but the Headquarters of the Western Strategic Direction.

It is significant that, already in peacetime, the Headquarters of the GSFG controls two Tank Armies and one Shock Army (essentially another Tank Army). For each Front can have only a single Tank Army and in many cases it does not have one at all. The presence in GSFG of three Tank Armies indicates that it has been decided to deploy at least three Fronts in the area covered by this Direction. Is this sufficient? Yes, for in a war the Commander-in-Chief of the Western Strategic Direction would have under his command not only all the Soviet troops in East Germany but all those in Czechoslovakia and Poland, together with the entire complement of the German, Czech and Polish armed forces, the Soviet Baltic Fleet and the Byelorussian Military District. This will be discussed in greater detail. For the present it is sufficient to note that the Group of Soviet Forces in Germany is an organisation which is regarded by the Soviet leadership as entirely different from any other Group of forces. No other force—in Poland, Czechoslovakia, Mongolia, Cuba, Afghanistan or, earlier, Austria or China— has ever been headed by a Commander-in-Chief. All these Groups were headed by a Commander.

Let us list the Generals and Marshals who have held the post of Commander-in-Chief of the Soviet Group of Forces in Germany:

Marshal G. K. Zhukov, the former Chief of the General Staff, who became First Deputy to the Supreme Commander and subsequently Minister of Defence and a member of the Politburo, the only man in history to have been awarded the title of Hero of the Soviet Union four times.

Marshal V. D. Sokolovskiy, former Chief of Staff of the Western Strategic Direction and later Chief of the General Staff.

General of the Army V. I. Chuykov, subsequently a Marshal and Commander-in-Chief of the Land Forces.

Marshal A. A. Grechko, later Minister of Defence and a member of the Politburo.

Marshal M. V. Zakharov, later Chief of the General Staff.

Marshal P. K. Koshevoy.

General of the Army V. G. Kulikov, later a Marshal, Chief of the General Staff and then Commander-in-Chief of the Warsaw Treaty Organisation.

Only one of this galaxy rose no higher—Marshal Koshevoy, who became seriously ill. But to reach the rank of Marshal is no mean achievement—and it was in Germany that he received the rank of Marshal, at a time when other Groups of forces were commanded only by Lieutenant-Generals and Colonel-Generals. Thus Koshevoy, too, stands out from the crowd.

One rule applied to all—anyone who held the post of Commander-in-Chief of the GSFG was either a Marshal already, was promoted to this rank on appointment or was given it shortly afterwards. Nothing of this sort has occurred with other Groups of forces.

The GSFG is a kind of springboard to the very highest military appointments. Commanders of other groups have never achieved such high standing. Moreover even the Commanders-in-Chief of the Land Forces, of the Air Forces, Fleet, Rocket Troops or Air Defence have never had such glittering careers or such future prospects as those who have been Commanders-in-Chief in Germany.

Surely this is enough to indicate that in wartime something far more powerful will be set up on the foundation represented by the GSFG than in the other, ordinary, Military Districts and Groups of forces?

None of the other Military Districts and Groups of forces have Commanders-in-Chief—only Commanders. Does this mean that in peacetime there are no Strategic Directions? Not at all. The Headquarters of the Western Strategic Direction (HQ,GSFG) is hardly concealed at all while the existence of the other Strategic Directions is only lightly camouflaged, as was "Colonel-General Vasilyev's Group." But it is easy to see through this camouflage.

It is sufficient to analyse the careers of those commanding Military Districts. One can then see that, for the overwhelming majority, command of a District represents the highest peak they will reach. Those who advance further are rare. In some

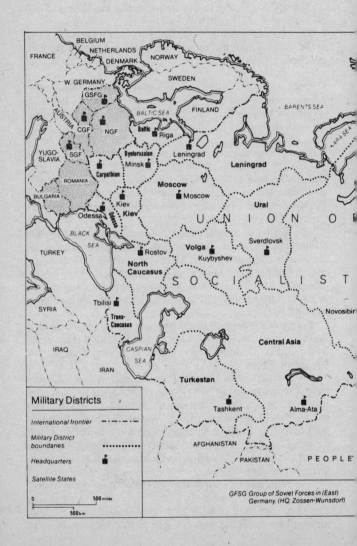

Military Districts

International frontier — · — · —
Military District
boundaries ....
Headquarters
Satellite States

0 _____ 500 miles
500 km

GFSG Group of Soviet Forces in (East)
Germany. (HQ: Zossen-Wunsdorf)

ARCTIC OCEAN

EAST SIBERIAN
SEA

LAPTEV SEA

S O V I E T

Siberian   Transbaykal

SEA OF OKHOTSK

R E P U B L I C S

Far East

Khabarovsk

Chita

Ulan Bator
Mongolia

SEA OF JAPAN

NORTH
KOREA   JAPAN

REPUBLIC OF CHINA

SOUTH
KOREA

NGF   Northern Group of Forces.   CFG   Central Group of Forces.   SGF   Southern Group of Forces.
      (Poland HQ: Legnica)   (Czechoslovakia HQ: Milovice)   (Hungary HQ: Budapest)

cases what follows is honourable retirement to posts such as Director of one Military Academy or another or an Inspector's post in the Ministry of Defence. Both these types of appointment are seen as "elephants' graveyards." They represent, in fact, the end of any real power.

However, one of the sixteen Military Districts is a clear exception. None of its former Commanders has ever left for an elephants' graveyard. On the contrary—the Kiev Military District is a kind of doorway to power. Here are the careers of all those who have commanded this District since the war:

Colonel-General A. A. Grechko became Commander-in-Chief of GSFG and a Marshal, Commander-in-Chief of Land Forces, Commander-in-Chief of the Warsaw Treaty Organisation, Minister of Defence and a member of the Politburo.

General of the Army V. I. Chuykov—C-in-C CSFG, Commander, Kiev Military District, Marshal, C-in-C of Land Forces and Deputy Minister of Defence.

Colonel-General P. K. Koshevoy—First Deputy to the C-in-C GSFG, Commander, Kiev Military District and General of the Army, C-in-C GSFG, and Marshal.

General of the Army I. I. Yakubovskiy—C-in-C GSFG, Commander, Kiev Military District, C-in-C of the Warsaw Treaty Organisation and Marshal.

Colonel-General V. G. Kulikov—Commander Kiev Military District, C-in-C GSFG and General of the Army, Chief of the General Staff, C-in-C of the Warsaw Treaty Organisation and Marshal.

Colonel-General G. I. Salmanov—Commander Kiev Military District, Commander of the Trans-Baykal Military District.

Surprisingly, as we have been following the brilliant careers of the Commanders of the Kiev Military District, we have come across some old friends, whom we met previously as C-in-C GSFG. Strangely, there has been an interchange of Generals between Wünsdorf and Kiev. Those who have gone to Kiev have later gone to GSFG. Those who have reached GSFG without going to Kiev have done so later. However, a Commander of the Kiev Military District does not see himself as junior to the C-in-C GSFG. The journey from GSFG to Kiev is not demotion and for many it has represented promotion.

Chuykov, for instance, was C-in-C GSFG as a General and was made a Marshal when he moved to Kiev.

But perhaps the Kiev Military District is of greater numerical strength than the others? Not at all—Byelorussia has more troops and the Far Eastern Military District has more than both the Kievan and Byelorussian put together. In territory Kiev is one of the smallest of the Districts. The Siberian District is sixty-seven times as large and Moscow District is far more important. But the Commander of the Moscow, Siberian, Far Eastern, Byelorussian and the other Military Districts cannot even dream of the prospects which stretch before Commanders in Kiev. In the last twenty years not one of the Commanders of Moscow District has become a Marshal, while all but one of those from Kiev have done so, the exception being the most recent who is still young and who will certainly soon be promoted.

Why is there such a sharp contrast between the Kievan and the fifteen other Districts? Simply because the organisation designated Headquarters Kiev Military District is in fact the Headquarters of the South-Western Strategic Direction, which in the event of war would take control not only of the troops already on its territory, but of those in Sub-Carpathia, Hungary (both Soviet and Hungarian) and also the entire armed forces of Romania and Bulgaria, with their fleets, and, finally, the Black Sea Fleet.

While relations with China were good there were only two High Commands of Strategic Directions—the Western and the South-Western—but as soon as the relationship deteriorated the Far Eastern Strategic Direction was re-established. It encompasses the Central Asian, Siberian, Trans-Baykal and Far Eastern Military Districts, part of the Pacific Fleet and the Mongolian armed forces. In peacetime the Headquarters of this Strategic Direction is merged with that of the Trans-Baykal Military District and is located in Chita. Clearly this is a most convenient location, occupying, as it does, a central position among the Military Districts bordering on China and protected by the buffer state of Mongolia.

PART TWO

TYPES OF
ARMED SERVICES

How the Red Army is divided
in relation to its targets

1

Over the centuries, the armed forces of most countries have traditionally been divided between land armies and fleets. In the twentieth century the third category of air forces was added. Each of the armed services is divided into different arms of service. Thousands of years ago, land forces were already divided into infantry and cavalry. Much later, artillery detachments were added, these were eventually joined by tank forces, and so the process continued.

Today's Red Army consists, unlike any other in the world, not of three, but of five different Armed Services:

The Strategic Rocket Forces
The Land Forces
The Air Defence Forces
The Air Forces
The Navy

Each of these Services, with the exception of the Strategic Rocket Forces, is made up of different arms of service. In the Land Forces there are seven, in the Air Defence Forces three, in the Air Forces three, and in the Navy six. The Airborne Forces constitute a separate arm of service, which is not part of the complement of any of the main Services.

In addition to these Services and their constituent arms of service, there are supporting arms of service—engineers, communications, chemical warfare and transport troops and others—which form part of the different Services and their component arms. In addition there are other services which support the operations of the whole Red Army. There are fifteen or so of these but we will examine only the most important: military intelligence and the disinformation service:

2

At the head of each of the Armed Services is a Commander-in-Chief. The standing of these Commanders-in-Chief varies. Three of them—those in command of the Land Forces, the Air Force, and the Navy—are no more than administrative heads. They are responsible for the improvement and development of their Services, and for ensuring that these are up to strength and properly equipped. Two of the others—the Commanders-in-Chief of the Rocket Forces and of the Air Defence Forces—are responsible not only for administrative questions but also for the operational control of their forces in action.

The discrepancy in the positions of Commanders-in-Chief results from the fact that, in combat, the Rocket Forces operate independently, without needing to work with any other Service. In the same way, the Air Defence Forces operate in complete independence. The Commanders-in-Chief of these two Services are subordinated directly to the Supreme Commander and are fully responsible for their forces both in peacetime and in war.

With the Land Forces, Air Forces and Navy the situation is more complex. In their operations they need to cooperate constantly and closely. If any of these three should decide to take independent action, the results would be catastrophic. For this reason the Commanders-in-Chief of these "traditional" Services are deliberately denied the right to direct their own forces in war. Their task is to supervise all aspects of the development and equipment of their Services.

Since the Land Forces, Air Forces and Navy can only operate in close conjunction, combined command structures have been devised to control them independently of their Commanders-in-Chief. We have already encountered these combined structures—they are the Fronts, which contain elements from both Land and Air Armies, and the Strategic Directions which incorporate Fronts and Fleets.

The establishment of these combined command structures and of systems of combat control, which are not subordinated to individual Commanders-in-Chief, has made it possible to solve most of the problems which result from the rivalry which has existed between the Services for centuries.

Let us take the case of a Soviet general who is slowly climbing the rungs of his professional ladder. First he commands a motor-rifle division, then he becomes deputy to the Commander of a Tank Army (it is normal practice to move officers from motor-rifle forces to tank forces and vice versa) and next he becomes an Army Commander. Until now he has always been a fierce champion of the interests of the Land Forces, which he supports fervently. So far, though, his position has been too lowly for his views to be heard by anyone outside the Land Forces. But now he rises a little higher and becomes Commander of a Front. He now has both an operational task, for the fulfilment of which his head is at stake, and the forces with which to carry it out—three or four Land Armies and one Air Army. The Commander-in-Chief of Land Forces supplies his Land Armies with all they require, the Commander-in-Chief of Air Forces does the same for his Air Army. But it is the Front Commander who is responsible for deciding how to use these forces in combat. In this situation every Front Commander forgets, as soon as he takes over his high post, that he is an infantry or a tank general. He has to carry out his operational task and for this all his Armies—Land and Air—must be appropriately prepared and supplied. If the Air Army is worse prepared and supplied than the All-Arms and Tank Armies, the Front Commander will either immediately take steps himself to restore the balance or will call on his superiors to do this. There are sixteen Front Commanders in all. All of them are products of the Land Forces, for these provide the basic strength of each Front, but they are in no way subordinate to the Commander-in-Chief of Land Forces in questions concerning the use of their resources. It is the Front Commanders who have the task of directing their forces to victory. For this reason, if the Land Forces were to be increased at the expense of the Air Forces, all the Front Commanders would protest immediately and sharply, despite their own upbringing in the Land Forces.

If our general should climb still higher and become Commander-in-Chief of a Strategic Direction, he will have a Fleet under his control, as well as four Fronts, each of which contains a mixture of Land Forces and Air Forces.

In wartime he will be responsible for combat operations

covering huge areas and he is already concerned, in peacetime, to ensure that all the forces under his command develop proportionately and in balance with one another. In this way yesterday's tank officer becomes an ardent champion of the development not only of the Land Forces but of the Air Forces and the Navy.

3

The Armed Services consist of arms of service. At the head of each arm of service is a Commander. However, in most cases the latter has purely administrative functions. For instance, the Commander-in-Chief of Land Forces has as one of his subordinates the Commander of Tank Forces. But tens of thousands of tanks are spread throughout the world, from Cuba to Sakhalin. Every reconnaissance battalion has a tank platoon, every motor-rifle regiment has a tank battalion, every motor-rifle division has a tank regiment, every Army a tank division, every Front a Tank Army, and each Strategic Direction has a Group of Tank Armies. Naturally, decisions on the use of all these tanks in combat are taken by the combat commanders as the situation develops. The Commander of Tank Forces is in no position to play any part in the control of each tank unit, and any such intervention would be a violation of the principle of sole responsibility for the conduct and results of combat operations. For this reason, the Commander of Tank Forces is strictly forbidden to intervene in combat planning and in questions of the use of tanks in combat. His responsibilities cover the development of new types of tank and their testing, the supervision of the quality of production of tank factories, ensuring that all tank detachments are supplied with the necessary spare parts and the training of specialists in the Tank Force Academies, in the five Tank High Schools and in training divisions. He is also responsible for the technical condition of tanks in all the armed forces and acts as the inspector of all tank personnel.

The Commander of the Rocket Forces and Artillery of the Land Forces, the Commander of the Air Defence of Land Forces, the Commander of Fleet Aviation and Commanders of other arms of service have similar administrative roles.

However, there are exceptions to this rule. It is possible that some arms of service may be totally (or almost totally) deployed in a single direction. The Commanders of these arms of service have both administrative and combat roles. These arms of service include the Air Forces' Long-Range (strategic missile-carrying) Aviation and Military Transport Aviation and the Airborne Forces. In wartime, and on questions concerning the use of their forces, the Commanders of these arms of service are subordinated directly to the Stavka.

The Strategic Rocket Forces

1

The Strategic Rocket Forces (SRF) are the newest and the smallest of the five Armed Services which make up the Soviet Army. They are also the most important component of that Army.

The SRF was established as an independent Service in December 1959. At its head is a Commander-in-Chief with the title of Marshal of the Soviet Union. Under his command are three Rocket Armies, three independent Rocket Corps, ten to twelve Rocket divisions, three sizeable rocket ranges and a large number of scientific research and teaching establishments. The total strength of the SRF is about half a million.

The SRF is both an operational and an administrative organisation. In peacetime its Commander-in-Chief is responsible to the Minister of Defence on all administrative questions and to the Politburo on all aspects of the operational use of rockets. In wartime the SRF would be controlled by the Defence Council, through the Supreme Commander. A final decision on the mass use of strategic rockets would be made by the Defence Council—i.e., the Politburo.

A Rocket Army consists of ten divisions. A division is made up of ten regiments and a technical base. A rocket regiment may have from one to ten launchers, depending on the type of rocket with which it is equipped. A strategic rocket regiment is the smallest in size of any in the Soviet Army. Its fighting strength is between 250 and 400 men, depending on the type of rocket with which it is equipped. Its basic tasks are to maintain the rockets, to safeguard and defend them and to launch them. Organisationally, a rocket regiment consists of the commander, his staff, five duty launch teams, an emergency repair battery and a guard company. This sub-unit is dignified with the title of regiment solely because of the very great responsibility which its officers bear.

Each regiment has an underground command post in which there is always a duty team of officers with direct communication links with the divisional commander, the Army commander, the commander-in-chief of the SRF and the Central command post. If this underground post goes out of action, the commander of the regiment immediately deploys a mobile control point working from motor vehicles. In a threatening situation two teams are on duty simultaneously—one in the underground command post and the other at a mobile one—so that either could take over the firing of all the regiment's rockets.

According to the situation, the duty teams at command posts are changed either every week or every month.

If a launcher is damaged, it is dismantled by the regiment's emergency repair battery. The guard company is responsible for the protection of the command posts and of the launchers. A large proportion of the regiment's personnel are involved in guard duties. Not one of them will have seen a rocket or know anything about one. Their job is to guard snow-covered clearings in pine forests, clearings which are surrounded by dozens of rows of barbed wire and defended by minefields. The guard company of a rocket regiment has fifty or so guard dogs.

The principal task of a rocket division is the technical supply of its regiments. For this, a divisional commander has under him a sub-unit known as a technical base, which has a complement of 3,000–4,000 and is commanded by a colonel. The technical base carries out the transport, maintenance, replacement, repair and servicing of the regiment's rockets.

The strength of a rocket division is 7,000–8,000.

The headquarters of each Rocket Army is responsible for coordination of the operations of its divisions, which will be deployed throughout a very large area. In a critical situation, the headquarters of a Rocket Army may make use of flying command posts to direct the firing of the rockets of regiments and divisions whose command posts have been put out of action.

The independent Rocket Corps are organised by the Rocket Armies, except that they have three or four rather than ten divisions. They are also armed with comparatively short-range rockets (3,000–6,000 kilometres), some of which are fired from mobile rather than from fixed underground launchers.

The existence of the rocket corps is due to the fact that while the three Rocket Armies come under the exclusive control of the Supreme Commander, they are needed to support the forces of the three main Strategic Directions and are at the disposal of the Commanders-in-Chief of these Directions. A whole Corps, or some of its divisions, can be used in support of advancing forces in any of the Directions.

Separate rocket divisions, subordinated directly to the Commander-in-Chief of the SRF, form his operational reserve. Some of these divisions are equipped with particularly powerful rockets. The rest have standard rockets and can be moved to any part of the Soviet Union, in order to reduce their vulnerability.

2

The Strategic Rocket Forces have a much revered father figure. If he did not exist neither would the SRF. His name is Fidel Castro: you may smile, but the SRF does not.

The story behind this is as follows. In 1959 Castro and his comrades seized power in Cuba. No one in Washington was alarmed by this and no reaction came from Moscow; it was seen as a routine Latin American coup-d'état. However, it was not long before Washington became uneasy and Moscow began to show interest. The Kremlin saw an unexpected chance to loosen the hold of its hated enemy, capitalism, on the Western hemisphere. This was obviously an excellent opportunity but one which it seemed impossible to exploit because of lack of strength on the spot. Hitherto, the Soviet Union had been able to support allies of this sort with tanks. But how could it help Fidel Castro at the other side of the ocean? At that time the Soviet Fleet could not dream of trying to take on the US Navy, particularly on the latter's own doorstep. Strategic aircraft existed but only for parades and demonstrations of strength. How could the United States be dissuaded from stepping in?

There was a simple, brilliant solution—bluff.

It was decided to make use of a weapon which had not yet come into service—what Goebbels would have called a "miracle weapon." For a miracle weapon was what the Politburo employed. Throughout 1959 there were top-priority firings of Soviet rockets and persistent rumours of extraordinary successes. In December rumours began to circulate about new, top-secret forces which were all-powerful, highly accurate, invulnerable, indestructible and so forth. These rumours were supported by the appointment of Marshal of Artillery M. I. Nedelin to a highly important position of some sort, with promotion to Chief Marshal of Artillery. In January 1960 Khrushchev announced the formation of the Strategic Rocket Forces, with Nedelin at their head. He followed this with claims that nothing would be able to withstand these forces, that they could reach any point on the globe, etc. Talking to journalists, Khrushchev revealed "in confidence" that he had been to a factory where he had seen rockets "tumbling off the conveyor belts, just like sausages." (Incidentally, then, as now, the supply of sausages was presenting the USSR with acute problems.) The West, unaccustomed to dealing with so high-level a charlatan, was duly impressed and consequently there was no invasion of Cuba. During the drama which took place, Khrushchev took to making fierce threats about "pressing the button."

At the moment when the establishment of the SRF was announced, a Force equal in standing to the Land Forces and said to far exceed the latter in striking power, at the moment when Marshal Nedelin's headquarters was established, with great show, the Soviet rocket forces consisted of four regiments armed with 8-Zh-38 rockets (copies of the German V.2) and one range, on which experiments with new Soviet rockets were being carried out. The figures for rocket production were negligible. All the rockets that were made were immediately used for demonstrations in space while the newly formed divisions received nothing but replicas, which were shown off at parades and in films. Empty dummies, resembling rockets, were splendidly designated "dimensional substitutes." Meanwhile, a hectic race was in progress to produce real, operational rockets. Accidents occurred, one after another. On 24 October, 1960, when an experimental 8-K-63 rocket blew up, the Commander-in-Chief of the Strategic Rocket Forces, Chief Marshal Nedelin, and his entire staff were burned alive . . .

However, the SRF had won its first battle, the battle for Cuba.

3

As time passed, the SRF became able to stand on its own feet. But the bluff continues. The American armed forces refer modestly to fifty intercontinental ballistic missiles as a Squadron. The Soviet Army builds at least five Regiments around this number of missiles. Alternately if the rockets are obsolescent they may form a Rocket Division or even a Rocket Corps.

The Americans do not classify a thousand rockets as a separate Service, or even as an individual arm of service. They are just part of the US Air Force's Strategic Air Command. In the USSR fifteen hundred rockets make up a complete Service, commanded by a Marshal of the Soviet Union.

At present, the Americans are armed, essentially, with a single type of intercontinental rocket, the "Minuteman." In the Soviet Union there are more than ten different types, amounting to approximately the same total as the Americans possess. Why this lack of coordination? Because not one of them is of really good quality. Some lack accuracy, and have too low a payload and too short a range, but they are kept in service because they are more reliable than other types. Others are retained because their accuracy is more or less acceptable. Others are neither accurate nor reliable but have a good range. But there is one other reason for this untidy situation, for this multiplicity of types. The fact is that the rocket forces have been developed piecemeal, like a patchwork quilt. Soviet industry is unable to turn out long production runs of rockets quickly. For this reason, while the factories are familiarising themselves with the manufacture of one type and beginning slowly to produce it, another type is being brought just as slowly into service. Familiarisation with this new type starts, in a dilatory way, and a small production run begins, with equal lack of haste, and thus, year by year, the Rocket Forces expand, gradually and in leisurely fashion. Often a really good rocket can only be produced in small numbers because the United States will only sell a small quantity of the parts needed for it. For example, if the Americans only sell seventy-nine precision fuel filters, the Soviets will be unable to produce more than this number of rockets. Some of these will be allocated for experimental use and the number available for operational deployment therefore becomes smaller still. It is then necessary to design a new rocket without high-precision filters but with electronic equipment to control the ignition process. But then, perhaps, it is only possible to purchase two hundred sets of this electronic equipment from the US. A first-class rocket, but no more than two hundred can be produced . . .

4

The SRF faces another, even more critical problem—its hunger for uranium. The shortage of uranium and plutonium has led the Soviet Union to produce extremely high-powered thermonuclear warheads with a TNT equivalent of scores of megatons. One of the reasons for this was the poor accuracy of the rockets; in order to offset this it became necessary to increase drastically the yield of the warheads. But this was not the most important consideration. The fundamental reason was that a thermonuclear charge, whatever its yield, needs only one nuclear detonator. The shortage of uranium and plutonium made it necessary to produce a comparatively small quantity of thermonuclear warheads and to compensate for this by increasing their yield.

The Soviet Union has put a lot of work into the problem of producing a thermonuclear warhead in which reaction is brought about not by a nuclear detonator but by some other means—for instance, by the simultaneous explosion of a large number of hollow charges. This is very difficult to achieve, for if just one charge functions a thousandth of a second early, it will scatter all the others. American electronic equipment is needed to solve the problem—high-precision timers, which will deliver impulses to all the charges simultaneously. There are some grounds for believing that timers of this sort may be sold to the Soviet Union and, if this happens, the SRF will acquire titanic strength. Meanwhile, not all Soviet rockets have warheads. There are not enough for every rocket, so that, at present, use is being made of radioactive material which is, quite simply, waste produced by nuclear power stations—radioactive dust. Rather than launch a rocket without a warhead, the wretched thing might as well be used to scatter dust in the enemy's eyes . . . Naturally, scattering small quantities of dust over wide areas of enemy territory, even if it is highly radio-active, will not do much damage and it will certainly not decide the outcome of a war. But what can one do if one has nothing better?

However, naturally, the SRF must not be underestimated. Rapid technical progress is being made and Soviet engineers are skilfully steering a course between the technological ice-bergs which confront them, sometimes achieving astounding successes, brilliant in their simplicity.

The technical balance could change very quickly, if the West does not press forward with the development of its own equipment as quickly and as decisively as the Soviet Union is doing.

The National Air Defence Forces

1

The National Air Defence Forces (ADF) are the third most important of the five Services which make up the Soviet Armed Forces, after the Strategic Rocket Forces and the Land Forces. However, we will examine them at this point, directly after the SRF, since like the latter they represent not simply an administrative structure but a unified, controlled combat organisation, subordinated directly to the Supreme Commander. Because they form a unified combat organisation, the ADF are always commanded by a Marshal of the Soviet Union. The Land Forces, which are five times the size of the ADF, and which represent the striking force of the Soviet Union in Europe, are headed only by a General of the Army.

2

In the armed forces of any other country, responsibility for air defence is laid upon its air forces. In the Soviet Union, the air defence system was so highly developed that it would be quite impossible to confine it within the organisational structure of the Air Forces. Moreover, the ADF are the third most important Service while the Air Forces occupy fourth place.

The independence of the ADF from the Air Forces is due not only to their size and to their technical development, but also to the overall Soviet philosophy concerning the allocation of wartime roles. In any country in which Soviet specialists are given the task of setting up or restructuring the armed forces, they establish several parallel systems of air defence. One is a static system, designed to defend the territory of the country and the most important administrative, political, economic and transport installations which it contains. This is a copy of the ADF. In addition, separate systems for self-defence and protection against air attack are set up in the land forces, the navy and the air force.

While the national defence system is static, those of the different armed services are mobile, designed to move alongside the forces which they exist to protect. If several systems find themselves operating in the same area, they work with one another and in such a case their collaboration is always organised by the national system.

3

The division of the ADF into a national system and another system for the protection of the armed services took place long before the Second World War. All anti-aircraft artillery and all searchlight and sound-ranging units were divided between those under the command of army and naval commanders and those covering the most important civil installations, which are not subordinated to army commanders but had their own control apparatus. The fighter aircraft available were divided in the same way. In 1939, for instance, forty air regiments (1,640 combat aircraft) were transferred from the strength of the Air Forces to that of the ADF, for both administrative and combat purposes. Mixed ADF units were formed from the anti-aircraft artillery, searchlight and air sub-units, which succeeded in co-operating very closely with one another.

During the war the ADF completed their development into a separate, independent constituent of the Armed Forces, on an equal footing with the Land Forces, the Air Forces and the Navy. During the war, too, the development of fighter aircraft designed specifically for either the Air Forces or the ADF was begun. Flying training schools were set up to train ADF pilots, using different teaching programmes from those of the Air Forces. Subsequently, anti-aircraft gunnery schools were established, some of which trained officers for anti-aircraft units of the Land Forces and Navy while others prepared officers for the anti-aircraft units of the ADF. After the war, the teams designing anti-aircraft guns for the Armed Forces were directed to develop especially powerful anti-aircraft guns for the ADF.

At the end of the war the total strength of the ADF was more than one million, divided into four ADF fronts (each with two or three armies) and three independent ADF Armies.

After the war the ADF was given official status as an independent Armed Service.

4

Today the ADF has more than 600,000 men. For administrative purposes they are divided into three arms of service:

> ADF Fighter Aviation
> ADF Surface-to-air Missile Forces
> ADF Radar Forces

For greater efficiency and closer cooperation, the sub-units of these three arms of service are brought together to form mixed units—ADF Divisions, Corps, Armies and Fronts (in peacetime Fronts are known as ADF Districts).

The fact that 3,000 combat aircraft, among them some of the most advanced, have no operational, financial, administrative or any other connection with the Air Forces, has not been grasped by ordinary individuals in the West, nor even by Western military specialists. It is therefore necessary to repeat that the ADF rate as a separate and independent Armed Service, with 3,000 supersonic interceptor aircraft, 12,000 anti-aircraft missile launchers and 6,000 radar installations.

It is because the ADF are responsible both for the protection of Soviet territory and of the most important installations in the USSR that they function independently. Since they are concerned mainly with the defence of stationary targets, the fighter aircraft developed for them differ from those with which the Air Forces are equipped. The ADF are also equipped with surface-to-air missiles and radar installations which differ from those used by the Land Forces and by the Navy.

The Air Forces have their own fighter aircraft, totalling several thousand. The Land Forces have thousands of their own anti-aircraft missile launchers, anti-aircraft guns and radar installations. The Navy, too, has its own fighters, anti-aircraft missiles and guns and radar, and all of these belong to the individual Armed Service rather than to the ADF, and are used to meet the requirements of the operational commanders of the Land Forces, Air Forces and Navy. We will discuss these independent air defence systems later; for the moment we will confine ourselves to the national defence system.

5

The fighter aircraft of the ADF are organised as regiments. In all, the ADF has more than seventy regiments, each with forty aircraft.

The ADF cannot, of course, use fighter aircraft built for the Air Forces, any more than the latter can use aircraft built to the designs fo the ADF. The Air Forces and the ADF operate under entirely different conditions and have different operational tasks and each Service therefore has its particular requirements from its own aircraft.

The ADF operates from permanent airfields and can therefore use heavy fighter aircraft. The fighter aircraft of the Air Forces are constantly on the move behind the Land Forces and must therefore operate from very poor airfields, sometimes with grass runways or even from sections of road. They are therefore much lighter than the aircraft used by the ADF.

ADF fighters are assisted in their operations by extremely powerful radar and guidance systems, which direct the aircraft to their targets from the ground. These aircraft do not therefore need to be highly manoeuvrable but every effort is made to increase their speed, their operational ceiling and range. The Air Forces require different qualities from their fighter aircraft, which are lighter, since they have to operate in constantly changing situations, and from their pilots, who have to work unassisted, locating and attacking their targets for themselves. The Air Force fighters therefore need to be both light and highly manoeuvrable but they are considerably inferior to those of the ADF in speed, range, payload and ceiling.

Let us look at an example of these two different approaches to the design of fighter aircraft. The MIG-23 is extremely light and manoeuvrable and is able to operate from any airfield, including those with grass runways. Clearly, it is an aircraft for the Air Forces. By contrast, the MIG-25, although designed by the same group, at the same time, is extremely heavy and unmanoeuvrable and can operate only from long and very stable concrete runways, but it has gained twelve world records for range, speed, rate of climb and altitude. For two decades this was the fastest operational aircraft in the world. It is easy to see that this is an ADF fighter.

Besides the MIG-25, which is a high-altitude interceptor, the ADF have a low-level interceptor, the SU 15, and a long-range interceptor, the TU 128, which is designed to attack enemy aircraft attempting to penetrate Soviet air space across the endless wastes of the Arctic or the deserts of Central Asia.

The Surface-to-air Missile (SAM) Forces of the ADF consist, organisationally, of rocket brigades (each with 10 to 12 launch battalions), regiments (3 to 5 launch battalions) and independent launch battalions. Each battalion has 6 to 8 launchers, according to the type of rocket with which it is equipped. Each battalion has between 80 and 120 men. First, all battalions were equipped with S 75 rockets. Then, to replace these, two rockets, the S 125 (low-altitude and short-range) and the S 200 (high-altitude and long-range), were developed. The S 200 can be fitted with a nuclear warhead to destroy enemy rockets or aircraft. Also introduced, to destroy the enemy's inter-continental ballistic missiles, was the UR 100, which has a particularly powerful warhead, but the deployment of this type has been limited by the US-Soviet ABM Treaty.

Each SAM battalion is equipped with several anti-aircraft guns of small (23mm) and large (57mm) calibre. These are used to repel either low-flying enemy aircraft or attacks by enemy land forces. In peacetime, these anti-aircraft guns are not classified as a separate arm of service of the ADF. However, in wartime, when the strength of the ADF would be increased three or four times, they would form an arm of service, deployed as anti-aircraft artillery regiments and divisions, equipped with 23, 57, 85, 100 and 130mm guns, which are mothballed in peacetime.

The Radar Forces of the ADF consist of brigades and regiments, together with a number of independent battalions and companies. They are equipped with several thousand radar installations, for the detection of enemy aircraft and space weapons and for the guidance towards these targets of ADF robot and interceptor aircraft.

In addition to these three main arms of service, the complement of the ADF includes many supporting sub-units (providing transport, communications, guard duties and administration), two military academies and eleven higher officers' schools, together with a considerable number of test-ranges, institutes for scientific research and training centres.

6

Operationally the ADF consists of a Central Command Post, two ADF Districts, which would become ADF Fronts in wartime, eight independent ADF Armies and several independent ADF Corps.

Up to regimental and brigade level ADF formations are drawn from a single arm of service—for example from SAM brigades, fighter regiments, independent radar battalions, etc. From division level upwards, each arm of service is represented in each formation and these are therefore called ADF Divisions, Corps, etc.

The organisation of each division, corps or other higher formation is decided in accordance with the importance of the installation which it is protecting. However, there is one guiding principle: each commander is responsible for the defence of one key point only. This principle is uniformly applied at all levels.

The commander of an ADF division is responsible for the protection of a single, highly important installation, for instance, of a large power-supply centre. He is also required to prevent incursions by enemy aircraft over his sector. The division therefore deploys one SAM brigade to cover the main installation, and moves two or three SAM regiments into the areas most likely to be threatened, ahead of the brigades, and a number of independent SAM battalions into areas which are in less danger. In addition, the divisional commander has one air regiment which may be used to make contact with the enemy at a considerable distance, for operations at boundaries or junctions not covered by SAM fire, or in the area in which the enemy delivers his main thrust. The operations of the SAM sub-units and of the interceptor aircraft are supported by radar battalions and companies which are subordinated both to the divisional commander himself and to the commanding officers of the division's SAM units.

An ADF corps commander organises coverage of the target he is protecting in precisely the same way. To protect the main installation itself he has one ADF division. Both he and his divisional commander are involved in the defence of the same installation. Two or three SAM brigades are moved forward to cover the sectors which are under greatest threat, while SAM regiments are deployed in less endangered areas. One air regiment is under the direct command of the corps commander, for long-range use or for operations in the area in which the enemy delivers his main attack. If the SAM sub-units are put out of action, the corps commander can at any time make use of his fighter regiment to cover an area in which a breakthrough is threatened. Thus there are two air regiments with each ADF Corps, one at the disposal of the ADF divisional commander, the other for use by the corps commander. A corps contains three or four SAM brigades, one with the ADF division, the others at the disposal of the corps commander, covering the approaches to the divisional position. In a corps there are five or six SAM regiments, two or three of which are used in the division's main sector, the remainder in the secondary sectors of the corps area. Lastly, the corps commander himself has a radar regiment, in addition to the radar forces of his subordinates.

An ADF Army commander, too, is responsible for the protection of a single key objective and has an ADF corps to cover it. In addition, an Army has two or three independent ADF divisions, each of which provides cover for its own key installation and also defends the main approaches to the key objective guarded by the Army. Independent SAM brigades are deployed in the secondary sectors of the Army's area. An Army commander also has two air regiments (one with aircraft for high-altitude operations, the other with long-range interceptors) and his own radar installations (including over-the-horizon radars).

An ADF District is similar in structure. The key objective is covered by an Army. Two or three independent ADF corps are deployed in the sectors under greatest threat while the less endangered areas are covered by ADF divisions, each of which, of course, has a key objective of its own. The District Commander also has two interceptor air regiments under his command and radar detection facilities, including very large aircraft equipped with powerful radars.

The nerve centre—Moscow—is, of course, covered by an ADF District: the main approaches to this District by ADF Armies and the secondary sectors by ADF corps. Each District and Army has, of course, the task of covering a key installation of its own.

The ADF contains two ADF Districts. Something must be said about the reasons for the existence of the second of these—the Baku District. Unlike the Moscow District, the Baku ADF District does not have a key target to protect. The fact that Baku produces oil is irrelevant; twenty-four times as much oil is produced in the Tatarstan area as in Baku. The Baku ADF District looks southwards, covering a huge area along the frontiers, which is unlikely to be attacked. Several of the armies of the ADF (the 9th, for instance), have considerably greater combat resources than the whole Baku District. It is, however, because of the need to watch such a huge area, a task for which an ADF Army has insufficient capacity, that a District was established there.

All in all, the ADF is the most powerful system of its sort in the world. It has at its disposal not only the largest quantity of equipment but in some respects the best equipment in the world. At the beginning of the 1980s the MIG-25 interceptor was the fastest in the world and the S-200 had the largest yield and the greatest range of any surface-to-air missile. In the period since the war the Soviet Air Defence Forces have shown their strength on many occasions. They did this most strikingly on 1 May, 1960, by shooting down an American U-2 reconnaissance aircraft, a type regarded until then as invulnerable, because of the incredible height at which it could operate. There is no doubt that the Soviet Air Defence Forces are the most experienced in the world. What other system can boast of having spent as many years fighting the most modern air force in the world as the Soviet ADF system in Vietnam?

In the mid-1970s some doubt arose as to its reliability when a South Korean aircraft lost its way and flew over Soviet Arctic territory for some considerable time before being forced down by a Soviet SU-15 interceptor. However, the reasons for this delay can be fully explained; we have noted that interceptor aircraft do not represent the main strength of the ADF, which lies in its surface-to-air missiles. The territory across which the lost aircraft flew was quite unusually well-equipped with SAMs, but there is simply no reason to use them against a civil aircraft. At the same time, because of the deep snow which lay in the area, hardly any interceptors were stationed there. Their absence was compensated for by an abnormally large number of SAMs, ready to shoot down any military aircraft. In this unusual situation, once the invader had been found to be a civil aircraft, it became necessary to use an interceptor brought from a great distance. This aircraft took off from Lodeynoye Polye and flew more than 1,000 kilometres, in darkness, to meet the intruder. In an operational situation it would not have been necessary to do this. It would be simpler to use a rocket.

Nevertheless, despite everything, the ADF has its Achilles heel. The fastest aircraft are flown by men who detest socialism with all their hearts. The pilot Byelenko is by no means unique in the ADF.

The Land Forces

1

The Land Forces are the oldest, the largest and the most diversified of the Services making up the Armed Forces of the Red Army. In peacetime their strength totals approximately 2 million, but mobilisation would bring them up to between 21 and 23 million within ten days.

They contain seven arms of service:

Motor-rifle Troops
Tank Troops
Artillery and Rocket Troops of the Land Forces
Air Defence Troops of the Land Forces
Airborne Assault Troops
Diversionary Troops (Spetsnaz)
Fortified Area Troops

The existence of the last three is kept secret.

In their organisation and operational strength, the Land Forces can be seen as a scaled-down model of the entire Soviet Armed Forces. Just take a look at their structure: the Strategic Rocket Forces are subordinated to the Stavka; the Land Forces have their own rocket troops; the Air Defence Forces are subordinated to the Stavka; the Land Forces have their own air defence troops. They also have their own aircraft, which are independent of the Air Force. The Air Defence Forces, in their numbers and equipment the strongest in the world, are subordinated to the Stavka; the Land Forces also have their own airborne troops which, using the same yardstick, are the second strongest in the world.

The Commander-in-Chief of the Land Forces has no more than an administrative function. His headquarters contains neither an Operational nor an Intelligence Directorate. All operational planning is carried out by the mixed commands of the Fronts, Strategic Directions or General Staff. The Commander-in-Chief's responsibilities are limited to the equipment, provisioning and training of his forces. However, despite the fact that he has no responsibility for the direction of operations the C-in-C Land Forces is still a highly influential administrator. Clearly, anyone who is responsible for the development and supply of forty-one Armies, including eight Tank Armies, deserves respect.

The Commanders of the various arms of service of the Land Forces, too, have purely administrative functions. The direction of operations, as we already know, is the function of mixed all-arms commands, which are not subordinated for this function to either the C-in-C or the Commanders of individual arms of service.

2

The Motor-Rifle Troops

Each motor-rifle section has a strength of eleven. One man acts as assistant to the rocket launcher and is jokingly referred to as the missile transporter. He does indeed carry three rockets, in a satchel. Each of these has a warhead capable of penetrating the armour of any modern tank, booster and sustainer engines, a spin stabiliser, a turbine, a fin assembly and a tracer compound.

His are not the only rockets in the section. It is also equipped with anti-aircraft rockets with seeker heads, which enable them to distinguish hostile aircraft from friendly ones and to destroy them. In addition, the section has four 9-M-14 "Malyutka" rockets which have an automatic guidance system. All this in one infantry section.

The section's BMP-1 combat vehicle has an automatic 73mm gun and three machine guns and has sufficient fire-power, manoeuvrability and protection to take on any modern light tank. The section also has three radio sets, sensors for the detection of radioactivity and gas and other complex devices in addition to its ordinary infantry equipment.

At this, the lowest, level, we find not a true infantry formation but a hybrid of tank, anti-tank, SAM, chemical, sapper and other sub-units.

The infantry is the oldest of the arms of service. All the remainder originated later and were developed as additions or reinforcements to the infantry. From our examination of the infantry section we see that the modern infantry is an arm of service which, even at its lowest level, has absorbed elements of many others.

The concept of the infantry, not as cannon fodder, but as the framework of the entire Armed Forces, the skeleton on which the whole of the remainder develops, has been held for a long time by Soviet generals. After the last war, all Soviet infantry officer training schools were renamed Officer Cadet Academies, and began to turn out, not run-of-the-mill platoon commanders, but commanders with a wide range of knowledge, able to organise cooperation between all arms of service in the battlefield, in order to ensure joint success.

It is for this reason that today's officers are not called either infantry or motor-rifle commanders, but all-arms commanders.

The organisation of a normal Soviet regiment which, by tradition, is still called a motor-rifle regiment, is as follows:

Command headquarters
Reconnaissance company
Signals company
Tank battalion (three companies)
Three motor-rifle battalions (each of three companies and one automatic mortar battery)
A battalion of self-propelled howitzers (three fire batteries and one control battery)
A battery of Grad-P multiple rocket launchers
A SAM battery
An engineer company
A chemical defence company
A maintenance company
A motor transport company

In all, the regiment has 27 companies, only 9 of which are motor-rifle companies. It is significant that, in a so-called "mo-

tor-rifle" regiment, there are 10 artillery battery commanders—
that is to say, one more than the number of motor-rifle company
commanders.

If we move a little higher, to the level of a division, we
find that, surprisingly, it is still referred to as a "motor-rifle"
division. We will look at the organisation of a motor-rifle
division later; for the present we will simply note that it contains
a total of 165 companies and batteries. Of these only 28 are
motor-rifle companies; it also has 23 tank companies and 67
artillery batteries (mortar, anti-aircraft and rocket). The remainder is made up of reconnaissance, signal and engineer,
chemical and other companies.

The motor-rifle troops make up the bulk of the Soviet forces.
Organisationally, they consist of 123 divisions and of an additional 47 regiments, which form part of the complement of
tank divisions. In addition, there are motor-rifle battalions serving in fortified areas and also with the Navy's marine infantry
brigades.

In peacetime motor-rifle sub-units are divided into those
with normal equipment (armoured personnel carriers) and those
equipped with infantry combat vehicles (BMPs). This is today's
version of the age-old division between light and heavy infantry, between grenadiers and chasseurs.

In theory all motor-rifle regiments in tank divisions and one
regiment in each motor-rifle division should be equipped with
BMPs. In practice, this depends upon the output of the defence
industries and upon their ability to supply combat equipment
to the forces. In many inland military districts divisions have
not received the BMPs allocated to them. By contrast, divisions
stationed in East Germany have two rather than one BMP
regiment.

Sub-units equipped with BMPs have much greater fire- and
striking-power than their normal motor-rifle equivalents. This
is not only because a BMP has better protection, armament
and manoeuvrability than an armoured personnel carrier. BMP
sub-units also have far more supporting weapons. For instance,
a motor-rifle battalion stationed on Soviet territory has a mortar
platoon. An equivalent BMP battalion has a battery instead of
a platoon. Moreover, these are not standard but automatic mortars, and they are self-propelled rather than towed. A standard
motor-rifle regiment has a howitzer battery, or in some cases
a battalion of towed howitzers. A BMP regiment has a howitzer

battalion equipped with self-propelled amphibious howitzers and a further battery of "Grad-P" multiple rocket launchers.

BMP sub-units are the first to receive new anti-tank, anti-aircraft, engineering and communications equipment. They are, in fact, the trump suit in the pack.

3

The Tank Forces

The Tank Forces represent the main striking power of the Land Forces. Their organisation is simple and well-defined. Every unit commander has his own tank assault force, of a size appropriate to his position. The commander of a motor-rifle division has a tank battalion at his disposal. The commander of a motor-rifle division has his own tank regiment. An Army commander has one tank division and a Front Commander a Tank Army. Finally, the Commander-in-Chief of a Strategic Direction has a Group of Tank Armies. Combat operations at each level are organised according to the established principles. An advance by a motor-rifle regiment is, essentially, an advance by a tank battalion which is supported by all the other battalions and companies of the regiment. This principle applies at all levels. You could, in fact, say that an advance by a Strategic Direction is really a break-through by a Tank Army Group supported by the operations of the three or four Fronts which belong to that Direction.

In addition to this basic striking force, Front Commanders and C-in-Cs of Strategic Directions may keep independent tank divisions in reserve, using them for rapid relief of the divisions which suffer the worst losses. Besides this, however, each commander, from divisional level upwards, has what might be called a personal tank guard. Besides the tank regiment which is his main striking force, a division commander has an independent tank battalion. Thus, a motor-rifle division has seven tank battalions in all: one in each of its three motor-rifle regiments, three in its tank regiment and the independent battalion. This battalion is entirely different from the others. Whereas the ordinary tank battalions have 31 tanks (3 companies of 10 each and one for the battalion commander), an independent battalion has 52 tanks (5 companies of 10 each, one for the battalion commander and the divisional commander's own tank). Unlike the others, an independent tank battalion has reconnaissance, anti-aircraft, engineer and chemical platoons. In its make-up it is more like a small, independent tank regiment than a large battalion. In addition, the independent tank battalions are the first to receive the latest equipment. I have seen many divisions equipped with T-44 tanks while the independent tank battalions had T-10Ms, which have then received T-55s, while the independent battalions got T-72s. The divisional commander will carefully and patiently assemble all his best crews in this battalion. The commander of a motor-rifle regiment will throw his tank battalion into the thick of a battle, and a divisional commander will do the same with his tank regiment but he will keep his independent tank battalions in reserve. These protect, respectively, the division's headquarters and the division's rocket battalion. These are not, of course, their main functions, but fall to the lot of the independent battalions because they almost always function as reserves.

But let us suppose that during a battle a situation arises in which a commander must throw in everything he has, a situation which can result in either victory or disaster. This is the moment at which he brings his own personal guard into the operation, a fresh, fully-rested battalion, of unusual size, made up of his best crews and equipped with the best tanks. At this moment a divisional commander is risking everything and for this reason he may head this, his own independent, tank battalion.

An Army Commander, too, in addition to the tank division which forms his striking force, has an independent tank battalion to act as his personal guard. He puts it into action only at the last possible moment and it may be with this battalion that he meets his own death in battle. In addition to his Tank Army, each Front Commander has an independent tank brigade, consisting of the best crews in the whole Front and equipped with the best tanks. Normally a Front's independent tank brigade has four or five battalions and one motor-rifle battalion. The commander of a Strategic Direction, too, has his personal tank guard, in addition to his Tank Army Group. This guard consists of a single independent tank division or, in some cases, of a tank corps made up of two divisions.

In all, the Tank Forces have 47 tank divisions, 127 regiments, serving with motor-rifle divisions and more than 500 battalions, either serving with motor-rifle regiments or acting as reserves for commanders of varying ranks. In peacetime their total strength is 54,000 tanks.

4

The Artillery and Rocket Troops of the Land Forces

After the end of the Second World War, the Rocket Troops were treated as a separate arm of service, not forming part of any one of the Armed Services but subordinated directly to the Minister of Defence. In 1959 they were split up. The Strategic Rocket Forces were established as a separate Armed Service. Those rocket troops who were not absorbed by the new Service were taken over by the Land forces and united with the Artillery to form the Artillery and Rocket Troops, as one of the constituent arms of service of the Land Forces.

At present this arm of service is equipped with four types of artillery—rocket, rocket launcher (multi-barrelled, salvo-firing), anti-tank and general purpose (mortars, howitzers and field guns). Each commander has at his disposal the artillery resources appropriate to his rank. Commanders of divisions and upwards have some of each of all four types of artillery weapon. Thus a motor-rifle division has one rocket battalion, one battalion of multi-barrelled rocket launchers, one anti-tank battalion and a howitzer regiment of three battalions for general support. We will discuss the quantity of fire weapons available to commanders of differing ranks when we come to talk about operational organisation.

5

The Air Defence Troops of the Land Forces

We have already spoken of the existence of two separate air defence systems—national and military. The two are unconnected: the difference between them is that the national system protects the territory of the Soviet Union and is therefore stationary while the military system is an integral part of the fighting services and moves with them in order to protect them from air attack.

Organisationally, each infantry section, with the exception of those which travel in platoon commanders' vehicles, contains one soldier armed with a "Strela 2" anti-aircraft rocket launcher. There are two such launchers in each platoon. The seeker heads with which they are fitted enable rockets fired from these launchers to shoot down enemy aircraft flying at heights of two kilometres and at distances of four kilometres. In every tank platoon, in addition to the anti-aircraft machine-guns carried by each tank, one of the leaders has three of these launchers, which are carried on the outside of the tank's turret.

Each motor-rifle and tank regiment has an anti-aircraft battery, armed with 4 ZSU-23-4 "Shilka" self-propelled rocket launchers and with 4 "Strela 1" launchers (known in the West as the SA-9). These two systems complement each other and are highly effective, the Shilka especially so. I have watched a Shilka working from a stony, ploughed field, belching out an uninterrupted blast of fire against small balloons released, without warning, from a wood a couple of kilometres away. The results it achieved were quite overwhelming. The British reference book, *Jane's,* is quite right to describe the Shilka as the best in the world.

The officer in charge of the anti-aircraft defence of each motor-rifle and tank regiment coordinates the operations of his battery and also those of all the Strela-2 launchers.

Each motor-rifle and tank division has one SAM regiment, armed with "Kub" (SA-6) or "Romb" (SA-8) rockets. Each Army has one SAM brigade, armed with "Krug" (SA-4) rockets.

In addition to all these, a Front Commander has under his command two SAM brigades with "Krug" rockets, several regiments with "Kubs" or "Rombs" and several AAA regiments, armed with 57mm and 100mm anti-aircraft guns.

6

The Airborne Assault Troops

Although the Airborne Assault troops wear the same uniform as airborne troops, they have no connection with them. Airborne troops are under the direct control of the Supreme Commander; they use transport aircraft and parachutes for their operations. By contrast, the Airborne Assault troops form part of the Land Forces and are operationally subordinate to a Front Commander. They are transported by helicopter and do not use parachutes. Moreover, their sub-units use helicopters not only as a means of transport but as fighting weapons.

In Soviet eyes, the helicopter has nothing in common with conventional aircraft; it is regarded virtually as a tank. At first this may seem a strange idea, but it is undeniably well founded. No aircraft can seize enemy territory; this is done by tanks, artillery and infantry working together. Helicopters are therefore regarded as belonging to the Land Forces, as tanks which do not fear minefields, mountains or water obstacles, as tanks with high fire-power and great speed but which have only limited protection.

The airborne assault troops were established in 1969. Their "father" and guardian angel was Mao. If he had never existed nor would they. Soviet generals had been pressing for their introduction since the beginning of the 1950s, but there were never sufficient resources for their creation and the decision to bring them into service was postponed from one five-year plan to another. However, in 1969, armed clashes took place on the frontier with China, and Soviet generals declared that they could only defend a line 7,000 kilometres in length with tanks which could be concentrated within a few hours at any one of the sectors of this enormous frontier. So the MI-24 made its appearance—a flying tank which no weapon has yet managed to shoot down in Afghanistan.

Military helicopters, which thus originated primarily as a weapon against China, actually made their first appearance with the Soviet forces in Eastern Europe. This was because the situation on the Chinese frontier improved; that on the frontiers with the West can never improve.

Organisationally, the airborne assault troops consist of brigades, subordinated to Front Commanders. Each brigade is made up of one helicopter assault regiment (64 aircraft), one squadron of MI-26 heavy transport helicopters and three airborne rifle battalions.

The airborne assault brigade is used in the main axis of advance of a Front in conjunction with a Tank Army and under cover provided by an Air Army.

In addition to this brigade, a Front also has other airborne assault sub-units, which do not represent part of its establishment. Each Army has one helicopter transport regiment, which is used to air-lift ordinary motor-rifle sub-units behind the enemy's front line. In each motor-rifle regiment, one battalion in three is trained, in peacetime, for operations with helicopters. Thus each division has three battalions trained for this purpose and each Army has thirteen such battalions.

Airborne assault forces are growing continually. Very soon we can expect to see airborne assault brigades with every Army and airborne assault divisions with every Front.

7

Diversionary Troops (SPETSNAZ)

Diversionary troops, too, wear the same uniform as airborne troops without having any connection with them. Unlike airborne assault troops, they are parachuted from aircraft into the enemy's rear areas. However, they differ from normal airborne troops in not having heavy equipment and in operating more covertly.

These SPETSNAZ forces form the airborne forces of the Land Forces. They are used in the enemy's rear to carry out reconnaissance, to assassinate important political or military figures and to destroy headquarters, command posts, communications centres and nuclear weapons.

Each all-arms or tank army has one SPETSNAZ company, with a complement of 115, of whom 9 are officers and 11 are ensigns. This company operates in areas between 100 and 500 kilometres behind the enemy's front line. It consists of a headquarters, three diversionary platoons and a communications platoon. Depending on the tasks to be carried out, the officers and men of the company divide into as many as 15 diversionary groups, but during an operation they may work first as a single unit, then split into 3 or 4 groups, then into 15 and then back again into one.

Usually, SPETSNAZ companies are dropped the night before an Army begins an advance, at a moment when the anti-aircraft and the other resources of the enemy are under greatest pressure. Thereafter, they operate ahead of the advancing sub-units of the Army.

Each Front has a SPETSNAZ brigade, consisting of a head-quarters company and three diversionary battalions. In peace-time the SPETSNAZ companies of the Armies of the Front are combined as a SPETSNAZ battalion, which explains why it is sometimes thought that there are four battalions in each diversionary brigade. In wartime this battalion would split into companies which would join their respective Armies.

Each of the Front's three battalions operates in the enemy's rear in exactly the same way as the SPETSNAZ companies of the Armies. Each battalion can split into as many as 45 diversionary groups and the three together can therefore produce a total of up to 135 small groups. But, if necessary, a SPETSNAZ brigade can operate at full strength, using between 900 and 1,200 troops together against a single target. Such a target might be a nuclear submarine base, a large headquarters, or even a national capital.

The headquarters company of a SPETSNAZ brigade is of particular interest. Unlike both the SPETSNAZ battalions and normal Army companies, it is made up of specialists—between 70 and 80 of them. This HQ company forms part of the SPETS-NAZ brigade and even many of the latter's officers may not be aware of its existence. In peacetime this company of specialists is concealed within the sports teams of the Military District. Boxing, wrestling, karate, shooting, running, ski-ing, parachute jumping—these are the sports they practice. As members of sports teams they travel abroad, visiting places in which they would kill people in the event of a future "liberation."

These Soviet sportsmen/parachutists, holders of most of the worlds' sporting records, have visited every national capital. They have made their parachute jumps near Paris, London and Rome, never concealing the fact that the sporting association which has trained them is the Soviet Army. When Munich,

Rome and Helsinki applaud Soviet marksmen, wrestlers and boxers, everyone assumes that these are amateurs. But they are not—they are professionals, professional killers.

In addition to these small companies within the diversionary brigades of the Fronts, there are also SPETSNAZ Long-Range Reconnaissance Regiments. The Commander-in-Chief of each Strategic Direction has one of these regiments. The best of these regiments is stationed in the Moscow Military District. From time to time this regiment goes abroad in full strength. On these occasions it goes under the title of the Combined Olympic Team of the USSR.

The KGB, as well as the Soviet Army, is training its diversionary specialists. The difference, in peacetime, between the two groups is that the Soviet Army contingent always belongs to the Central Army Sports Club while those from the KGB are members of the "Dynamo" Sports Club. In the event of war, the two diversionary networks would operate independently of one another, in the interests of reliability and effectiveness. But a description of the diversionary network of the KGB lies outside our field.

8

The Fortified Area Troops

For many decades, the problem of defence was not the Soviet Union's first priority. All its resources were devoted to strengthening its striking power and its offensive capabilities. But then China began to present a challenge. Of course, both Soviet and Chinese leaders knew that Siberia could never provide a solution to China's territorial problems. Siberia looks large on the map but even the great conqueror Jenghiz Khan, who had defeated Russia, China and Iran, by-passed Siberia, which is nothing more than a snowy desert. Both Soviet and Chinese politicians realise—as do their Western opposite numbers—that the solution of the Chinese territorial problem lies in the colonisation of Australia. Nevertheless, the Soviet Union takes steps to strengthen its frontiers, even though it is certain that the West will be the first victim of China, as it was the first victim of Hitler and of the Iranian students.

The Soviet Union knows from its own experience how peace-loving a socialist country becomes when its economy, and consequently its army, is weak. But it also knows what can be achieved by a country whose whole economy has been nationalised—a country in which everything of value belongs solely to the government and in which all resources can therefore be concentrated in order to achieve a single goal. Knowing this, the Soviet Communists are preparing for every possible contingency in good time.

In 1969 the problem of defending the 7,000 kilometre frontier with China became particularly acute. The calculation involved was a simple one: one division can hold a sector of 10 or, at the outside, of 15 kilometres of the frontier. How many divisions would be needed to defend 7,000 kilometres?

Since there was no question of using the old methods of conducting operations, new methods—new solutions—were found. We already know that one of the most important of these was the establishment of the airborne assault troops. A second was the introduction of a second arm of service—the Fortified Area Troops. This represented a return to the age-old idea of building fortresses.

Today's Soviet fortresses—the Fortified Areas—are either completely new or are established in areas in which there were old defences, built before the Second World War, which withstood repeated attacks by the Japanese army.

Modern Fortified Areas are, of course, so constructed as to survive a nuclear war. All fortifications have been strengthened against nuclear attack and contain automatic systems for the detection of poisonous gas and air filtration plants.

Today, the old reinforced concrete structures are hardly ever used for operational purposes. Instead, they serve as underground command posts, stores, barracks, assembly points, communications centres, or hospitals. All operational structures are being newly built. Here the Soviet Union finds itself in a very favourable situation, because it has retained tens of thousands of old tanks. These are now installed in reinforced concrete shelters so that only the turrets appear above the ground. The turrets themselves are strengthened with additional armour plating, often taken from obsolete warships. Sometimes the tops of turrets are covered with an additional shield made of old railway lines; the whole is then carefully camouflaged. Under the hull of the tank is a reinforced concrete magazine for several hundred shells and a shelter for personnel. The whole forms an excellent firing point, with a powerful (often 122mm) tank gun, two machine guns, an excellent optical system, reliable defence against a nuclear blast and an underground cable connecting it with the command post. With these resources, two or three soldiers can defend several kilometres of frontier. Since these tank turrets cover one another and since, in addition to them, the fortified areas contain thousands of gun turrets taken from obsolete warships, some of which contain quick-firing 6-barrelled 30mm guns, which are uniquely effective against infantry and aircraft, it would clearly be extremely difficult to break through such a line of defence. The Soviet Union has bitter memories of the way little Finland was able to halt the Soviet advance in this way in 1940.

Each fortified area is spaciously set out, to increase its ability to withstand the effects of nuclear weapons. Organisationally, each fortified area is manned by five or six battalions of troops, a tank battalion and an artillery regiment and is able to cover a frontier sector of 30 to 50 kilometres or more. Clearly, it is not possible to fortify the entire frontier in this way and fortified areas are therefore set up in the most threatened sectors, the intervening territory being covered by nuclear and chemical mines and by airborne assault sub-units, located in bases protected by the fortified areas. This whole arrangement has already enabled the Soviet Union to establish a defensive system covering enormous stretches of territory, without having to move a single one of the divisions earmarked for the liberation of Western Europe from capitalist oppression.

The Air Forces

1

The Air Forces are the fourth most important of the Armed Services. There are two reasons for this low rating.

In the first place, the Commander-in-Chief of the Air Forces does not control all aircraft. Those of the Air Defence Forces—which are the fastest—are completely independent of the Air Forces. Those of the Navy, which include the most modern bombers, also have no link with the Air Forces. The airborne assault troops, as an integral part of the Land Forces, have nothing to do with the Air Forces either.

Secondly, unlike the Commanders-in-Chief of the Strategic Rocket Forces and the Air Defence Forces, the C-in-C of the Air Forces is not an operational commander but an administrator.

Subordinated to the C-in-C of the Air Forces in peacetime are:

Sixteen Air Armies
The Commander of the Long-Range Air Force
The Commander of Military Transport Aviation
Two military academies, officers' training schools, scientific research establishments, and test centres, administrative and supply echelons.

The total peacetime strength of the Air Forces is half a million men and 10,000 military aircraft and helicopters. However, the apparent strength of the C-in-C of the Air Forces is illusory. He is responsible for all questions concerning the functioning of the Air Forces, from the development of new aircraft to the allocation of rations for guard dogs, from the training of cosmonauts to the propagation of experience acquired in Vietnam, but he is in no way involved in questions concerning the operational use of the aircraft under his command. This means that he is not an operational Marshal, but an official and administrator, albeit one of very high rank.

In wartime all sixteen Air Armies become integral components of the Fronts. Each Front has an Air Army, which it uses as it considers necessary. Only the highest operational commanders—the C-in-C of a Strategic Direction or the Supreme Commander—may interfere in a Front's operational planning problems (including those of the Air Army belonging to it). The C-in-C of the Air Forces may only advise the Supreme Commander if his advice is sought; if not, his task is solely to ensure that the Air Armies receive all the supplies they need to carry out their operations.

Nor is the Long-Range Air Force operationally controlled by the C-in-C of the Air Forces. It is subordinated exclusively to the Supreme Commander, who can either make use of its entire strength or allocate part of it, temporarily, to the Commanders-in-Chief of Strategic Directions.

The same arrangement applies to Military Transport Aviation which is entirely under the control of the Supreme Commander.

When control of all these forces is taken from the C-in-C of the Air Forces, he is left only with military academies, training schools, research centres, administrative echelons, hospitals and supply depots. He supplies operational units with reinforcements of equipment and men, oversees the supply of ammunition, fuel, and spare parts, investigates reasons for catastrophes and does a thousand other useful jobs, but he does not direct operations.

Even in peacetime the range of his responsibilities is similarly limited. His Air Armies are deployed in Military Districts and are used in accordance with the plans of their staffs. The General Staff decides how the Long-Range Air Force and Military Transport Aviation are to be used.

2

In peacetime there are sixteen Air Armies. In wartime there would be rather more, since some of them would be divided in two. An Air Army has a strictly regulated organisation. It consists of:

Three fighter divisions
Two fighter-bomber divisions
One bomber division
One regiment of fighter/reconnaissance aircraft
One regiment of bomber/reconnaissance aircraft
One or two regiments of light transport aircraft

Fighter, fighter/reconnaissance and fighter-bomber sub-units have the same organisational form: A flight has 4 aircraft, a squadron 12 (three flights), a regiment 40 (three squadrons and a command flight), a division 124 (three regiments and a command flight).

Bomber and bomber/reconnaissance sub-units, too, are identically organised: A flight has 3 aircraft, a squadron 9 (three flights), a regiment 30 (three squadrons and a command flight), a division 93 (three regiments and a command flight).

In all, an Air Army has 786 combat aircraft and between 40 and 80 light transport aircraft. In the fighter, fighter-bomber and bomber regiments of its divisions, the first squadron contains the best pilots, bomb-aimers and air crew. It is a great honour to serve in such a squadron. The second squadron is trained in reconnaissance duties as well as in its main functions. If necessary, the commander of an Air Army can put in the air, besides two reconnaissance regiments (70 aircraft), 18 squadrons, of what might be called "amateur" reconnaissance aircrew (207 aircraft). Each third squadron is made up of young airmen. After the latter have put in some years of service in this third squadron, the commander of the regiment decides who shall join the "aces" in the first squadron, who shall go to the second, for reconnaissance duties, and who shall stay in the third, among the novices. The best crews from the second squadron graduate to the reconnaissance regiments, where they become professionals rather than amateurs.

3

This is all very well, the informed reader may say, but in the 37th Air Army, which is stationed in Poland, there are two rather than six divisions, while the 16th Air Army, in East Germany, has eight divisions. Moreover, neither of these has a regiment of light transport aircraft; instead they have helicopter regiments. What is the significance of this?

It is quite simple. In wartime a Front would be deployed in Poland. It would contain an Air Army. The Army's headquarters and two Soviet divisions are already there. In wartime the complement would be brought up to strength with divisions of the Polish Air Forces. In peacetime the latter should be allowed to believe themselves independent.

In East Germany two Fronts would be deployed and the 16th Air Army would therefore be split into two (this is always done during exercises). Each Army would contain four Soviet divisions, the complement being made up with divisions of the East German Air Forces. In peacetime the two Armies are combined because of the need for unified control over all air movement in East German air space and also in order to conceal the existence of two Fronts.

In wartime each Soviet motor-rifle and tank division will have 4 helicopters and every all-arms and tank Army will have 12. In peacetime it is best to keep them together, which reduces supply and training problems. This is why there are helicopter regiments in Air Armies. But at the outbreak of war the helicopters would fly off to their respective motor-rifle or tank divisions and Armies. The commanders of helicopter regiments would then be left without jobs. At this point they would be sent light transport aircraft, which would come from the civil air fleet. The pilots of these would be only half-militarised but highly experienced; the commanders are already military men. In wartime these regiments would be used to drop the diversionary sub-units of the Front and of its Armies behind the enemy's lines. For experienced civil pilots this is not a particularly difficult task and the aircraft which they would be flying would be those they fly in peacetime.

4

The Long-Range Air Force (LRAF) consists of three Corps, each of three divisions. Some Western sources mistakenly refer to these Corps as Armies.

Each LRAF division has approximately 100 combat aircraft and a corps consists, on average, of 300 strategic bombers, which can carry air-to-ground missiles.

The commander of the LRAF is subordinated to the C-in-C of the Air Forces only for administrative purposes. Operationally he is subordinate solely to the Supreme Commander.

There are three Strategic Directions. There are also three LRAF corps, which are deployed in such a way that each Strategic Direction can have access to one corps. During combat operations an LRAF corps may be temporarily subordinated to the C-in-C of a Strategic Direction or it may carry out operations to support him, while remaining under the command of the Supreme Commander.

However, the Soviet marshals would not plan to conduct operations in every sector simultaneously, but would concentrate on one. It is therefore possible that in wartime all 900 strategic bombers might be concentrated against one opponent.

5

Military Transport Aviation

The Military Transport Aviation (MTA) force consists of six divisions and several independent regiments. It has approximately 800 heavy transport and troop-carrying aircraft. Its main task is to land airborne forces in the enemy's rear.

Like the LRAF, the MTA is subordinated to the C-in-C of the Air Forces for administrative purposes only. Operationally, the MTA is subordinated to the Supreme Commander and it can be used only on his instructions, in accordance with the plans of the General Staff.

The MTA has a huge reserve organisation—Aeroflot, the largest airline in the world. Even in peacetime, the head of Aeroflot has the rank of Marshal of the Air Force and the function of Deputy to the C-in-C of the Air Forces. Organisationally, even in peacetime, Aeroflot is divided into squadrons, regiments and divisions and all its aircrew have ranks as officers of the reserve. In wartime Aeroflot's heavy aircraft would automatically become part of MTA, while its light aircraft would become transport regiments for the Air Armies of the Fronts. Even in peacetime Aeroflot helicopters are painted light green, as they would be in the divisions of an operational army.

Why does the West consider Admiral Gorshkov a strong man?

1

Of the five Armed Services the Navy ranks as fifth and last in importance. This certainly does not mean that the Navy is weak—simply that the other armed services are stronger.

In all, the Soviet Navy has four fleets: Northern, Pacific, Baltic and Black Sea, in order of strength.

Each of the four fleets has six arms of service:

Submarines
Naval Aviation
Surface Ships
Diversionary SPETSNAZ naval sub-units
Coastal Rocket and Artillery Troops
Marine infantry

The first two of these are considered the primary arms of service; the remainder, including surface ships, are seen as auxiliary forces.

The Commander-in-Chief of the Navy has a purely administrative function, since the Northern Fleet is subordinated, for operational purposes, to the Stavka and the three other fleets to the C-in-Cs of the respective Strategic Directions. In addition to his administrative function, however, the C-in-C of the Navy is the Stavka's main adviser on the operational use of the Navy. In certain situations, too, on the instructions from the Stavka, he may direct groups of ships operating in the open sea. But he has no independent operational planning function; this is entirely the responsibility of the General Staff.

2

Soviet naval strength is based on submarines. These are divided by function, into submarines used for:

    command
    ballistic rockets
    cruise missiles
    torpedoes

They are further classified according to their method of propulsion—nuclear or diesel-electric. The building of diesel-electric submarines (except for some used for diversionary or reconnaissance purposes) has been halted. Henceforth all Soviet submarines will have nuclear propulsion.

Nuclear submarines are grouped in divisions, each of 8 to 12. All the submarines in a division have the same type of armament. A flotilla consists of 4 to 5 divisions. They have mixed complements and may consist of between 35 and 64 nuclear submarines with varying functions.

Diesel-electric submarines are organised in brigades each of 8 to 16. Brigades may form divisions (2 to 3 brigades) or squadrons (4 to 6 brigades).

3

Each fleet has a naval aviation component designated, for instance, "Naval Aviation of the Northern Fleet." Each such component is made up of air divisions and of independent regiments and is the equivalent of an Air Army. Each fleet's naval aviation normally includes a division armed with long-range air-to-surface missiles, for operation against enemy aircraft carriers, one or two divisions of long-range anti-submarine aircraft and independent regiments with anti-submarine seaplanes, torpedo-bombers, reconnaissance aircraft and supply and transport aircraft. In the last few years regiments of deck-landing aircraft and helicopters have been formed.

4

The Soviet Navy must be the only one in the world in which a nuclear-propelled cruiser, armed with missiles, is relegated to an auxiliary category. In fact, every Soviet surface ship, whether it is a battleship or a missile-cruiser, ranks as auxiliary (the exception is the aircraft carrier which is considered as a part of the naval air force). Perhaps this is correct; in a global war submarines and aircraft would play the primary roles. All other forces would work to support them. And, no matter how the number of Soviet surface ships may grow, Soviet submarines will always outnumber them. Moreover there has recently been a noticeable trend towards an increase in the displacement of submarines and it is quite possible that they will eventually surpass the surface ships in tonnage, too, and will maintain their superiority permanently.

Soviet surface ships are organised in groups (for small ships only), brigades (medium-size ships and groups of smaller ones), divisions and squadrons.

In the next few years, the Soviet Navy will be enlarged by the acquisition of a series of large nuclear-propelled missile cruisers. Intensive work is being put into the design and building of large nuclear-propelled aircraft carriers. Ships like the *Moskva* and the *Kiev* have only been built in order to acquire the experience needed before really large ships are built. Particular attention will be paid to the building of large landing ships which are capable of a high degree of independence. The construction of small surface ships will continue. Despite the enormous progress which has been made in building surface ships, however, they will continue to be classified as auxiliary forces.

5

The presence of diversionary SPETSNAZ sub-units in the Soviet Navy is a closely guarded secret. Yet they exist and have done so for a long time. Already by the end of the 1950s each

Fleet had its own SPETSNAZ diversionary brigade, under the direct command of the Third Department of the Intelligence Directorate at Naval Headquarters.

A diversionary brigade has one division of miniature submarines, two or three battalions of frogmen, a parachute battalion and a communications company. It forms an entirely independent combat unit and an independent arm of service within the fleet. For camouflage purposes, its members sometimes wear the uniform of the marine infantry. In other circumstances they may wear any other type of uniform, again as camouflage. The parachutists wear Naval Aviation uniform, the crews of the miniature submarines, of course, that of ordinary submarine crews, the remainder that of seagoing personnel, coastal artillery forces, etc.

Again for camouflage purposes, the personnel of a diversionary brigade is dispersed between several naval bases. This does not prevent it from functioning as a unified combat organisation. In wartime these brigades would be used against enemy naval installations, in the first place against nuclear submarine bases. Groups of diversionary troops may operate from surface ships or from large submarines or may be landed from aircraft. In addition, a unit of large fishing trawlers would be mobilised in wartime to launch and to support operations by miniature submarines. The compartments of these trawlers, designed to hold large catches, are ideal for the rapid launch or recovery of miniature submarines and small diversionary craft.

The diversionary SPETSNAZ brigades of the Navy, like those serving with Fronts, each have as part of their complement a headquarters company of specialists, whose primary task is the assassination of political and military leaders. These companies are disguised as naval athletic teams. These "sportsmen" are, naturally, keen on rowing, swimming and scuba-diving as well as on shooting, boxing, wrestling, running and karate.

As a well-known example we can quote Senior Lieutenant Valentin Yerikalin, of the SPETSNAZ brigade of the Black Sea Fleet, who won a silver medal for rowing at the Olympic Games held in Mexico City. There was no attempt to conceal the fact that Yerikalin was a naval officer and a member of the Central Army Sports Club. Some years later this "sportsman" turned up in Istanbul, having now become a diplomat. He was arrested by the Turkish police for trying to recruit a Turkish subject to work for the Black Sea Fleet, or, more precisely, for the diversionary brigade of this Fleet.

6

The Navy's coastal rocket and artillery troops consist of regiments and independent battalions. They are equipped with both stationary and mobile rocket launchers and with artillery weapons. Their task is to cover the approaches to principal naval bases and ports.

7

Each Fleet has Marine Infantry contingents, consisting of regiments and brigades. In their organisation, these regiments are similar to the motor-rifle regiments of the Land Forces. They differ from the latter in receiving special training for operating in varying conditions and also in being allocated personnel of a higher calibre. Generals from the Land Forces who have watched exercises carried out by the marine infantry often say, with some envy, that a regiment of marine infantry, with the same equipment as that issued to the Land Forces, is the equivalent in its operational potential of one of the latter's motor-rifle divisions.

The Soviet Navy has only one brigade of marine infantry. This belongs to the Pacific Fleet. It consists of two tank and five motor-rifle battalions and is equipped with especially heavy artillery. This brigade is sometimes mistakenly taken for two independent regiments of marine infantry.

The Soviet marine infantry has a very promising future. In the next few years it will receive new types of equipment which will enable it to put large units into action against distant targets. Special combat equipment is being developed for such operations by the marine infantry.

In our examination of the Soviet Navy we must bear in mind a myth which is widely believed in the West—"The Soviet Navy was weak until a strong man, Gorshkov, arrived and brought it up to its proper strength." This presumption is untrue in several respects.

Until the Second World War, Soviet Communist expansion was directed at states adjacent to the USSR—Finland, Estonia, Latvia, Lithuania, Poland, Germany, Romania, Turkey, Iran, Afghanistan, Mongolia, China. Understandably, in this situation, the senior officers of the Navy wielded little influence, for no one would allow them to build up the Navy at the expense of the Land or Air Forces. For the USSR, the Second World War was a land war, and during the first few years after the war, Communist aggression, too, remained entirely land-based—Czechoslovakia, Romania, Hungary, Turkey, Greece, Korea, China. If Gorshkov had appeared during this period, no one would have allowed him to become all-powerful. During the first few years after the war too, there was another problem of overriding urgency—that of catching up with the United States in the fields of nuclear weapons and of delivery systems for them. Until this problem was solved, there could be no question of allowing Gorshkov to build a navy.

The situation changed radically at the end of the 1950s.

Throughout the world, Communist land-based aggression was running into opposition from a wall of states bonded together in military blocs. At this point, the acquisition of a navy became necessary if the campaign of aggression was to continue. Expansion was continuing beyond the seas and across oceans—in Indonesia, Vietnam, Laos, Africa, Cuba and South America. In this situation, even if the Commander-in-Chief of the Navy had not wished to expand his fleets, he would have been forced to do so. Until the war, the main threat to the USSR had come from continental powers—from Germany, France and Japanese-occupied Manchuria. After the war the United States became the main enemy. Of course, anyone occupying Gorshkov's position would have received billions of additional rubles to use in the struggle against the USA. At the beginning of the 1960s it was established that a nuclear submarine provided an excellent platform for rockets. A start was made with their production. Of course, they would not be at Gorshkov's disposal but he was given the green light to develop conventional naval forces with which to protect them.

One final point. The Politburo had realised quite clearly, early on and without help from Gorshkov, that the great sea powers, Great Britain, the United States and Japan, would take the place of Germany and France as the main enemies of the Soviet Union. It was for this reason that in July 1938 the Politburo adopted a resolution "On the construction of an ocean-going fleet." (At that time Gorshkov was only the commander of a destroyer.) In accordance with the resolution, a start was made with the building of aircraft carriers like the *Krasnoye Znamya* and with giant battleships like the *Sovetskiy Soyuz* and cruisers like the *Shapayev*.

Germany entered the Second World War with 57 submarines, Great Britain with 58, Japan with 56 and the United States with 99. According to its own figures, the Soviet Union had 212 when it came into the war, although American engineers, who built these submarines, estimate that it had 253. The Soviet Navy had 2,824 aircraft in 1941, the coastal artillery had 260 batteries, including some 406mm guns. All this was before Gorshkov. The war put a brake on the shipbuilding programme and after its end the building of all the large ships laid down before the war was discontinued, since they had become obsolete.

However, the Politburo understood the need for an ocean-going navy; and a new shipbuilding programme, of which we can see the results today, was approved in September 1955. This programme pre-dated Gorshkov. He was simply empowered to carry out a programme which had been authorised before his time.

There is no doubt that Gorshkov is a strong-willed and purposeful admiral, but this counts for little in the USSR. No admiral would be allowed to advocate this or that step if the Politburo thought differently from him.

Finally, no matter how powerful the West may consider Gorshkov, the fact remains that the Soviet Navy ranks as fifth of the five Armed Services.

The Airborne Forces

1

The Airborne Forces (ABF) do not rank as one of the Armed Services but as an arm of service. However, they are an independent arm of service, and do not belong to any of the Armed Services. In peacetime they are subordinated directly to the Minister of Defence and in wartime to the Supreme Commander.

At present there are only 13 formations in the world which one can call "Airborne Divisions." The US, West Germany, France, China and Poland each have one. The remaining 8 belong to the Soviet Union.

The airborne divisions are directed, for both administrative and operational purposes, by a Commander. His post is of unique importance. Although he commands only 8 divisions, he has the rank of General of the Army, the same as that held by the Commander-in-Chief of the Land Forces, who has 170 divisions under his command.

In peacetime, all the ABF divisions are up to their full wartime complement and staffed by the best troops. The ABF have first choice of personnel, before even the Strategic Rocket Forces and the Navy's submarine detachments.

ABF troops may operate under the control of the C-in-C of Strategic Directions, in groups of 1 to 3 divisions, or they may function independently.

If 1 to 3 divisions are to be used for an airdrop in a particular sector their operations are coordinated by an ABF corps command group, which is established temporarily for this purpose. One of the ABF Commander's deputies commands the corps. If 4 or 5 divisions are to be used, a temporary ABF Army command group is established. This may be headed by the Commander of the ABF himself, or by one of his deputies.

The entire strength of Military Transport Aviation of the Air Forces is controlled by the Commander of the ABF while an airborne assault operation is taking place.
Each ABF division consists of:

Three parachute regiments
A reconnaissance battalion (18 armoured reconnaissance vehicles)
A battalion of self-propelled artillery (32 airborne assault guns)
An anti-tank battalion (18 85mm guns)
A howitzer battalion (18 122mm guns)
A battalion of multiple rocket launchers (18 BM 27-Ds)
An anti-aircraft battalion (32 ZSU-23-4s)
A communications battalion
A motor transport battalion
A battalion responsible for the storage and packing of supply-dropping parachutes
A chemical warfare company
An engineer company

A parachute regiment has three battalions and mortar, anti-aircraft, anti-tank, and self-propelled artillery batteries.
All the battalions in one regiment of a division are equipped with BMD-1 armoured personnel carriers. Two other regiments have one battalion each of BMD-1s and two of light motor vehicles. Thus, of the nine parachute battalions in a division, five have armoured vehicles of great manoeuvrability and considerable fire-power, the remaining four have light vehicles. In all, a parachute division has 180 armoured personnel carriers, 62 self-propelled guns, 18 multiple rocket launchers, 36 field guns, 45 mortars, 54 anti-aircraft guns, more than 200 anti-aircraft rocket launchers and more than 300 anti-tank rocket launchers. The division is fully motorised, with more than 1,500 vehicles. Its average peacetime complement is 7,200.

2

There has been discussion for some considerable time, in both the Soviet General Staff and the Central Committee, of the question of transforming the ABF into a sixth, independent Armed Service.

It is envisaged that such a Service would have four or five parachute divisions, a large contingent of transport aircraft, several newly-established divisions of marine infantry, units of landing ships and several aircraft carriers with fixed-wing aircraft and helicopters.

Experience has shown that the USSR has not enough forces equipped and trained for armed intervention in a territory which is separated from it by an ocean and that it is unprepared for such an undertaking. There are many examples—Cuba, Indonesia, South Africa, Chile, Central America. A new Armed Service of the sort described would enable the Soviet Union to intervene effectively in such areas.

As its internal crises become more acute, the aggressiveness of the Soviet Union increases. For this reason it appears probable that the sixth Armed Service will be created in the next few years.

Military Intelligence
and its Resources

1

Soviet Military Intelligence is neither an Armed Service nor an Arm of Service. It has no uniform or identifying badge or emblem. Nor are these needed. Intelligence is a logistical support service, like the services concerned with nuclear warheads or camouflage or disinformation.

All these services are secret and do not need publicity. Each of them adopts the appearance of the unit in which it finds itself and becomes indistinguishable from it.

Soviet military intelligence is a gigantic organisation, which performs a vast range of tasks. In numbers and technical equipment it is approximately the size of the Bundeswehr—the entire armed services of the Federal German Republic.

In action, decisions are taken by commanding officers, ranging from those in charge of sections to the Supreme Commander. The plans on which these decisions are based are prepared for the commanding officer by his staff. He then either approves the plan or rejects it and orders that another one should be prepared. All commanding officers from battalion level upwards have staffs. The chief of staff is both his commander's principal adviser and his deputy. Staffs vary in size according to the importance of the unit—a battalion has a staff of two, and the General Staff numbers tens of thousands. In spite of this, the work of any staff proceeds according to the same plan.

The first officer on the staff plans operations, the second officer provides him with the information he needs about the enemy. The chief of staff coordinates the work of these two, helps them, checks their work, prepares a plan with their help and presents it to the commander, who either accepts or rejects it.

On a battalion staff the chief of staff and the first officer are one and the same. The staff of a regiment consists of a chief of staff, a first officer and a second officer, who is in charge of intelligence work. On a divisional staff the first and second officers have their own working groups. An Army staff has first and second departments. The staff of a Front and of a Strategic Direction has First and Second Directorates. The General Staff has First and Second Chief Directorates.

Staffs also have other departments, directorates or Chief Directorates but the work of the first component—planning—and of the second—intelligence—form the backbone of any staff.

All intelligence work (which includes reconnaissance) from battalion level to the very top, is thus wholly in the hands of the staff officers concerned and represents one of the most important components of the work of the staff.

Those employed on intelligence and reconnaissance work can be divided into "professionals"—those whose basic function it is—and "amateurs"—those who are employed on intelligence work from time to time and for whom it is an additional rather than their main occupation.

The intelligence and reconnaissance resources of a battalion are not large. A motor-rifle battalion has a mortar battery, with a command platoon, which includes an artillery reconnaissance section. This section works for the mortar battery, reporting all the results which it obtains both to the battery commander and to the second officer on the battalion's staff, who is responsible for all reconnaissance work in the battalion. This is all. All the personnel involved are "professionals." In a tank battalion there is no mortar battery and therefore no "professionals." But there are "amateurs." In each motor-rifle or tank battalion the second company, besides carrying out its normal duties, is trained for reconnaissance operations behind the enemy's lines. During an action any of the platoons of the second company may be detailed for reconnaissance tasks for the battalion. Sometimes the whole second company may be detached to carry out reconnaissance tasks for the regiment.

2

The second officer on the staff of a regiment has the title "Regimental Intelligence Officer." He is a major and the resources at his disposal are not inconsiderable.

Directly under his command is the regiment's reconnaissance company, which has 4 tanks, 7 armoured vehicles (BMP "Korshun" or BRDM-3) and 9 motorcycles.

In addition the regiment has an artillery battalion, anti-tank, rocket and anti-aircraft batteries. All these have resources sufficient to meet their own requirements for artillery reconnaissance and observation and the information which they produce is also sent to regimental headquarters.

The regiment also has an engineer company with a reconnaissance platoon and a chemical warfare company with a CW reconnaissance platoon. The specialised reconnaissance activities of these platoons are of primary benefit to the engineer and CW companies but since they are engaged in reconnaissance they are controlled by the regimental intelligence officer (RIO).

Finally, the latter is in charge of the second officers on the staffs of the regiment's battalions. These officers work for their battalions but are subordinated to and fully controlled by the RIO. During combat operations, at the direction of the commander of the regiment, the "amateur" companies from any of the battalions can be subordinated to the RIO, to work for the regiment as a whole. Thus, the regiment's "professional" reconnaissance company may be joined at any time by a second tank company and by the three second companies from the motor-rifle battalions.

In a battle, a regiment's reconnaissance companies operate at ranges of up to 50 kilometres away. Both the "professional" and the "amateur" companies have BMP or BRDM vehicles for CW, engineer and artillery reconnaissance work. The fact that these vehicles are always with what are purely reconnaissance sub-units has led to the idea that they are an integral part of these units. But this is not so. The CW reconnaissance platoon is taken from the CW company, the engineer reconnaissance platoon from the engineer company and so forth.

113

Quite simply, it would be both pointless and dangerous to send special reconnaissance sub-units behind the enemy lines unprotected. For this reason they always operate with normal tank and motor-rifle reconnaissance sub-units, which protect and are temporarily in command of them.

During reconnaissance operations, all reconnaissance sub-units work covertly, keeping away from concentrations of enemy troops and always avoiding contact. They operate to achieve surprise, working from ambushes to capture prisoners and documents and they also carry out observation of the enemy. They accept battle only when they clash unexpectedly with the enemy, and if it is impossible to avoid contact or to escape. If they do find themselves in contact with superior numbers of the enemy they will often disperse, meeting again some hours later at an agreed spot in order to resume their mission.

There is one situation in which reconnaissance sub-units would accept battle, whatever the circumstances. If they encountered enemy nuclear forces (missile launchers, nuclear artillery, convoys or stores of nuclear warheads) they would report that they had located the target, would discontinue their reconnaissance mission and would launch a surprise attack on the enemy, with all their resources, whatever this might cost and whatever the strength of the enemy's defences.

3

A divisional intelligence officer—the second officer on a divisional staff—has the rank of lieutenant-colonel. He has very considerable resources at his disposal. In the first place he is in charge of all the regimental intelligence officers, in the division, with all their subordinates, both "professional" and "amateur." He supervises artillery reconnaissance and observation, which in a division is already of sizeable proportions. He is also in charge of the engineer reconnaissance company of the division's sapper battalion and of the CW reconnaissance company in the division's CW protection battalion. In addition, he has personal control of the division's reconnaissance battalion.

To coordinate the workings of all these resources (more than a thousand "professionals" and more than fifteen hundred "amateurs") a divisional intelligence officer has a group of officers, which has the designation "Second Group of the Divisional Staff."

The reconnaissance battalion of a division is made up of the division's best soldiers and officers—the fittest, toughest, most quick-witted and resourceful. It has four companies and auxiliary sub-units.

The first of these, a long-range, reconnaissance company, is the smallest and the most ready for battle of the 166 companies and batteries in the division. It has a strength of 27, 6 of whom are officers and the remainder sergeants. It has a commander, a company sergeant-major and five long-range reconnaissance groups each consisting of an officer and four sergeants. These groups can operate far behind the enemy lines. They may be landed by helicopter or may push through into the enemy's rear in jeeps or light armoured vehicles after following close behind their own troops and then passing them and moving on far ahead. Long-range reconnaissance groups are used both to gather intelligence and to carry out diversionary and terrorist operations.

The battalion's second and third companies have the same organisational structure as the reconnaissance companies of regiments and use the same equipment and tactics, but unlike them they operate at distances of up to 100 kilometres ahead of the front line.

The fourth company is the "radio and radar reconnaissance" or signals intelligence company. Its function is to detect and locate enemy radio transmitters, to intercept and decipher their transmissions and to locate, identify and study the enemy's radar stations. In peacetime, the great majority of these companies are already on an operational footing. In the Group of Soviet Forces in Germany, for instance, there are 19 tank and motor-rifle divisions. These contain 19 reconnaissance battalions, each of which has one signals intelligence company. All these companies have been moved, in peacetime, up to the border with West Germany and are working at full stretch, twenty-four hours a day, collecting and analysing any radio signal which is transmitted in their operational area. The same applies to all the other, similar companies of the divisions which are stationed on Soviet territory and in all the frontier military districts. In a number of cases, the signals intelligence companies of divisions in military districts away from the frontier have been moved into frontier districts and are working operationally, supplementing and duplicating the work of other similar companies.

4

The second officer of the staff of an Army has the rank of colonel. To control the Army's reconnaissance work he has his own department, the Second Department of the Army Staff. Because an Army has so many reconnaissance resources and because these differ so widely one from the other, the department is divided into four groups.

The first group is concerned with the reconnaissance activity of the motor-rifle and tank divisions of the Army and also of the Army's independent brigades and regiments.

Army reconnaissance departments have no second group.

The third group is concerned with diversionary and terrorist operations. Under its control is an independent SPETSNAZ company, the organisation and functions of which have already been discussed.

The fourth group deals with the processing of all the information which is received.

The fifth group directs radio and radar reconnaissance. It controls two electronic intelligence battalions. It also coordinates the operations carried out in this field by the Army's divisions. Needless to say, all signals intelligence battalions are working operationally in peacetime. In East Germany, for instance, there are 5 Soviet Armies, that is to say 10 electronic intelligence battalions, which keep a constant watch on the enemy, in addition to the 19 companies which are on the strength of the divisions of these Armies.

5

A Front is made up of two or three all-arms armies and of a tank and an air army. It possesses a large quantity of reconnaissance resources—enough to equal the intelligence services of a large European industrial state.

The second officer of a Front's staff is a major-general. To control the reconnaissance and intelligence activities of the Front he has a reconnaissance directorate (the Front's Second Directorate), which has five departments.

The first of these controls the reconnaissance work of all the Armies belonging to the Front, including that carried out by the Air Army, which we have already discussed.

The second department carries out agent work, for which it maintains an Intelligence Centre, working on behalf of the Armies making up the Front, since these do not run agents, and three or four intelligence outposts. The centre and the outposts are hard at work, in peacetime, obtaining intelligence in the territory in which the Front would operate in wartime. The Soviet Army has a total of 16 military districts, 4 groups of forces, and 4 fleets. Each of these has a staff with a Second Directorate, which itself has a second department. There are thus 24 of these; each of them constitutes an independent agent-running intelligence organisation, which is active on the territories of several foreign countries, working separately from any other similar services. Each of them has four or five individual agent-running organisations which seek to recruit foreigners who will work for the Front or for its tank armies, fleet, flotilla or all-arms armies.

The third department of each of these 24 Reconnaissance Directorates concerns itself with diversionary and terrorist activities. The department supervises activity of this sort in the armies of the Front but also has its own men and equipment. It has a SPETSNAZ diversionary brigade and a SPETSNAZ diversionary agent network of foreign nationals, who have been recruited to work for the Front in the latter's operational area in wartime. Thus, in both peace and wartime the officer in charge of the reconnaissance and intelligence work of a Front or Fleet has two completely separate secret networks, one, which gathers intelligence, controlled by the second department of the Directorate and another, concerned with diversionary and terrorist operations, which is subordinated to the third department.

The fourth department collates all the reconnaissance and intelligence material which is produced.

The fifth department is concerned with the radio and reconnaissance work of the divisions and armies and also has two regiments and a helicopter squadron of its own which also carry out signals intelligence operations.

6

A Strategic Direction is made up of four Fronts, one Fleet and a Group of Tank Armies. Its staff contains a Reconaissance Directorate, headed by a lieutenant-general. We already know that he has at his disposal a diversionary SPETSNAZ long-range reconnaissance regiment, containing Olympic medal-winners, most of whom are not only professional athletes but professional killers. The Reconnaissance Directorate also has an entire range of reconnaissance and intelligence-gathering equipment, one of which deserves special mention.

This is the "Yastreb" pilotless rocket aircraft, which is launched from a mobile rocket launcher and which carries out photo- and radio-reconnaissance at heights of more than 30 kilometres, flying at speeds in excess of 3,500 kilometres per hour. From Byelorussia the "Yastreb" has successfully carried out photographic reconnaissance over Spain, Great Britain and the French Atlantic seaboard. Its appearance at the beginning of the 1970s caused alarm at NATO headquarters. It was mistakenly identified as a MIG-25R. After a MIG 25 had appeared in Japan and had been carefully examined, the experts came to the conclusion that this aircraft had insufficient operational radius to fly over Western Europe. It was realised that there had been a false alarm and in order not to cause another one the Soviet Union discontinued flights by the "Yastreb" in peace-time. However, it is still being used over China, Asia and Africa and over the oceans. Having the invulnerability of a rocket and the precision of an aircraft, the "Yastreb" would also make an excellent vehicle for a nuclear warhead. Unlike a rocket it can be used again and again.

7

The second officer of the General Staff has the title of Head of the Chief Intelligence Directorate (GRU). He is a full General of the Army. Besides controlling the intelligence and reconnaissance resources subordinated to him, he has his own, incomparably huge intelligence network. The GRU works for the Supreme Commander. It carries out espionage on a scale unparalleled in history. It is enough to record that during World War II the GRU was able, with its own resources, to penetrate the German General Staff from Switzerland and to steal nuclear secrets from the United States, and that after the war it was able to induce France to leave NATO, besides carrying out many less risky operations. The work of the GRU's agent networks is controlled by the first four Directorates, each of which is headed by a lieutenant-general. The processing of all information reaching the GRU is carried out by an enormous organisation which is grouped into six Information Directorates. Today the Head of the GRU has two separate, worldwide, intelligence organisations, a colossal number of electronic intelligence centres, centrally controlled diversionary units and so on and so forth.

However, the Chief Intelligence Directorate of the General Staff is a subject which calls for a substantial book to itself.

8

Staffs are of different types. The smallest is that of a battalion, the largest is the General Staff. But each has its own intelligence and reconnaissance resources, just as each brain has its own eyes and ears. The higher staffs control the lower ones and the corresponding higher intelligence organisations direct those below them. At all levels, the intelligence and reconnaissance organisations work for their respective staffs, but if intelligence which is received is of interest to either a higher or lower echelon, it is passed on immediately.

Here is a particularly interesting example of such coordination.

In the summer of 1943, the Red Army was preparing to halt the enormously powerful German advance. In the Kursk salient seven Soviet Fronts were simultaneously preparing their defences.

The overall coordination of operations in the Strategic Direction was in the hands of Marshal G. K. Zhukov. Never in the history of warfare had such a defence system been set up, on a front more than a thousand kilometres in length. The overall depth of the obstacles erected by the engineers was 250–300 kilometres. On an average, 7,000 anti-tank and anti-personnel mines were laid along every kilometre of the front. For the first time the AT artillery density reached 41 guns per kilometre. In addition, field guns and anti-aircraft guns were brought up for use against tanks. It was already impossible to break through such a front. Nevertheless, the German command decided to try to do so. But, they were only able to bring together a million men and officers to carry out the operation, and they were unable to achieve surprise. On the night of 5 June a reconnaissance group from one of the thousands of Soviet battalions captured a German lance-corporal who had been clearing a passage through barbed wire obstacles. The Soviet battalion was immediately put on the alert and the second officer on its staff decided to inform the regimental intelligence officer of what had happened. The regiment was brought to battle readiness straight away and the news of the capture of the lance-corporal was transmitted to the intelligence group of the divisional staff and from there to the staff of the corps, to the staff of the 13th Army, straight from there to the Central Front headquarters and thence to the Headquarters of the Strategic Direction, to Marshal Zhukov and finally to the Chief Intelligence Directorate of the General Staff. It took twenty-seven minutes for the message to pass from the battalion staff to the Chief Intelligence Directorate. The news was astonishing. If the enemy was clearing passages through barbed wire, he must be preparing to advance. But only an immense offensive could be contemplated against such a mighty defensive system. And immense it was—but it ended in complete disaster.

The Distorting Mirror

1

At the time of the siege of Sevastopol, Nicholas I attempted to make the shameful Crimean war seem more acceptable. But nothing came of his efforts: the Russian newspapers printed not what the government wanted but what their journalists saw with their own eyes. More than that—it was not only journalists who wrote in the Russian newspapers and journals about the war but officers of the Russian army—actual participants in the war.

Lev Tolstoy, then a very young officer, wrote *Sevastopol Stories,* in which, in contrast to the government's propaganda, he described the war as he saw it for himself. At that time, of course, there was no freedom, let alone democracy. Yet, surprisingly, the young officer was not hanged, or disembowelled with a ramrod or banished to Siberia—he was not even dismissed from the army. He continued his military career, most successfully.

Tolstoy was not an exception. Look at the newspapers from that time and you will be surprised to see how Russian officers, even generals, wrote in almost every issue criticising their own government for lethargy and clumsiness and for their inability to rule the country or direct the army. Lev Tolstoy stood out from all the critics of the regime only because he was more talented than the rest.

During the Russo-Japanese war the Tsarist government tried once again to make the war seem attractive. It was hopeless. The Russian newspapers totally rejected all attempts to embroider reality. They published not what the Tsar wanted but what eye-witnesses had seen. One of them, an uneducated sailor from the battleship *Orel,* Novikov, gathered a mass of material about the blunders of the Russian Naval Staff and of the admirals who had taken part in the war and, without any fear of the consequences, began to publish it. It sold like hot cakes and Novikov made a lot of money out of his criticisms of the Russian government and of the Tsar himself. Did they cut off his head? Not at all; he bought a large house by the sea in Yalta, right next door to the Tsar, and lived there, writing his books, the best of which is *Tsushima*.

By the time of the First World War, the government was no longer making any great efforts to colour reality. A certain Vladimir Ulyanov, a student who had not obtained his degree, and who concealed his identity behind the pseudonym "Lenin," began to publish Communist newspapers, in editions of millions, exposing every attempt to mislead the public. His newspapers were free, although it cost millions of gold roubles to print them. Where did such a half-educated man lay his hands on so much money?

But then the anarchy came to an end. The Tsar was overthrown, the bourgeoisie were driven off and the people inherited everything. Publishing houses, being large undertakings, were immediately nationalised. From then on the newspapers began to contain not whatever might come into someone's head but what the people really needed, and whatever would benefit the people. Since, naturally, the people as a whole cannot run a newspaper, it is run by the best representatives of the people. They take great care that no one uses the newspapers against the people. If a young officer, an uneducated sailor or a student without a degree should approach the editors, these representatives would immediately ask—do our people need this? Is it necessary to frighten or disillusion them? Should they be corrupted? Perhaps it is not such immature, subjective writings, which are detrimental to the popular interests, which should be published, but what the people need.

That is how things developed—if an article or story did not serve the people's interests it was not published in the people's newspapers. Everything had been nationalised, everything belonged to the people. That being so, why should their representatives waste public money on the publication of a harmful article or a story?

It is said that nationalised undertakings belong to the whole community. But try sitting in the compartment of a nationalised train without a ticket—you will be made to get out and will be fined. In other words, the nationalised railways are not yours or mine or his or ours. They belong to the people who run it— in the final instance, to the government. The same applies to a nationalised newspaper. It, too, belongs to the government. In the Soviet Union all newspapers are nationalised and thus all belong to the government. Is it necessary for the government to criticise its own actions in its own newspaper? That is the reason why there is absolutely no criticism of the government in the Soviet newspapers. That is why no unqualified student would be able, nowadays, to voice criticisms of any representative of the Soviet people. On the other hand, the government has acquired excellent facilities to publish anything they wish, without risking public exposure; the whole press now belongs to it. And it is this freedom from control which allows the government and all its institutions to make daily, even hourly, use of an exceptionally powerful and effective weapon—bluff.

2

Soviet leaders use bluff on a large scale in international politics and they use it in masterly fashion. They employ it with particular skill in the military field: everything is secret—just try to find out what is true and what is not.

During the Cuban crisis Khrushchev threatened to reduce capitalism to ashes by pressing a button; this was at a time when Soviet rockets were still blind, having completely unreliable guidance systems, which meant that they could only be launched on strictly limited courses, otherwise no one could be sure where they would end up.

After Khrushchev all work directed at deception of the enemy was centralised. I have already mentioned the Chief Directorate for Strategic Deception, which is commanded by General N. V. Ogarkov. Here is an example of its work.

The Soviet Union had been alarming the rest of the world with its rockets for some time before the United States began to deploy a system for anti-missile defence. For the Soviet Union this American system was like a knife at its throat— because of it Soviet rockets had lost much of their power to terrorise. The USSR was quite simply unable to deploy its own similar system and it had no intention of doing so—it does not hold defensive systems in any great esteem. But it was essential somehow to stop the Americans.

So the whole Soviet (nationalised) press began saying—in unison—"We have been working on this question for a long time and we have had some success." Then, casually, they showed the whole world some lengths of film showing one rocket destroying another. A very primitive trick. A circus clown who knows the precise trajectory characteristics of a rocket and its launch-time could hit it with an airgun. If a trick like this was shown to Soviet schoolchildren in a circus, they would not be taken in. They would know quite well that there are no miracles and that the clown must have fixed it somehow. In Western capitals, too, they knew that there are no miracles, and that until the US gave the USSR computers no system of the sort could be built there.

But the tricks continued. A gigantic rocket appeared in a Moscow parade, not in the contingent from the Strategic Rocket Forces but in that of the National Air Defence Forces—obviously, therefore, it must be an anti-ballistic missile. Finally, the USSR set about erecting a most important building—an ABM guidance station. A station of this sort built by the Americans would be fully automated, needing a team of more than a thousand, with high engineering qualifications, to run it. This station looks like the Pyramid of Cheops, although it is much larger.

They began to build it right in the outskirts of Moscow, directly on the ring-road round the capital. Let all the foreign diplomats take a good look at it. Occasionally incomprehensible high-powered signals would be transmitted by the station which careful analysis showed to be exactly the sort of signals such a station would transmit. But, inside, the building was empty, without its most essential component—a computer and command complex.

However, the dimensions of the building, the incomprehensible transmissions, the lengths of film and various dark hints dropped by Soviet generals produced the required effect. And the Soviet press provided further evidence—defence against missiles, it said, is a very expensive and not very effective business, although we are putting every effort into it. Soviet intelligence agents suddenly received orders to suspend all their efforts to acquire information on American ABM systems. The display of such disrespect for and such lack of interest in America's first-class electronic industry was calculated to indicate clearly that the Soviet Union enjoyed enormous superiority in this field. The West's nerve failed and the SALT I talks followed. At the signing ceremony the American President sat at the conference table with Brezhnev—and signed. The world sighed with relief and applauded the treaty as a victory for common sense, as a step forward taken by two giants, together.

But did the American President know that he was sitting at the table with the head of an organisation which calls itself the Communist Party of the Soviet Union? Did he know that this organisation has shot 60 million people in its own country and that it has set itself the goal of doing the same throughout the world? Not even the American Mafia could dream of doing things on this scale. When he made his quick decision to hold talks with the ringleader of the most terrible band of gangsters in the history of civilisation, did he not realise that they might simply fool him, as they would a naive schoolchild? Did he take appropriate steps against this? Were his advisers sufficiently alert?

When, next day, the Soviet newspapers published photographs of the smiling faces of the participants in the conference, the Soviet Army could not believe its eyes. Imagine: the US President with his closest advisers, Brezhnev and—right behind Brezhnev—General Ogarkov!

Unbelievable! How could such a thing happen? What were the American presidential advisers thinking of? Did they learn nothing from Pearl Harbor? Could anyone be more negligent than these people were at the signing of this treaty? Why did none of them realise that behind Brezhnev there stood not the chief ideologist, not the Politburo member responsible for scientific research, not the Politburo member responsible for the world's largest military industrial system, not the Minister of Defence, not the Chief of the General Staff, not even the Commander-in-Chief of the National Air Defence Forces, who should be in charge of the anti-missile defence system? Why was nobody there except Ogarkov, head of the Chief Directorate of Strategic Deception? This Chief Directorate is the most powerful in the Soviet General Staff. It is even more powerful than either the First or the Second Chief Directorate. Strategic Deception is that part of the General Staff which is responsible for all military censorship—for all censorship in the fields of science, technology, economics and so forth. This directorate makes a careful study of everything that is known in the West about the Soviet Union and fabricates an enormous amount of material in order to distort the true picture. This most powerful organisation supervises all military parades and any military exercises at which foreigners are to be present; it is responsible for relations with the service attachés of all foreign countries, including those with "fraternal" ties with the Soviet Union. This octopus-like organisation runs *Red Star, Soviet Union, Standard Bearer, Equipment and Armament* and a hundred other military newspapers and journals. The Military Publishing House of the Soviet Ministry of Defence is part of this Chief Directorate. Nothing can be published in the USSR without a permit from its head, no film can appear without one, not a single troop movement can take place without permission from the Chief Directorate, no rocket-base, no barracks—even for the troops of the KGB—can be built without its agreement, nor can a single factory, collective farm, pipe-line or railway be constructed without its prior permission. Everything in this huge country must be done in such a way that the enemy always has a false impression of what is going on. In some fields achievements are deliberately concealed; in others—as was done with anti-missile defence—they are exaggerated out of all recognition. In addition, of course, representatives of the Chief Directorate, helped by Soviet military intelligence, have recruited a collection of mercenary hack journalists abroad, through which it spreads false information, disguised as serious studies. Its representatives attend negotiations concerned with détente, peace, disarmament, etc. For instance, the head of the 7th Department of the Chief Directorate, Colonel-General Trusov, is a permanent member of the Soviet delegation attending the SALT discussions. When the stakes were at their highest, the head of the Chief Directorate, General Ogarkov himself, joined the delegation. He made a brilliant success of the operation to fool the American delegation. For this he was made Chief of the General Staff and at the same time he was promoted to Marshal of the Soviet Union. It is significant that his predecessor, Kulikov, reached the rank of Marshal only when he left the General Staff.

Ogarkov's presence in the delegation produced no reaction. The American delegation did not break off the negotiations when he appeared, did not leave the conference hall as a sign of protest, did not slam the door. On the contrary, it was his arrival which got the talks, which had come to a standstill, going again, after which they moved quickly to a triumphant conclusion. Both sides exchanged applause and threw their cards on the table, having agreed on a drawn game.

But, for heaven's sake, if the agreement was shortly going to halt the further growth of anti-missile systems, if the game was almost over, surely this was the moment to take a peep at the enemy's cards? Just as a precaution, against what might happen in the future? What was the point of simply signing the agreement, after which nothing could be put right, without letting a small group from each side catch a brief glimpse of things as they were in the enemy camp? The agreement should not have been signed without some arrangement of this sort.

Or if only, once the agreement had been signed, the Soviets had shown their American opposite numbers something, not a film in a cinema, but something real—in the most general terms, by all means, and without giving any details away. The Soviet delegation, too, would have been not uninterested to see something of the American achievements. But the Soviet card-sharpers knew in advance that the Americans had at least three aces in their hand, and that is why the Soviet side threw their cards on the table, without showing them, and quickly proceeded to shuffle the pack.

Incidentally, shortly after this, having exploited the credulity of America, the Soviet Union built an excellent rocket, with the industrial index number 8-K-84 and the military designation UR-100. UR means "universal rocket." It can be used both to deliver a nuclear strike and to repel one. It is the largest of the Soviet strategic rockets. Its manufacture is an out-and-out violation of the SALT I agreement, but no protest has come from the American side. This is because Ogarkov's organisation succeeded in concealing the rocket's second function, so that it is officially regarded as a purely offensive weapon. The SALT I agreement was got round in another way, too. An excellent Soviet anti-aircraft rocket, the S-200, which was developed to destroy enemy aircraft, was modernised and made suitable—with certain limitations—for use against enemy missiles. Ogarkov's organisation never allowed this rocket to appear at parades, even in its original, anti-aircraft variant. The Chief Directorate of Strategic Deception is strict in its observance of the principle: "The enemy should see only what Ogarkov wishes to show them." This is the reason why all foreign diplomats were enabled to see the huge construction right in the very outskirts of Moscow.

3

Ever since I first found myself in the West, I have been soaking up information of all kinds. I have visited dozens of libraries, seen hundreds of films. I have taken in everything, indiscriminately—James Bond, Emmanuelle, Dracula, the Emperor Caligula, the Godfather, noble heroes and crafty villains. To someone who had only seen films about the need to fulfil production plans and to build a brighter future, it was impossible even to imagine such variety. I kept on and on going to films. One day I went to an excellent one about the burglary of a diamond warehouse. The thieves broke into the enormous building with great skill, put a dozen alarms out of action, opened enormously thick doors and finally reached the secret innermost room in which the safes stood. Of course, in addition to all the transmitters, alarm devices and so on, there were TV cameras, through which a guard kept constant watch on what was happening in the room where the safes were. But the thieves, too, were ingenious. They had with them a photograph of the room, taken earlier. They put this in front of the cameras and, using it as a screen, emptied the safes. The guards sensed that something was happening. They began to feel vaguely uneasy. But looking at the television screen they were able to convince themselves that everything was quiet in the safe room.

I am sometimes told that the American spy-satellites are keeping a careful watch on what is happening in the Soviet Union. They take infra-red photographs of the country from above and from oblique angles, their photographs are compared, electronic, heat and all other emissions are measured, radio transmissions are intercepted and painstakingly analysed. It is impossible to fool the satellites. When I hear this, I always think of the trio of sympathetic villains who hid from the cameras behind a photograph, using it as a shield behind which to fill their bags with diamonds. Incidentally, the film ended happily for the thieves. When I remember the cheerful smiles they exchanged at the end of their successful operation, I also think of Ogarkov's beaming countenance at the moment the agreement was signed.

The Chief Directorate of Strategic Deception does exactly what the sympathetic trio did—they show the watchful eye of the camera a reassuring picture, behind the shelter of which the gangsters who call themselves the Communist Party of the Soviet Union, the Soviet Army, Military Industry and so forth go about their business.

This is the way it is done in practice. A huge American computer, which has been installed at the Central Command Post of the Chief Directorate of Strategic Deception, maintains a constant record of all intelligence-gathering satellites and orbiting space stations and of their trajectories. Extremely precise short- and long-term forecasts are prepared of the times at which the satellites will pass over various areas of the Soviet Union and over all the other territories and sea areas in which the Armed Services of the USSR are active. Each Chief Directorate unit serving with a military district, a group of armies or a fleet makes use of data provided by this same American computer to carry out similar work for its own force and area. Each army, division and regiment receives constantly up-dated schedules showing the precise times at which enemy reconnaissance satellites will overfly their area, with details of the type of satellite concerned (photo-reconnaissance, signals intelligence, all-purpose, etc.), and the track it will follow. Neither the soldiers nor most of the officers know the precise reason for daily orders, like "From 12.20 to 12.55 all radio transmissions are to cease and all radars are to be switched off," but they must obey them. At the same time, each division has several radio transmitters and radars which work only during this period and which are there solely to provide signals for the enemy's satellites.

The Chief Directorate has its own intelligence-gathering satellites, but, unlike those working for the Chief Intelligence Directorate, they maintain a watch over Soviet territory, looking constantly for radio transmitters and radars which fail to observe the timetables laid down for communication security. Severe punishments await divisional or regimental commanders who are found to be ignoring the timetables.

In addition to these bogus signals, the Chief Directorate is constantly organising flights by aircraft, tests of rockets, troop movements and other operations to take place as the satellites' cameras pass overhead, with the aim of emphasising one aspect of activity while concealing others. Thus, in the period running up to the SALT I negotiations, every sort of attempt was made to present a picture of Soviet activity and success in anti-missile operations. After the negotiations, great pains were taken to hide activity and success in this field, since these represented a violation of the agreements which had been reached.

The Chief Directorate differs from our resourceful burglars in presenting false pictures not for a few hours but for decades. It has at its disposal not three crooks but tens of thousands of highly-qualified specialists and almost unlimited powers in its dealings with generals, marshals and those who run the military industries over the concealment of the true state of affairs.

There is no doubt that these activities enable the Politburo, without great difficulty, to empty the pockets of those in the West who will not understand that they are dealing with organised crime, committed by a state which is operating on a world-wide scale.

PART THREE

COMBAT ORGANISATION

The Division

1

We have already seen that the unit known as a "motor-rifle regiment" in the Soviet Army is in fact an all-arms unit with half the numerical strength of brigades in Western armies, which is nevertheless equal or even superior to the latter in fire-power and striking-power. This position is reached through the merciless exploitation of Soviet solders, who are regarded solely as fighting machines, rather than as human beings who require rest, good food, recreation and so forth.

Having a strength of 2,000, a motor-rifle regiment is equipped with 41 battle tanks, 3 reconnaissance tanks, 100 armoured personnel carriers, 6 130mm heavy assault guns, 18 122mm self-propelled howitzers, 6 "Grad-P" multiple rocket launchers, 18 self-propelled mortars, 18 automatic grenade launchers, 4 self-propelled anti-aircraft guns, 4 surface-to-air missile complexes, 100 light anti-aircraft and several hundred light anti-tank weapons, including the "Mukha," and the RPG-16 anti-tank rocket launchers, both portable and mounted on vehicles, together with the requisite engineer, chemical warfare, medical, repair and other supporting sub-units.

A modern Soviet tank regiment is organised along almost exactly the same lines as a motor-rifle regiment, except that it has three tank battalions rather than one and one motor-rifle battalion instead of three. Its other sub-units are exactly the same: a battalion of self-propelled artillery, a battery of multiple rocket launchers, an anti-aircraft battery, reconnaissance, communications, engineering, chemical warfare and repair companies. The strength of such a regiment is 1,300. It has considerably fewer light anti-tank weapons than a motor-rifle regiment, reasonably enough in a regiment with a total of 97 tanks, since tank guns are the best of all anti-tank weapons.

2

A Soviet motor-rifle division is more of an all-arms unit than a motor-rifle regiment, containing, as it does, sub-units with the most varied functions and capabilities.

The organisation of a division is simple and well-balanced.

The strength of a motor-rifle division is 13,000. It is commanded by a Major-General. It is made up of:

A headquarters staff.

A communications battalion—the division's nerve-system, used for communications with all its elements, with the higher command and with neighbouring divisions.

A reconnaissance battalion—the eyes and ears of the division.

A rocket battalion—the most powerful weapon in the hands of the divisional commander, with six launchers which can fire chemical and nuclear weapons for distances of up to 150 kilometres.

An independent tank battalion—the divisional commander's bodyguard, which protects divisional headquarters and the rocket battalion, and which can be used in battle when the divisional commander needs all his resources.

A tank regiment—the division's striking force.

Three motor-rifle regiments, two of which are equipped with armoured personnel carriers and light weapons and which attack on a wide front during an offensive, probing for weak spots in the enemy's defences. The third regiment, equipped with infantry combat vehicles and with heavy weapons, is used with the tank regiment to attack the enemy at his weakest point— "in the liver" as the Soviet Army says.

An artillery regiment—the main fire-power of the division—which consists of three battalions of 152 self-propelled howitzers and one battalion of BM-27 heavy multiple rocket launchers. In all, the regiment has 54 howitzers and 18 heavy rocket launchers. The full strength of the regiment is used in the division's main axis of advance, in which the tank and

heavy motor-rifle regiments are also active—that is, in the area
in which the enemy has been proved to be most vulnerable.

The anti-aircraft (SAM) regiment has as its primary task the
protection of the divisional headquarters and of the rocket battalion. It must also provide protection for the division's main
battle group, even though this is already capable of defending
itself against enemy aircraft. The regiment has five batteries,
each with six rocket launchers. In peacetime, two of the launchers of each battery are held in reserve and the fact that they
exist must not in any circumstances be disclosed until the outbreak of war. This has led Western experts to underestimate
the defence capabilities of Soviet divisions, believing that each
regiment has only 20 launchers whereas in fact it has 30. In
order to maintain this illusion, the armies of all the Soviet allies
actually do have only 20 launchers in each regiment.

The anti-tank battalion acts as the divisional commander's
trump card when he finds himself in a critical situation. Until
then it is kept in reserve. It is brought into action during a
defensive action, when the enemy's tanks have broken through
fairly deeply and once the direction of his main thrust can be
clearly identified. In an offensive it is used when the division's
main battle force has broken through in depth and the enemy
is attacking its flank and rear. The battalion is armed with 18
100 or 125mm anti-tank guns and six anti-tank missile complexes.

The engineer battalion is used, together with the anti-tank
battalion, to lay minefields rapidly in front of enemy tanks
which have broken through, in order to stop them or at least
to slow them down in front of the division's anti-tank guns. It
also clears mines ahead of the division's advancing troops during an offensive and helps them to cross water obstacles.

The chemical warfare battalion carries out the measures
necessary for defence against nuclear, chemical or biological
attacks by the enemy.

The transport battalion supplies the division with fuel and
with ammunition. Its 200 vehicles enable it to move 1,000 tons
of fuel and ammunition at the same time.

The repair battalion recovers and replaces combat equipment.

The medical battalion does the same, but for the division's
personnel.

The helicopter flight, which has 6 helicopters, is used for

command and communications duties and to land the division's diversionary troops behind the enemy's lines.

The division has a total of 34 battalions. Those battalions which are subordinated directly to the divisional commander are given the designation "independent"—for instance "Independent Communications Battalion of the 24th Division." This system is also used in all higher formations. For instance, an Army consists of divisions. But it also contains regiments and battalions which do not form part of its complement, which are called "independent" as, for instance, in the "41st Independent Pontoon Bridge Regiment of the 13th Army."

The total complement of a Soviet motor-rifle division is 287 tanks, 150 infantry combat vehicles, 221 armoured personnel carriers, 6 rocket launchers, 18 130mm heavy assault guns, 18 anti-tank guns, 126 self-propelled and towed howitzers, 96 mortars and multiple rocket launchers, 46 mobile anti-aircraft missile complexes, 16 self-propelled automatic anti-aircraft guns, and hundreds of light anti-tank and anti-aircraft weapons.

3

A tank division is organised in the same way as a motor-rifle division, except that it has three tank regiments rather than one and one motor-rifle regiment instead of three. In addition, a tank division has no independent tank or anti-tank battalions, since its anti-tank strength is much greater than that of a motor-rifle division.

A tank division has 10,500 men. It is equipped with 341 tanks, 232 infantry combat vehicles, 6 rocket launchers, 6 heavy assault guns, 126 self-propelled howitzers, 78 mortars and multiple rocket launchers, 62 self-propelled anti-aircraft missiles and artillery complexes and hundreds of light anti-aircraft and anti-tank weapons. While it has fewer personnel, a tank division has far greater striking power than a motor-rifle division.

The Army

1

Until the mid-1950s, divisions were organised in corps, and a number of corps made up an Army. However, because of the greatly increased combat strength of the divisions, and also because an Army Commander had acquired the means to control all his divisions simultaneously, the corps came to be considered unnecessary as an intermediate formation and was therefore abolished.

Today, however, a relatively small number of corps are left in the Soviet armed forces. They exist where a division is too small a unit for the task in hand and an Army too large.

From time to time in this book we have used the term "All-Arms Army." This has been done in order to distinguish this type of Army from Tank Armies, Air Armies, Air Defence Armies and Rocket Armies. However, in normal usage the expression "all-arms" is not used; instead, the units concerned are simply referred to as the 13th or the 69th Army. Some have honorary titles, such as "2nd Shock Army" or "9th Guards Army." These titles add nothing to the present-day strength of these armies—they are simply reflections of past glory. For instance, the 3rd Army, which has no honorary title, is considerably better equipped than the 11th Guards Army.

Sometimes Armies evolve along new lines but keep their former designations, which do not fit their present functions. Thus, the 2nd Tank Army is now an All-Arms Army. By contrast, the 3rd Shock Army, despite its designation, is in fact a Tank Army.

During the Second World War the Red Army had a total of 18 Air Armies, 11 Air Defence Armies, 6 Guards Tank Armies, and 70 other armies, of which 5 were known as Shock Armies and 11 as Guards Armies.

Today there are fewer armies but their strengths vary considerably. The Soviet Armed Forces now have 3 Rocket Arm-

ies, 10 Air Defence Armies, 16 Air Armies, 8 Guards Tank
Armies and 33 other armies, a number of which are still referred
to as either Shock or Guards Armies.

2

In the West it is firmly believed that today's Soviet Armies
lack a clear organisational structure. A superficial analysis of
the complement of each of the Soviet Armies seems to confirm
this: some Armies have 7 divisions while others have only 3.
The proportion of tank and motor-rifle divisions which they
contain also varies constantly.

In fact, though, Armies do have quite clear organisational
structures. However, the Soviet Union does not think it advis-
able to display this clarity in peacetime; this would throw too
much light on their plans for war. Divisions have a high degree
of administrative autonomy and can be quickly regrouped from
one Army to another. In peacetime the system certainly does
seem illogical, but once a war began each Army would take
on an entirely clear shape.

There is one further cause for this apparent confusion. This
is that the Soviet Union has forbidden its East European allies to
establish Armies in either peacetime or wartime. If a homoge-
neous mass becomes too large it may explode. The Soviet High
Command avoids this danger within the Soviet Army itself, by
constantly moving the various nationalities around, to produce a
featureless grey mass of soldiery, unable to understand one another. In peacetime, the armed forces of the East European countries only have divisions. In wartime these divisions would
immediately join Soviet Armies which were under strength. This
is precisely what happened in the summer of 1968.

In peacetime, these East European divisons see themselves as
part of their own national armed forces. In wartime they would
be distributed throughout the Soviet Armies; for administrative
purposes they would come under their national Ministries of Defence and, ultimately, under the Commander-in-Chief of the
Warsaw Treaty Organisation. For military purposes they would
be subordinated to the Soviet Armies, Fronts and Strategic Directions and, ultimately, to the Soviet Supreme Commander and
to his General Staff. It is because of this that the Staff of the Warsaw Treaty Organisation is a bureaucratic institution rather than
operational headquarters. And this is why, in peacetime, many

Soviet Armies appear unstructured. In wartime they would be brought up to strength with East European contingents and they would then assume their proper forms.

3

In wartime an Army consists of five divisions, one of which is a tank division, and the remaining four motor-rifle divisions. In various instances in which the mass use of tanks would be difficult, an Army may have nothing but motor-rifle divisions, which have only a limited number of tanks. But the Armies which are earmarked to operate in Western Europe are made up in this way—one tank and four motor-rifle divisions.

Besides these five divisions each Army has:

A headquarters staff—the brain of the Army.

A communications regiment—its nervous system.

An independent SPETSNAZ diversionary company and two signals intelligence battalions—its eyes and ears.

A rocket brigade—the most powerful weapon in the hands of the Army's commander, which enables him to deliver nuclear and chemical attacks. Earlier each rocket brigade had 9 launchers, with a range of up to 300 kilometres. Today a brigade has 18 launchers, with a greatly increased range.

An independent tank battalion—the Army Commander's personal guard. This defends the Army's control post and the rocket brigade and is brought into action only in the most critical situations, when everything is at stake.

An artillery brigade—the main fire-power of the Army. This consists of five battalions—three with 18 130mm guns each, one with 18 152mm gun-howitzers and one with 18 BM-27 multiple rocket launchers.

An anti-aircraft brigade, which covers the Army's command Post and Rocket Brigades with its fire and which also operates in the Army's main axis of advance, supplementing the anti-aircraft coverage which the divisions can provide for themselves. This brigade consists of a command battalion, a supply battalion and three fire-battalions, each with three batteries.

The camouflage service has decreed that one of the launchers in each of these batteries is never to show itself. It therefore appears to observers that these batteries consist of three launchers, whereas in fact they have four, one of which is always kept in reserve. An anti-aircraft brigade is therefore generally believed to have 27 launchers, whereas in fact it has 36.

An anti-aircraft regiment, which has 30 57mm S-60 anti-aircraft guns. Experience in Vietnam and in wars in the Middle East has shown that conventional anti-aircraft artillery has by no means outlived its usefulness and that there are many situations in which the effectiveness of anti-aircraft rockets falls off sharply and that anti-aircraft guns can supplement these most usefully.

An anti-tank regiment, which consists of three battalions. This has 57 heavy anti-tank guns and 18 anti-tank missile complexes.

An independent anti-tank battalion, which has 40 IT-1 tracked anti-tank rocket launchers. The existence of these battalions, and of the IT-1 itself, is a carefully guarded secret. These batteries do not form part of the anti-tank regiment, and there is a sound reason for this, since they carry out operations using quite different tactics. The independent anti-tank battalions, with their highly mobile launchers, harass the enemy constantly, making surprise attacks from vehicles and manoeuvring from area to area under the pressure exerted by the enemy's superior forces. Meanwhile the anti-tank regiment, armed with more powerful but less manoeuvrable guns, has the task of stopping the enemy tanks, at absolutely any cost, when they reach a previously defined line. Thus the more mobile battalion goes into action against the enemy's tanks from the moment the latter break through, while the anti-tank regiment, deep in the rear, is preparing an impassable barrier, behind which it will fight to the last man.

The helicopter squadron is used for communications and for control, and sometimes to land troops behind the enemy lines. It has 16 medium and 4 heavy helicopters.

The Army's supporting sub-units include:

An engineer regiment
A pontoon bridge regiment
An independent assault crossing battalion
A transport regiment
An independent pipe-laying battalion
A chemical warfare battalion

A medical battalion
A mobile tank-repair workshop, with a tank recovery company

In wartime the complement of an Army is 83,000. It has 1,541 tanks, 48 rocket launchers, 832 infantry combat vehicles, 1,100 armoured personel carriers, 1,386 guns, mortars and multiple rocket launchers, 376 heavy anti-aircraft missile launchers and anti-aircraft guns, 40 transport helicopters and thousands of light anti-aircraft and anti-tank weapons.

4

A Tank Army, like an All-Arms Army, has a permanent complement which is strictly observed. Its organisation is standardised with that of an All-Arms Army. It is therefore simpler not to list the rocket brigade, the diversionary company and so forth but simply to pick out the features which distinguish a Tank Army from an All-Arms Army. There are three such features:

(1) An All-Arms Army has five divisions, one of which is a tank division. A Tank Army has only four, all of which are tank divisions.

(2) A Tank Army does not break through the enemy's defences. This is done for it by the All-Arms Armies. Therefore a Tank Army does not have an artillery brigade, of which it has no need. But while it is operating deep in the defences of the enemy it may suddenly encounter strong enemy forces against which massed intense fire must be brought down very quickly. For this purpose, in place of an artillery brigade, a Tank Army has a regiment of BM-27 multiple rocket launchers.

(3) A Tank Army does not fight to hold areas or lines: its task is solely to attack the enemy. It therefore has no anti-tank regiment (which holds territory) or independent anti-tank battalion (which harasses the advancing enemy). It has no need of these sub-units, which would contribute nothing to its proper function.

In the near future there will be one further special feature in the organisation of a Tank Army. It will include an airborne assault brigade, which has the function of seizing and holding bridges, crossing points and road junctions ahead of the avalanche of advancing tanks. At present only Fronts have these brigades. Temporarily, until they come into service, Tank Armies are forced to use motor-rifle regiments, or sometimes divisions, which have battalions with special training in helicopter assault landings. Once the airborne assault brigades join the Tank Armies, the need for such motor-rifle regiments and divisions will disappear.

In all, in wartime, a Tank Army has 54,000 men, 1,416 tanks, 993 infantry combat vehicles, 894 guns, mortars and multiple rocket launchers, 42 rocket launchers, 314 heavy anti-aircraft missile launchers and anti-aircraft guns, 64 combat and 34 transport helicopters and thousands of light anti-aircraft and anti-tank weapons.

5

If we compare the weapons available to an All-Arms Army with those of a Tank Army, we discover an apparently paradoxical situation; the Tank Army has fewer tanks than the All-Arms Army, but more infantry combat vehicles than the latter, whose very foundation is its motor-rifle sub-units!

In fact, though, this is not a paradox. An All-Arms Army is a combination of tanks, of heavy and light motorised infantry, artillery and other forces whose job is *to break through the enemy's lines*.

A Tank Army is far smaller than an All-Arms Army. It is a combination of tanks and *heavy* infantry, with artillery and operational helicopter sub-units, whose job it is *to operate deep in the enemy's rear*.

An All-Arms Army has more than 1,000 armoured personnel carriers (for light infantry) and a Tank Army has practically none.

A Tank Army, being smaller, has far better cross-country performance, and greater manoeuvrability and striking power. It has fewer tanks than an All-Arms Army, but they are far more highly concentrated. This gives the Tank Army a clearly defined offensive character, while the All-Arms Army is essentially a universal weapon.

The Front

1

The Front is a group of Armies, unified under a single command to carry out combat operations in wartime. It is set up either during or immediately before the outbreak of a war. It is an all-arms formation in every respect, incorporating elements of the various Armed Services.

The Commander of a Front has an operational, not an administrative function. He possesses very considerable authority and the forces under his command are not subordinate to the Commanders-in-Chief of their respective Services. The different Services from which the forces making up a Front are drawn are not permitted to interfere in the operational use of these forces. A Front Commander has sole and personal responsibility for the preparation, conduct and outcome of combat operations. He is subordinated either to the Commander-in-Chief of a Strategic Direction who is in control of operations or directly to the Supreme Commander himself. The Armed Services from which the forces making up a Front are taken are concerned only with the reinforcement, reequipment, provisioning and supply of these forces.

This clear differentiation between operational and administrative functions makes it possible to concentrate complete authority in individual hands, to avoid duplication of control, to ensure proper cooperation between sub-units of different Armed Services and to avoid friction between them.

At the beginning of the war between the Soviet Union and Germany, five Fronts were created. In the course of the war their number was increased to fifteen. During its final stages the Fronts operating in the Central Direction were made up of 1 or 2 Air Armies, 2 or 3 Tank Armies, 8 or 9 All-Arms Armies and a considerable number of independent tank, artillery and motor-rifle corps. These Fronts had strengths of up to a million soldiers, three thousand tanks, three thousand aircraft, and up to fifteen thousand guns and mortars.

2

After the war, because of the introduction of nuclear weapons and as part of the continuous technical improvement of the Armed Forces, it was decided that in any future war more powerful, more compact and therefore more easily controlled Fronts would be used.

Contrary to the belief held in the West, Fronts have a quite clearly defined combat organisation, like battalions, regiments, divisions and armies.

A Front comprises:

A command staff.

A communications regiment—the nerve system.

A diversionary "SPETSNAZ" brigade, a signals intelligence regiment and a radar battlefield surveillance regiment— the eyes and ears of the Front.

An Air Army.

A Tank Army—the Front's striking force.

Two All-Arms Armies.

An independent tank brigade—the Front Commander's personal guard, which defends his command post and the Front's rocket brigades. This brigade is only brought into action in the most critical situations.

Two rocket brigades. One has 12 launchers with a range of 9-1,200 kilometres and is used in accordance with the plans of the Front Commander. The second brigade is similar in composition and armament to an Army's rocket brigade and is used to strengthen the Army which is having the greatest success.

An artillery division, consisting of six regiments and an anti-tank battalion. Three of the regiments have 54 130mm M46 guns each and two of the remainder have 54 152mm D20 howitzers each. The other regiment has 54 240mm mortars. The artillery division, in its entirety, is used to strengthen the artillery of the Army which is having the greatest success.

A specially strengthened artillery brigade, consisting of five battalions. The first three each have 12 180mm S-23 guns, the other two each have 12 203mm B-4M howitzers. The brigade is used to strengthen the Army which is having the greatest success.

A tank-destroyer brigade, of five battalions, armed with 90 heavy anti-tank guns and 30 anti-tank rocket complexes.

Two anti-aircraft missile brigades and two anti-aircraft artillery regiments, equipped and organised like similar sub-units in an Army.

An airborne assault brigade, used for the rapid capture of important lines, bridges, crossings and mountain passes in support of the Front's advancing forces. In the next few years commanders of the Tank Armies of a Front will also each have one such brigade.

Several penal battalions, which are used to negotiate minefields and for attacks on strongly fortified enemy positions. The number of penal battalions available depends on the numbers of soldiers and officers who are unwilling to fight for socialism.

The supporting sub-units include:

An engineer brigade.

A pontoon bridge brigade.

An assault-crossing battalion.

A transport brigade.

A pipe-laying regiment.

A CW protection regiment.

Several field and evacuation hospitals.

A mobile tank repair workshop.

A tank transport regiment.

In territories in which it is difficult to use tanks, a Front will have no Tank Armies. Instead of these it may have an independent tank division but it may not have this either. This does not, of course, apply to Western Europe.

Fronts earmarked for operations in Western Europe will have up to 5,600 tanks, 772 combat aircraft, 220 helicopters, 3,000 infantry combat vehicles, 3,000 armoured personnel carriers, and up to 4,100 guns, mortars and salvo-firing rocket-launchers together with a large quantity of other arms and combat equipment.

3

It will, of course, be pointed out that the forces stationed on East German territory are precisely twice as strong as those I have listed, having:

Not one Tank Army, but two
An Air Army which has a considerably larger number of aircraft than I have shown
Two airborne assault brigades, rather than one
Not one diversionary brigade, but two
Four rocket brigades, instead of two
Two engineer brigades, not one
Two pontoon bridge brigades, rather than one
An artillery division which has more than 700 guns, as against the 324 listed above

How can this be explained? There is nothing mysterious about it. A Front advancing against a strong enemy may have a zone of advance of 200–250 kilometres. In East Germany there is thus room for two Fronts. In Czechoslovakia there is room for only one.

Two routes lead from East Germany to the West, separated from each other by a considerable distance. Because of this, it is convenient to employ two different Fronts; control over a single Front advancing in two different directions is bound to produce difficulties. If the Soviet forces are supplemented with East German units there will be precisely two Fronts in the GDR. No publicity is given to this intention in peacetime, in order to keep it secret. Besides, it is quite simply inconvenient to keep two generals of equal seniority in the same country. For the senior Soviet officer in the GDR is not only a military commander, he is also the administrative head of a Communist colony. For this reason the staffs of the Fronts are unified, although even for annual exercises they separate, as do the Air Armies and the artillery divisions. A single telephone call is all that is needed to set up two separate fronts—everything else has been arranged already.

Why are there 20 Soviet Divisions in Germany, but only 5 in Czechoslovakia?

1

The Soviet Union maintains 10 motor-rifle, 1 artillery and 9 tank divisions in East Germany. In Poland it has 2 tank divisions, in Czechoslovakia it has 2 tank and 3 motor-rifle divisions. In the Byelorussian Military District, which borders on Poland, it has 9 tank and 4 motor-rifle divisions; Poland has 5 tank and 8 motor-rifle divisions, Czechoslovakia has 5 tank and 5 motor-rifle divisions.

At first sight, these figures seem to be an arbitrary and nonsensical jumble.

However, let us recall the basic fact that the East European divisions, brigades and regiments are not permitted to form their own Armies or Fronts. They simply form parts of various Soviet Armies, taking the place of missing elements. We should therefore not regard Soviet and East European divisions as separate entities. Instead, we should see them as forces of the Warsaw Treaty Organisation, without national distinctions. Once we do this, we see an entirely harmonious picture.

Let us take Czechoslovakia as an example. In Prague there is a Soviet Colonel-General, who commands the Central Group of Forces. Under him are the staffs of an Air Army and of two All-Arms Armies. The Air Army has a complement of only 150 Soviet combat aircraft, but, if we add to these 500 Czech combat aircraft, we have a complete Air Army, with a Soviet general at its head.

Altogether in Czechoslovakia there are 7 tank and 8 motor-rifle divisions. This is exactly the number needed to make up a Front. 4 of the tank divisions constitute a Tank Army. 2 of the remaining tank divisions and the 8 motor-rifle divisions form two Armies and the remaining tank division acts as a

reserve. In peacetime, Czechoslovakia has two artillery brigades and two anti-tank regiments. This is exactly what is
needed to complete two Armies, but the Tank Army does not
need these sub-units. Czechoslovakia has three rocket brigades
and this is precisely what is needed—one brigade for each
Army, including the Tank Army. All the front-line sub-units
are Soviet.

The Soviet Colonel-General in Prague is the Commander
of the Central Front. The commanders of the Air Army and of
the two All-Arms Armies are also Soviet, while the divisions,
brigades and regiments are both Soviet and Czech, but all are
entirely under Soviet control. Already in peacetime, there is a
complete Front in Czechoslovakia; only one element is lacking—a headquarters staff for the Tank Army. Everything else
is there. However, five hundred kilometres from the Soviet-
Czech frontier, in the small Ukrainian town of Zhitomir, is the
staff of the 8th Guards Tank Army. This staff has no one under
its command. So that the generals should not become bored,
they frequently make trips to Czechoslovakia to inspect the
tank divisions. Then they return home. All that would be needed
to move them to Czechoslovakia is a two-hour flight by pas-
senger aircraft. Once this is done the Central Front is ready
for battle.

In Warsaw, too, there is a Soviet Colonel-General. He also
has at his disposal the headquarters staff of an Air Army (the
37th Air Army which has 360 combat aircraft) but he has only
two Soviet tank divisions. There are no staffs for land armies,
for it would be odd to have three Army staffs for two tank
divisions. So the Soviet Colonel-General has a huge staff in
Legnica on which there are sufficient generals to form both the
headquarters staff of a Front and those of three Armies. And
in Poland, too, there are just the right number of divisions to
form a Front—7 tank and 8 motor-rifle. As in Czechoslovakia,
there are 4 tank divisions—a Tank Army—2 tank and 8 motor-
rifle divisions—two Armies—and one tank division, to act as
a reserve. There are exactly the number of auxiliary sub-units
needed for the Front and for the Armies from which it is made
up. The number of combat aircraft is sufficient to reinforce
both the 37th Air Army and the Air Army in Czechoslovakia.

In peacetime there is already a complete Front in Poland;
it needs no further strengthening. The transformation of the
Soviet staff in Legnica into a headquarters staff for a Front and

staffs for three Land Armies can take place automatically. In 1968 it was completed in a matter of minutes. What appears to be one staff, in fact, functions, even in peacetime, as four independent staffs; they are all located in one place in order to camouflage this fact.

In East Germany there are two Fronts. The overall total of Soviet and East German aircraft is precisely the number needed to make up two Air Armies. The staff of the 16th Air Army is already stationed in East Germany; that of the 1st Air Army can be brought from Byelorussia in a single transport aircraft within a couple of hours and once this has been done the two Fronts have their complete contingent.

In peacetime, there are two Tank Army staffs in East Germany—each Front has one—and three staffs for All-Arms Armies. In other words, one more is needed. This, too—the staff of the 28th Army—would come from Byelorussia, in a single aircraft and within two hours. There would then be two Fronts, each with one Air Army, one Tank Army and two All-Arms Armies. The move of the staffs can be accomplished so quickly because it is only necessary to move five generals and twelve colonels for each staff—the remainder are already in East Germany.

In all, there are 11 tank and 14 motor-rifle divisions in East Germany. Each Front needs a minimum of 6 tank and 8 motor-rifle divisions. Thus only three more divisions are needed and they, too, would come from Byelorussia. This would take twenty-four hours. The two Fronts could begin combat operations without them and they, too, would be in action within a day.

But what about poor Byelorussia, robbed of the staff of an Air Army, the staff of an All-Arms Army and three divisions—one tank and two motor-rifle? She has plenty left.

To be specific, she has a Colonel-General and his staff, two rocket brigades, two anti-aircraft SAM brigades, a diversionary brigade, an airborne assault brigade, the staffs of the 5th and 7th Guards Tank Armies and eight tank divisions—four with each Tank Army.

2

With a very small number of moves—three Army staffs and three divisions—we have produced a structure which has the precision and harmony of a mathematical formula.

We now have the following picture:

In the first echelon there are three Fronts, two in East Germany, one in Czechoslovakia.

In the second echelon—one Front in Poland.

In the third echelon—a Group of Tank Armies.

The seaward flank is covered by the Soviet Baltic Fleet which in wartime would incorporate all the ships of the Polish and East German Navies.

At the head of each of these formations is a Commander. Above him is the Commander-in-Chief, whose headquarters is at Zossen-Wünsdorf. There could be no better place for a headquarters anywhere in the world. It is very close to West Berlin which, with its immediate surroundings, would, of course, be immune from Western nuclear attacks. The C-in-C makes use of West Berlin as a hostage and as a safeguard; he is thoroughly protected against conventional weapons by concrete shelters and by Tank Armies.

Each Army has one tank and four motor-rifle divisions. Each Tank Army has four tank divisions. Each Front has one Air Army, one Tank Army and two All-Arms Armies. The Group of Tank Armies has two Tank Armies. In all, each Front has six tank and eight motor-rifle divisions. There are a total of six Tank Armies and eight All-Arms Armies. The Strategic Direction has four Fronts (All-Arms) and one Group of Tank Armies.

The Armies of this Strategic Directorate have a total of 32 tank divisions and 32 motor-rifle divisions.

In addition, the C-in-C of the Western Strategic Direction has at his disposal two tank divisions, one in Poland, the other in Czechoslovakia and two airborne divisions (the 6th Polish and the 103rd Guards division, which is in Byelorussia).

Also at the disposal of the C-in-C of the Strategic Direction are a diversionary long-range reconnaissance SPETSNAZ regiment, a regiment of pilotless "Yastreb" reconnaissance aircraft, a Guards communications brigade, a transport brigade, a division of railway troops, a pipe-laying brigade, a CW protection brigade, an engineer brigade, a pontoon bridge brigade and other sub-units.

For the duration of a particular operation he may have temporary command of:

> One Corps from the Strategic Rocket Forces
> One—or in some cases all three—Corps from the Long Range Air Force
> One Army from the National Air Defence Forces
> The whole of Military Transport Aviation

3

The Western Strategic Directorate is the mightiest grouping of forces on this planet. It has the task of breaking through the West's defences to rescue the West Europeans from the fetters of capitalism. The plan for its operational use is simple—a simultaneous attack by all three Fronts. The Front which is most successful will be immediately strengthened by the addition of the second echelon Front from Poland, which has the task of smashing through the enemy's defences, after which the Group of Tank Armies will be used to widen the breach, supported by parachute drops by the airborne divisions. Divisions which suffer heavy losses will not be reinforced but will be immediately withdrawn from battle and replaced by fresh divisions from the Moscow, Volga or Urals Military Districts. In the event of a breakthrough into France, the Western Strategic Direction may be allocated a further Group of Tank Armies, which is located in the Kiev Military District in peacetime and is made up of the 3rd and 6th Guards Tank Armies.

It must be emphasised that the task of the C-in-C of the Western Strategic Direction is to advance swiftly westwards and to concentrate all his efforts on this and this alone. He is covered on the south by neutral Austria and Switzerland, which, it is planned, will be liberated somewhat later, while on the north of the Strategic Directorate lie the West German "Land" of Schleswig-Holstein and Denmark. A plan has been devised to prevent the forces of the Directorate from moving northwards

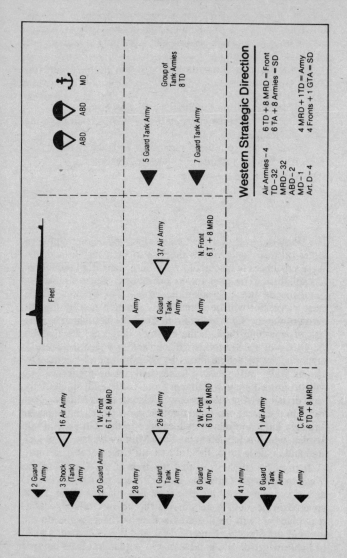

ABD   ABD   MD

Fleet

2 Guard Army
3 Shock (Tank) Army
16 Air Army
20 Guard Army
1 W. Front
6 T + 8 MRD

28 Army
1 Guard Tank Army
26 Air Army
8 Guard Army
2 W. Front
6 TD + 8 MRD

41 Army
8 Guard Tank Army
1 Air Army
Army
C. Front
6 TD + 8 MRD

Army
4 Guard Tank Army
37 Air Army
Army
N. Front
6 T + 8 MRD

5 Guard Tank Army
7 Guard Tank Army
Group of Tank Armies
8 TD

Western Strategic Direction

Air Armies – 4   6 TD + 8 MRD = Front
TD – 32   6 TA + 8 Armies = SD
MRD – 32
ABD – 2   4 MRD + 1TD = Army
MD – 1   4 Fronts + 1 GTA = SD
Art. D – 4

as well as westwards. The Baltic Military District will become the Baltic Front in wartime. It will not come under the command of the Western Strategic Directorate but will be independent—in other words it will be subordinated directly to the Supreme Commander. This Front will cross Polish territory into Germany and will deploy northwards, with the task of covering the northern flank of the Western Strategic Directorate, of liberating Denmark and of seizing the Baltic Straits. Because it will have to work on a very narrow front and to carry out operations on islands, the composition of the Front has been somewhat modified. It will include:

The 30th Air Army

The 9th and 11th Guards Armies, each consisting of one tank division and of three motor-rifle divisions instead of four

One tank division, rather than a Tank Army

An artillery division and all the remaining units which ordinarily constitute a Front.

As compensation for the divisions it lacks, the Front has one most unusual component—a Polish marine infantry division. In addition, the Soviet 107th Guards Airborne Division will operate in support of the Front, although it will not be subordinated to it.

To the north another Front will operate, independently of any Strategic Direction, subordinated directly to the Supreme Commander. This Front will be established on the base provided by the Leningrad Military District. It will be made up of one Air Army, two All-Arms Armies and an independent tank division. An airborne division based in the Leningrad Military District, but not subordinated to it, will provide operational support. This Front will operate against Norway and, possibly, Sweden.

The Organisation
of the South-Western
Strategic Direction

1

The South-Western Strategic Direction stands shoulder to shoulder with the Western and is organised in exactly the same way: three Fronts in the first echelon, one Front in the second echelon, a Group of Tank Armies in the third echelon, and a seaward flank protected by the Black Sea Fleet, which would be joined in wartime by all the ships of the Bulgarian and Romanian navies.

Unlike its Western equivalent, the South-Western Strategic Direction covers terrain which is unsuitable for the deployment of a large quantity of tanks. In addition, of course, the enemy is not as strong here as he is in the West. The Fronts of the South-Western Strategic Direction therefore have no Tank Armies. Each Front consists of an Air Army and two All-Arms Armies. The staffs for all the Armies are brought from military districts in the USSR.

In order to examine the structure of this Strategic Direction, we will do two things: we will assume five Bulgarian tank brigades to equal two tank divisions—an equation which any military specialist will confirm is reasonable. We will also move one Soviet motor-rifle division forward just 200 metres from the town of Uzhgorod on to Hungarian territory. We will then have the following picture:

In Hungary there are 3 tank and 8 motor-rifle divisions. The Front there will consist of two Armies each of 1 tank and 4 motor-rifle divisions, with 1 tank division in reserve.

In Romania there are 2 tank and 8 motor-rifle divisions—these will also form a Front of two standard Armies together with an Air Army.

In Bulgaria there are 2 tank and 8 motor-rifle divisions.

In the second echelon is the Carpathian Military District,

consisting of the 58th Air Army and the 13th and 38th Armies. We already know that the staff of the 8th Guards Tank Army has no one under its command and is to move to Czechoslovakia in the event of war. Having made this assumption and after moving one motor-rifle division forward 200 metres, the Front will have 3 tank and 8 motor-rifle divisions—2 Armies with one division in reserve.

Finally, in the third echelon, there is the Kiev Military District, in which are located the staff of the C-in-C of the Strategic Direction and the Group of Tank Armies (the 3rd and 6th Guards Tank Armies, with a total complement of 8 tank divisions).

In reserve the C-in-C has two tank divisions (in Hungary and Czechoslovakia), four motor-rifle divisions and the 102nd Guards Airborne division. In addition he has a diversionary regiment and the variety of supporting formations and units which the C-in-C of the Western Strategic Direction also has.

Of course, it is no accident that the Group of Tank Armies is located in the Kiev Military District. From here the Group can move quickly forward to the Front by which it is most needed. But it could also be quickly brought under the command of the Western Strategic Direction and, by violating the neutrality of Austria from Hungary, could attack the undefended Austro-German frontier.

2

The proportions laid down for the South-Western Direction are observed as precisely as those of its Western counterpart.

In each Army there are 4 motor-rifle divisions and 1 tank division. In the Strategic Direction there are 4 All-Arms Fronts and 1 Group of Tank Armies.

In each Front there are 2 tank and 8 motor-rifle divisions. In all there are 2 Tank Armies and 8 All-Arms Armies made up of 16 tank and 32 motor-rifle divisions. You will recall that in the Western Direction there are 32 tank and 32 motor-rifle divisions.

The South-Western Strategic Direction can be strengthened with forces from the Odessa and North Caucasus Military Districts.

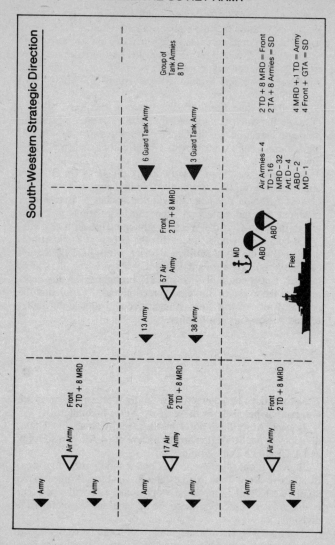

South-Western Strategic Direction

Air Army

Army

Army

Front
2 TD + 8 MRD

Army

Army

17 Air
Army

Front
2 TD + 8 MRD

13 Army

57 Air
Army

Front
2 TD + 8 MRD

6 Guard Tank Army

3 Guard Tank Army

Group of
Tank Armies
8 TD

Air Army

Army

Army

Front
2 TD + 8 MRD

38 Army

MD

ABD   ABD

Fleet

Air Armies – 4
TD – 16
MRD – 32
Art. D – 4
ABD – 2
MD – 1

2 TD + 8 MRD = Front
2 TA + 8 Armies = SD

4 MRD + 1 TD = Army
4 Front + GTA = SD

PART FOUR

MOBILISATION

Types of Division

1

The Soviet Army is armed with dozens of types of artillery weapons: guns, howitzers, gun-howitzers, and howitzer-guns, ordinary and automatic mortars, multi-barrelled, salvo-firing rocket launchers, anti-tank and anti-aircraft guns. In each of these classes of weapons there is a whole array of models—from very small to very large—and most of these exist in many variants—self-propelled, auxiliary-propelled, towed, assault, mountain and static.

But despite the wide variety of artillery systems, all of these have one feature in common; no matter how many men there are in the crew of a gun—three or thirty—only two qualified specialists—the commander and the gunlayer—are needed. All the rest of the crew can perform their duties without any kind of specialised training. Any No 2 loader, rammer number, fuse-setter, ammunition handler or other member of a gun's crew, can have his duties explained in three minutes and the crew can be working like automata within a few hours. The same applies to the driver of a self-propelled gun or of a gun tractor. If he was previously a tractor driver he too will quickly master his new functions.

Soviet generals know that it is possible to teach a bear to ride a bicycle—and very quickly. Why, they reason, do we need to maintain a peacetime army of hundreds of thousands of soldiers whose wartime tasks would be so simple? Surely it is easier to replace the thirty men in a two-gun howitzer platoon with five—the platoon commander, two gun-commanders and two loaders and to moth-ball both guns and their tractors? If war comes, the others—the bears—can be trained very quickly.

For the present let them occupy themselves with peaceful work—casting steel (armoured, of course) or building electrical power-stations (for the production of aluminium, which is used only for military purposes in the USSR).

2

In peacetime the great majority of Soviet artillery regiments, brigades and divisions therefore have only 5% of the soldiers they would need in wartime. Only those units (an insignificant minority) stationed in the countries of Eastern Europe or on the Chinese frontier are up to full strength.

This principle applies not only to the artillery but to most of the land forces and indeed to the bulk of the whole Soviet Armed Forces. It is almost impossible to apply it to certain categories—to tank forces or to submarines, say. But it does apply in many cases, particularly to the infantry, to the marine infantry, to repair, transport and engineer sub-units and to units manning Fortified Areas.

Because of this, the enormous Soviet land forces, with their peacetime strength of 183 divisions as well as a very large number of independent brigades, regiments and battalions, have a laughably small numerical strength—little more than one and a half million men.

This astonishingly small figure is deceptive. Simply bringing the existing divisions and the independent brigades, regiments and battalions up to strength on the first day of mobilisation will raise the strength of the land forces to 4,100,000. But this is just the first stage of mobilisation.

3

Soviet divisions are divided into three categories, depending on the number of "bears" absent in peacetime:

Category A—divisions which have 80% or more of their
           full strength

Category B—those with between 30% and 50%
Category C—those with between 5% and 10%

Some Western observers use categories 1, 2 and 3 in referring to Soviet divisions. This does not affect the crux of the
matter, but is not quite accurate. Categories 1 to 3 are used in
the USSR only when referring to military districts. Divisions
are always referred to by letters of the alphabet. This is because
it is simpler to use letters in secret abbreviations. For instance,
"213 C MRD" refers to the 213th motor-rifle division, which
falls in category C. The use of a numerical category in such a
message could lead to confusion. In referring to military districts, which have titles but no numbers, it is more convenient
to use figures to indicate categories.

Some Western observers overestimate the number of soldiers on the strength of category B and C divisions. In fact
there are considerably fewer soldiers than it would appear to
an outside observer. These overestimates presumably result
from the fact that in many military camps, in addition to the
personnel of divisions which are below strength, there are other
sub-units and units, also below strength but not included in the
complement of the division. The Soviet land forces have some
300 independent brigades, more than 500 independent regiments and some thousands of independent battalions and companies, which do not belong to divisions. In most cases their
personnel are quartered in the barracks of divisions which are
below strength, which gives a misleading impression of the
strength of the division itself. In many cases, too, for camouflage purposes, these sub-units wear the insignia of the divisions with which they are quartered. This applies primarily
to rocket, diversionary and reconnaissance/intelligence personnel but is also the case with units concerned with the delivery,
storage and transport of nuclear and chemical weapons.

About a third of the divisions in the Soviet Army fall into
category A. They include all divisions stationed abroad and a
number of divisions on the Chinese frontier.

Categories B and C, too, account for approximately a third
of all Soviet divisions. In recent years there has been a constant
shift of divisions from category B to category C, because of
the introduction of such new arms of forces as airborne assault
troops and fortified area troops. The new sub-units and units

need entirely new troops, which are always taken from category B divisions. They cannot be taken from category A divisions, because these represent the minimum number of troops who must be kept at readiness, or from category C divisions because these have no one to spare.

It must also be noted that in category B divisions the three most important battalions—rocket, reconnaissance and communications—are kept at category A strength. In category C divisions these battalions are maintained at category B strength.

The same applies to similar sub-units serving with Armies and Fronts. All rocket, reconnaissance, diversionary and communications sub-units of Armies and Fronts are maintained at a strength one category higher than that of all the other elements of the particular Army or Front.

4

It must be emphasised that the category allocated to a division has no effect whatsoever upon the extent to which it is supplied with new weapons. Divisions stationed abroad, which are all, without exception, in category A, take second place when new combat equipment is being issued.

The newest equipment is issued first of all to the frontier Military Districts—Baltic, Byelorussian, Carpathian, Far Eastern and Trans-Baykal.

Only five or seven, sometimes even ten years after a particular piece of equipment has first been issued, is it supplied to divisions stationed abroad. Third to be supplied, after them, are the Soviet Union's allies. Once the requirements of all these three elements have been fully satisfied, the new production of the particular model is discontinued. Once production of a new version has begun, the re-equipment of the frontier military districts begins once again, and the material withdrawn from them is used to bring units located in the rear areas up to the required scale. Once the Soviet frontier military districts have been re-equipped, the process of supplying their used equipment to Category C divisions follows. Then the whole process begins again—to the second echelon, then to the first, then from the second via the first to the third.

Such a system of supplying combat equipment has undeniable advantages.

Firstly, secrecy is greatly increased. Both friends and enemies assume that the equipment issued to the Group of Forces in Germany is the very latest available. Enemies therefore greatly underestimate the fighting potential and capabilities of the Soviet Army. Friends, too, are misled and it therefore becomes possible to sell them a piece of equipment which is being issued in East Germany as if it were the most up-to-date model.

Secondly, it becomes far more difficult for a Soviet soldier to defect to the enemy with details of the newest equipment— or even, perhaps, to drive across the border in the latest tank or fighting vehicle. It is practically impossible to do this from the Baltic or Byelorussian Military Districts. The Soviet command does not worry at all about the Trans-Baykal or Far Eastern Military Districts. It knows very well that every Soviet soldier hates socialism and that he would therefore defect only to one of the capitalist countries. No one would ever think of defecting to socialist China.

Thirdly, in the event of war, it is the first echelon forces which would suffer the greatest losses in the first few hours— good equipment must be lost, of course, but it should not be the very latest. But then, after this, the Carpathian, Byelorussian and Baltic divisions go into battle equipped with the new weapons, whose existence is unsuspected by the enemy.

This system of re-equipment has been in existence for several decades. It is significant that the T-34 tank, which went into mass production as early as 1940, was issued only to military districts in the rear areas. Although the USSR was unprepared for Germany's surprise attack, these security measures were taken automatically, simple as they were to enforce. The surprise onslaught made by the Germans destroyed thousands of Soviet tanks, but there was not a single T-34 among them. Nor, despite the fact that the Soviet Army had some 2,000 of these tanks, did they appear in battle during the first weeks of the war. It was only after the first echelon of the Soviet forces had been completely destroyed that the German forces first met the excellent T-34. It is also significant that German Intelligence did not suspect even the existence of the tank, let alone the fact that it was in mass production.

The Invisible Divisions

1

On 31 December, 1940, the German General Staff finished work on a directive on the strategic deployment of the Wehrmacht for the surprise attack on the USSR. A top-secret appendix to the directive was prepared from data provided by German Intelligence, containing an appreciation of the fighting strength of the Red Army. The German generals believed that the Soviet land forces possessed 182 divisions, of which only 141 could be brought into a war against Germany. Because of the tense situation on the Asian frontiers of the USSR, a minimum of 41 divisions must at all costs be left guarding these frontiers. The whole plan for the war against the USSR was therefore based on an estimate of the speed with which 141 Soviet divisions could be destroyed.

On 22 June Germany attacked, taking everyone in the USSR, Stalin included, by surprise. The way the war developed could not have been better for Germany. In the first few hours, thousands of aircraft were blazing on Soviet airfields while thousands of Soviet tanks and guns did not even succeed in leaving their depots. In the first days of the war, dozens of Soviet divisions, finding themselves encircled and without ammunition, fuel or provisions, surrendered ingloriously. German armoured spearheads carried out brilliant encirclement operations surrounding not just Soviet divisions or corps but entire Armies. On the third day of the war the 3rd and 10th Soviet Armies were surrounded near Bialystok. Immediately after this an equally large encirclement operation was carried out near Minsk, Vitebsk and Orsha, near Smolensk. Two Soviet armies were destroyed after being surrounded near Uman' and five Armies in a huge pocket near Kiev.

However, already, even while the bells were ringing for their victories, the sober-minded German generals were biting their fingernails, as they bent over maps; the number of Soviet divisions was not diminishing—on the contrary, it was rising fast. Already in mid-August General Halder was writing in his diary; "We underestimated them. We have now discovered and identified 360 of their divisions!" But Halder was only talking about the Soviet divisions which were directly involved at that moment in fighting in the forward areas—that is, first echelon divisions. But how many were there in the second echelon? And in the third? And in the reserves of the Armies and the Fronts? And in the internal military districts? And in the Stavka's reserve? And how many divisions had the NKVD? How many were there in all?

The miscalculation proved fatal. 153 German and 37 allied divisions proved insufficient to destroy the Red Army, even given the most favourable conditions.

The German generals' miscalculation was twofold. Firstly, the Red Army consisted, not of 182 but of 303 divisions, without counting the divisions of the NKVD, the airborne forces, the marine infantry, the frontier troops, the Fortified Area troops and others.

Secondly, and this was most important, the German generals knew absolutely nothing about the "second formation" system—the system which splits Soviet divisions into two in the course of one night. This is a system which enables the Soviet General Staff to increase the number of its divisions by precisely one hundred per cent, within a remarkably short time.

2

The system of "invisible" divisions was adopted by the Red Army at the beginning of the 1930s. It saved the Soviet Union from defeat in the Second World War. It is still in use today.

The process, which enables the Soviet leadership to expand the fighting strength of its Armed Forces with great speed, is simple and reliable and uses almost no material resources.

In peacetime every divisional commander has not one but two deputies. One of these carries out his duties continuously, the other does so only from time to time, since he has an additional series of responsibilities. He also has a secret designation—"Divisional Commander—Second Formation."

The chief of staff of a division, a Colonel, also has two deputies, Lieutenant-Colonels, one of whom also has a secret designation—"Divisional Chief of Staff—Second Formation."

The same system applies in every regiment.

Every battalion has a commander (a Lieutenant-Colonel) and a deputy, who is secretly designated "Battalion Commander—Second Formation."

Let us imagine that a conflict has broken out on the Soviet-Chinese frontier. A division receives its stand-to signal and moves off immediately to its operational zone. The divisional commander has only one deputy—the officer who has been carrying out this function, with all its responsibilities, in peacetime. His chief of staff and his regimental commanders, too, have only one deputy apiece. The battalion commanders have no deputies, but in a situation of this sort one of the company commanders in each battalion immediately becomes deputy to the battalion commander and one of the platoon commanders automatically takes his place.

Such unimportant moves of officers do not reduce the fighting efficiency of the division in any way.

So, the division leaves its camp at full strength, with all its soldiers and equipment. If it has less than its complement of soldiers and junior officers, it will be brought up to strength as it moves to the operational zone. The absorption of reservists is an operation which has been very carefully worked out.

However, after the departure of the division the military camp is not left empty. The Colonel who functioned as deputy to the division's chief in peacetime has remained there. There, too, are six Lieutenant-Colonels, who were the deputies of the regimental commanders, together with the deputy battalion commanders and with one third of the platoon commanders, who now become company commanders.

Thus, an entire command staff remains in the camp. Their previously secret titles become overt. Within twenty-four hours this new division receives 10,000 reserve soldiers and the military camp from which one division has only just set out is already occupied by a new one. Unquestionably, of course, the new division is inferior in fighting power to the one which has just departed for the front. Of course, the reservists have long ago forgotten what they were taught during their army

service many years earlier. It is understandable that the platoons, companies and battalions have not shaken down and are
not yet capable of obeying the orders of their commanders
promptly and accurately. Nevertheless, this is a division. At
its head is a trained and experienced officer who for several
years has been, essentially, an understudy to the commander
of a real operational division and who has often performed the
latter's functions. Those in command of the new regiments,
battalions and companies, too, are all operational officers, rather
than reservists. Each of them has worked constantly with real
soldiers and with up-to-date equipment, has taken part in battle
exercises and has borne constant, heavy responsibility for his
actions and for those of his subordinates. In addition, all the
officers of the new division from the commander downwards
know one another and have worked together for many years.

But where does enough equipment for so many new divisions come from? This question is simple. These "invisible"
divisions use old equipment. For instance, immediately after
the end of the war, Soviet infantrymen were armed with PPSh
automatic weapons. These were changed for AK-47 assault
rifles. Each division received the number of new weapons which
it needed and the old ones were mothballed and stored in the
division's stores for the "invisible divisions." Then the AKM
rifle replaced the AK-47s, which were taken to the divisional
store, from which the old PPSh weapons were sent (still fit for
use) to government storehouses or were passed on to "national
liberation movements." The same path has been followed by
the RPG-1, RPG-2, RPG-7 and then the RPG-16 anti-tank
rocket launchers. As new weapons are received, those of the
previous generation remain in the division's store, until the
division receives something completely new. Then the contents
of the store are renewed.

The same happens with tanks, artillery, communications
equipment and so forth. I have myself seen, in many divisional
stores, mothballed JS-3 tanks (which were first issued to units
at the end of the Second World War) at a time when the whole
division was equipped with the T-64, which was then brand
new. When the Soviet artillery began to be re-equipped with
self-propelled guns, the old, towed guns were certainly not sent
away to be melted down. They were mothballed for the "second
formation division."

So, you say, these "invisible divisions" are not only staffed with reservists who have grown fat and idle, but are equipped with obsolete weapons? Quite correct. But why, Soviet generals ask, reasonably, would we issue fat reservists with the latest equipment? Would they be able to learn to use it? Would there be enough time to teach them in a war? Is it not better to keep the old (in other words simple and reliable) equipment, which is familiar to the reservists? Weapons which they learned to use eight or ten years ago, when they were in the army? Mothballing an old tank is a thousand times cheaper than building a new one. Is it not better to put ten thousand old tanks into storage than to build ten new ones?

Yes, the "invisible divisions" are old-fashioned and they don't bristle with top-secret equipment, but it costs absolutely nothing to maintain 150 of them in peacetime. And the arrival of 150 divisions, even if they are old-fashioned, at a critical moment, to reinforce 150 others who are armed with the very latest equipment, could nonplus the enemy and spoil all his calculations. That is just what happened in 1941.

The system of "second formation" is not restricted to the land forces. It is also used by the airborne forces, the frontier troops, the marine infantry, in the Air Forces and by the National Air Defence Forces.

Here is an example of the use of this system.

At the end of the 1950s the anti-aircraft artillery regiments and divisions of the National Air Defence Forces began to be rapidly re-equipped with rocket weapons, in place of conventional artillery. All the anti-aircraft guns were left with the anti-aircraft regiments and divisions as secondary weapon systems, in addition to the new rockets. It was intended that, in the event of war, an anti-aircraft artillery regiment could be set up as a counterpart to each anti-aircraft rocket regiment and that the same could be done with each anti-aircraft rocket brigade and division. Khrushchev himself came out strongly against the system. Those commanding the National Air Defence Forces suggested that Khrushchev should withdraw amicably but Khrushchev refused, rejecting what he saw as a whimsical idea by a handful of conservative generals who were unable to understand the superiority of anti-aircraft rockets over obsolete anti-aircraft guns. But then the war in Vietnam began. Suddenly, it was realised that rockets are useless against aircraft which are flying at extremely low altitudes. It also became clear, that there are conditions in which it is quite impossible to transport rockets into certain areas, that during mass attacks it is almost impossible for rocket launchers to reload so that after the first launch they are completely useless, that the electronic equipment of rocket forces is exposed to intense countermeasures by the enemy, and that those may seriously reduce the effectiveness of missile systems. It was then that the old-fashioned, simple, reliable, economical anti-aircraft guns were remembered. Thousands of them were taken out of mothballs and sent to Vietnam to strengthen the anti-aircraft rocket sub-units. The results they achieved are well known.

This makes it quite clear why old anti-aircraft guns (tens of thousands of them) are still stored, today, by the anti-aircraft rocket sub-units of the Soviet Army. All of them have already been collected together for the "invisible" regiments, brigades and divisions. If it should become necessary, all that needs to be done is to call upon those reservists who have once served in units equipped with these systems and the numerical strength of the National Air Defence Forces will be doubled. Of course, its fighting strength will not be increased in proportion to this numerical growth, but in battle any increase in strength may change the relative positions of the combatants.

Why is a Military District commanded by a Colonel-General in peacetime, but only by a Major-General in wartime?

1

No single aspect of the organisation of the Soviet Army gives rise to so many disagreements and misunderstandings among specialists as the question of Military Districts. One expert will assert that a district is under the command of the Commander-in-Chief of Land Forces. Others will immediately reject this. The commander of a military district has an Air Army at his disposal and he is in command of it, but the C-in-C Land Forces is not entitled to exercise command over an Air Army. The commander of a military district may have naval, rocket or flying training schools in his area and he must command them, but the C-in-C Land Forces has no authority over such institutions.

In order to understand the role of the military district in the Soviet Army, we must once again return to wartime and remember what its function was then.

Before the war, the territory of the Soviet Union was divided into 16 military districts. The same organisational structure still exists today, with minor changes. Before the war military districts were commanded by Colonel-Generals and Generals of the Army. Today the situation remains exactly the same. During the war the forces from these districts went to the front, under the command of these same Colonel-Generals and Generals. But the military districts remained in existence. During the war they were commanded by Major-Generals or, in a few instances, by Lieutenant-Generals.

During the war the military districts were nothing but territorial military administrative units. Each military district was responsible for:

Maintaining order and discipline among the population, and ensuring the stability of the Communist regime.

Guarding military and industrial installations.

Providing and guarding communications.

Mobilising human, material, economic and natural resources for use by the fighting armies.

Training reservists.

Of course these activities did not fall within the scope of the C-in-C Land Forces. For this reason, the military districts were subordinated to the Deputy Minister of Defence and through him to the most influential section of the Politburo.

The military districts contain training schools for all Services and arms of service and it is in these that new formations for all the Armed Services are assembled. For example, ten armies, one of them an Air Army, were formed in the Volga Military District during the war, together with several brigades of marine infantry, one Polish division and a Czech battalion. In any future war, the military districts would perform the same function. While military units and formations were being assembled and trained they would all come under the orders of the commander of the military district. He would himself be responsible to the C-in-C Land Forces for all questions concerning the latter's armies, to the C-in-C of the Navy on all matters concerning marine infantry, for air questions to the C-in-C of the Air Forces and for questions relating to foreign units to the C-in-C of the Warsaw Treaty Organisation. Because the overwhelming majority of the units in a district comes from the Land Forces, it has come to be believed that the C-in-C Land Forces is the direct superior of the commanders of the military districts. But this is a misapprehension. Each C-in-C controls only his own forces in any given military district. He has no authority to become involved in the wide range of questions for which the commander of the military district is responsible, in addition to the training of reservists. As soon as new formations have completed their training, they pass from the responsibility of the commander of the military district to the Stavka and are sent to the front. Thus, the commander of a military district is simply the military governor of a huge territory. As such, he is in command of every military formation located on his territory, whichever Armed Service it comes from.

2

At the end of the war staffs and fighting units would be dispersed throughout the country in accordance with the plans of the General Staff. It would be normal for a Front, consisting of a Tank, an Air and two All-Arms Armies, to be located in a military district. By virtue of his position, the Front Commander, who has the rank of Colonel-General or General of the Army, is of considerably greater importance than the wartime commander of a military district. In peacetime, in order to avoid bureaucracy and duplication, the staffs of the Front and of the military district are merged. The Front Commander then becomes both the military and the territorial commander, with the peacetime title of Commander of the Forces of the District. The general, who acted as a purely territorial commander during the war, becomes the Deputy Commander of the district in peacetime, with special responsibility for training. The Front's chief of staff becomes the peacetime chief of staff of the district and the officer who held the function in the district in wartime becomes his deputy.

Thus, in peacetime a military district is at one and the same time an operational Front and an enormous expanse of territory. However, it can split into two parts at any moment. The Front goes off to fight and the district's organisational framework stays behind to maintain order and to train reservists.

In some cases something which is either larger or smaller than a Front may be located in a particular military district. For instance, only a single Army is stationed in the Siberian Military District, while the Volga and Ural Military Districts, too, have only one Army, which in both cases is of reduced strength. In peacetime the staffs of these Armies are merged with the staffs of the districts in which they are located. The Commanders of these Armies act as district commanders while the generals who would command the district in wartime function as their deputies. Since these particular districts do not contain Fronts, they have no Air Armies. The C-in-C Land Forces therefore has the sole responsibility for inspecting these troops and this is what has led to the belief that these Districts are under his command.

No two districts are in the same situation. The Kiev Military District contains the staff of the Commander-in-Chief of the South-Western Strategic District and a Group of Tank Armies. The staffs of the Kiev Military District, of the Group of Tank Armies and of the C-in-C have been merged. In peacetime, too, the C-in-C goes under the modest title of Commander of the Kiev Military District. We have already seen how different the position is in other districts.

In the Byelorussian Military District the staffs of the District and of a Group of Tank Armies are merged. Although he has more forces than his colleague in Kiev, the Commander of the District is nevertheless two steps behind him, since he is not the C-in-C of a Strategic Direction but only the Commander of a Group of Tank Armies.

In the Trans-Baykal Military District the District staff, that of the C-in-C of the Far Eastern Strategic Direction and the staff of the Front are merged.

Depending on the forces stationed on its territory, a military district is assigned to one of three categories, category 1 being the highest. This classification is kept secret, as are the real titles of the generals who, in peacetime, each carry the modest title of Commander of a Military District.

The System for Evacuating
the Politburo from the Kremlin

1

The Kremlin is one of the mightiest fortresses in Europe. The thickness of the walls in some places is as much as 6.5 metres and their height reaches 19 metres. Above the walls rise eighteen towers, each of which can defend itself independently and can cover the approaches to the walls.

In the fourteenth century the Kremlin twice withstood sieges by the Lithuanians and during the fifteenth century the Mongolian Tartars made two unsuccessful attempts within the space of fifty years to capture it.

After the Tartar yoke had been shaken off, the Kremlin was used as a national treasury, as a mint, as a prison and as a setting for solemn ceremonies. But the Russian Tsars lived in Kolomenskoye and in other residencies outside the town. Peter the Great left Moscow altogether and built himself a new capital, opening a window on Europe. An unheard-of idea—to build a new capital on the distant borders of his huge country, right under the nose of the formidable enemy with whom Peter fought for almost his whole reign. And all in order to have contact with other countries.

After Peter the Great, not a single Tsar built behind the Kremlin's stone walls. Go to the capital he built, to Tsarkoye Syelo, to Peterhof, to the Winter Palace, and you will note that all of them have one feature in common—enormous windows. And the wider the windows of the imperial palaces became, the more widely the doors of the empire were thrown open. The Russian nobility spent at least half of their lives in Paris, some of them returning home only long enough to fight Napoleon before rushing back there as quickly as possible. After the 1860 reforms, a Russian peasant did not even have to seek permission before emigrating. If he wanted to live in Amer-

ica—well, if he didn't like being at home, to hell with him!
Even today in the United States and in Canada millions of
people still cling to their Slavonic background. Foreigners were
allowed into the country without visas of any sort—and not
just as tourists. They were taken into Government service and
were entrusted with almost everything, given posts in the War
Ministry, the Ministry of Foreign Affairs, the Ministry of the
Interior . . . The ministries, the crown and the throne were entrusted to Catherine the Great, who was honoured as the mother
of the country, everybody having forgotten that she was a
German. There is no need even to mention the freedom given
to foreign business undertakings which set themselves up on
Russian territory. It was, in short, an idyllic state of affairs,
or perhaps not quite idyllic but certainly something entirely
different to the state of affairs which exists today.

Under Lenin, everything changed. He began by closing all
the frontiers. Before the First World War more than 300,000
people went to Germany alone, each year, for seasonal work.
Vladimir Ilyich soon put a stop to that. And having closed the
country's frontiers he soon became aware that it would be no
bad thing to shut himself away from the people behind a stone
wall. He suddenly thought of the Kremlin. Lenin realised quite
clearly that he would be shot at more often than the Emperors
of Russia had ever been and without a moment's hesitation he
abandoned the wide windows of the imperial palaces for the
blank walls of the Kremlin.

Having shut his people in behind a wall of iron and having
put a stone one between them and himself, Lenin then took a
precaution which had not been resorted to in Russia for a
thousand years. He brought in foreign mercenaries to guard
the Kremlin—the 4th Latvian rifles to be precise. Lenin did
not trust Russians with this job—he must have had his reasons.

These mercenaries claimed, as one man, that they were
guarding Lenin out of purely ideological motives, since they
were convinced socialists. Despite this, however, not one of
them would acknowledge the validity of Soviet bank notes;
they demanded that Lenin should pay them in the Tsar's gold.
Thanks to Lenin, there was enough of this available. At the
same time, a brave preacher in Riga prophesied that the whole
of free Latvia would one day pay with its blood for these
handfuls of gold.

The Kremlin also had a great appeal for Stalin, who inherited

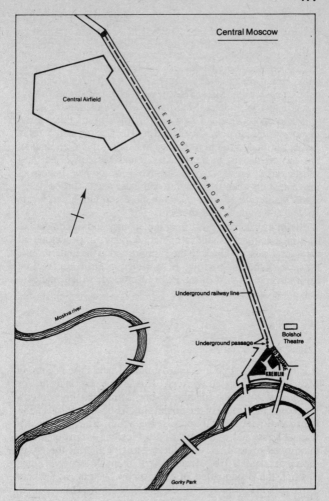

Central Moscow

Central Airfield

LENINGRAD PROSPEKT

Moskva river

Underground railway line

Underground passage

Bolshoi Theatre

KREMLIN

Gorky Park

it from Lenin. He strengthened and modernised all its buildings thoroughly. Among the first of the changes he was responsible for was a series of large-scale underground constructions—a secret corridor leading to the Metro, an underground exit on to Red Square and an underground command post and communications centre. Stalin threw Lenin's foreign mercenaries out of the Kremlin. Many of them were executed straight away, others many years later—before the seizure of Latvia itself.

Stalin chose to spend a large proportion of his thirty years in power immured in the Kremlin. He also arranged for a number of underground fortresses to be built in the grounds of his various dachas in the country round Moscow. The most substantial of these was at Kuntsevo. His complex pattern of movement between the Kremlin and these dacha fortresses enabled Stalin to confuse even those closest to him about where he was at any particular moment.

Stalin's system of governing the country and of controlling its armed services is still in operation today. In peacetime all the threads still lead back to the Kremlin and to the underground fortresses around Moscow. In wartime, control is exercised from the control post of the High Command, which, incidentally, was also built by Stalin.

2

It is quite impossible to acquire a plot of land in the centre of Moscow—even in a cemetery. This is not surprising if you visualise a city which contains seventy Ministries. For Moscow is not only the capital of the Soviet Union but also of the RSFSR (Russian Soviet Federal Socialist Republic), which means that it must house not only Soviet ministries but dozens of republican ones as well. Besides these Moscow houses the KGB, the General Staff, the Headquarters of the Moscow Military District, the Headquarters of the Moscow District Air Defence Forces, the Headquarters of the Warsaw Treaty Organisation, CMEA, more than one hundred embassies, twelve military academies, the Academy of Sciences, hundreds of committees (including the Central Committee), and of directorates (including the Chief Intelligence Directorate—GRU), editorial offices, libraries, communications centres, etc.

Each of these wishes to put up its buildings as close as possible to the centre of the city and to build accommodation for its thousands of bureaucrats as close to its main buildings as it can.

A fierce battle goes on for every square metre of ground in the centre of Moscow and only the Politburo can decide who should be given permission to build and who should be refused.

And yet, almost in the centre, a huge, apparently endless field lies fallow. This is Khodinka, or, as it is known today, the Central Airfield. If this field were built on there would be room for all the bureaucrats. Their glass skyscrapers would rise right along the Leningradskiy Prospekt, which runs into Gorky Street and leads straight to the Kremlin. Many people look enviously at Khodinka musing about ways of cutting small slices out of it—after all this "Central Airfield" is not used by aircraft: it simply lies there, empty and idle.

For several years the KGB made efforts to acquire a small piece of land at Khodinka. The Lubyanka could not be enlarged any further, but the KGB was still growing. A vast new building was needed. But all attempts by the KGB to persuade the Politburo to allocate it some land at Khodinka were unsuccessful. That was how the huge new KGB building came to be built right out beyond the ring-road—a highly inconvenient location. Meanwhile the endless field still stretches through the centre of Moscow, lying empty as it always has done. Once a year rehearsals for the Red Square military parade are held there and then the field sinks back into lethargy. Naturally this valuable piece of ground is not being kept just for these rehearsals. The troops could be trained on any other field—there are enough of them around Moscow.

Why does the Politburo refuse even the KGB, its favourite offspring, permission to cut the smallest corner off this vast unused field? Because the field is connected to the Kremlin by a direct underground Metro line—Sverdlov Square (under the Kremlin itself)—Mayakovskaya—Byelorusskaya—Dinamo —Aeroport. Muscovites know how often and how quickly this line is closed during any kind of holiday or celebration, or any other event which breaks the normal rhythm of life in the Soviet capital.

Why do the Soviet leaders particularly like this Metro line? Already before the war many spacious underground halls had been built for Moscow Metro stations and the ceremonies to mark the anniversary of the revolution, on 6 November, 1941, were actually held in the Mayakovskiy Metro station. Everyone invited to attend had to reach the station from above, because the line had been closed. Once they were there a special Metro train appeared carrying Stalin, Molotov and Beriya. They came from the Sverdlov Square Metro station. To reach this, they do not, of course, leave the Kremlin. They have their own secret corridor leading to the Metro from right inside the buildings.

Stalin's route out of the Kremlin has existed unchanged for several decades. If necessary, any or all of the members of the Politburo can be taken underground, in complete secrecy and security, to Khodinka, where government aircraft await them in well-guarded hangars. With normal organisation, the Politburo can leave the huge, traffic-laden city within fifteen minutes, during which no outsider will spot official cars speeding along streets in the centre or helicopters flying out of the Kremlin.

North-west of Moscow is another government airfield—Podlipki. (Incidentally, just beside this airfield is the centre at which cosmonauts are trained.) The sub-unit stationed at Podlipki is known as the 1st Task Force of the Civil Air Fleet. In fact it has virtually nothing to do with the Civil Air Fleet—it is a group of government aircraft. Ordinary official flights begin and end at Podlipki. Special official flights, involving ceremonial meetings and escorts, make the brief flight to Sheremetyevo or to one of Moscow's other large airports.

In an emergency the Politburo could be evacuated in various ways:

—from the Kremlin in official cars to Podlipki and from there by air to the Supreme Command Post; this is a long and inconvenient route. In addition all Moscow can see what is happening.

—from the Kremlin by Metro to Khodinka and from there by helicopter to Podlipki; this, too, is a fairly long route, involving as it does changing from the helicopter to a fixed-wing aircraft.

—the shortest variation—an aircraft of the 1st Task Force of the Civil Air Fleet is either permanently stationed at Khodinka or makes the short flight there from Podlipki, takes the members of the Politburo on board, and vanishes.

3

The special aircraft soars up into the early morning mist over sleeping Moscow. As it gains height it makes a wide turn and sets course for the SCP—the Supreme Command Post, built by Stalin and modernised by his successors. Where is the SCP? How can it be found? Where would Stalin have chosen to site it?

Most probably it is not in Siberia. Today the eastern regions are threatened by China, as they were before the war by Japan. Of course the SCP would not be located in any area which might be threatened, even theoretically, by an aggressor, so it cannot be in the Ukraine, in the Baltic region, in the Caucasus or in the Crimea. Common sense suggests that it must be somewhere as far away as possible from any frontier—in other words in the central part of the RSFSR, which could hardly be over-run by enemy tanks and which could scarcely be reached by enemy bombers, or by aircraft carrying airborne troops. And if hostile aircraft were to reach the spot they could only do so without fighter cover, so they would be defenceless.

Secondly, the SCP cannot, of course, be sited in an open field. There must be a minimum of 200 metres of solid granite above its many kilometres of tunnels and roads. This being so, it can only be in either the Urals or Zhiguli.

Thirdly, it stands to reason that it must be surrounded by natural barriers which are so impenetrable that no hunter who happens to enter the area, no geologist who loses his way, no gaol-breaker, no pilot who has survived a crash and wandered for weeks through the taiga can come across the SCP's huge ventilator shafts, descending into terrifying chasms or its gigantic tunnels, their entrances sealed by armoured shields weighing thousands of tons. If Stalin set out to keep the location of the SCP secret he would not have chosen the Urals, whose gentle slopes were being completely worn away by the feet of tens of millions of prisoners. Where could one build a whole town, so that no trace of it would be found by a single living soul? The only possible place is Zhiguli.

Would it be possible to find a better place, anywhere on earth, to build an underground town? Zhiguli is a real natural miracle—a granite monolith 80 kilometres long and 40 wide.

Some geolists maintain that Zhiguli is one single rock, crumbling slightly at the edges but retaining the original, massive unity of all its millions of tons. It rises out of the boundless steppes, almost entirely encircled by the huge river Volga, which turns it into a peninsula, with rocky shores which stretch for 150 kilometres and fall sheer to the water's edge. Zhiguli is a gigantic fortress built by nature, with granite walls hundreds of metres high, bounded by the waters of the great river. From the air, Zhiguli presents an almost flat surface, overgrown with age-old, impenetrable forest.

The climate is excellent—a cold winter, with hard frosts, but no wind. The summer is dry and hot. This would be the place to build sanatoriums! Here and there in clearings in the virgin forests there are beautiful private houses, fences, barbed wire, Alsatian dogs. One of Stalin's dachas was built here, but nothing was ever written about it, any more than about those at Kuntsevo or Yalta. In the vicinity were the villas of Molotov and Beriya and later of Khrushchev, Brezhnev and others.

Anyone who has travelled on the Moscow Metro will say that there is no better underground system in the world. But I would disagree with this—there is a much better one. In Zhiguli. It was built by the best of the engineers who worked on the Moscow Metro—and by thousands of prisoners.

In Zhiguli tens of kilometres of tunnels have been cut, hundreds of metres deep into the granite monolith and command posts, communications centres, stores and shelters have been built for those who will control the gigantic armies during a war.

In peacetime, no aircraft may fly over this region. Not even the most friendly of foreigners may enter the Zhiguli area, which is protected by a corps of the National Air Defence Forces and by a division of the KGB. Nearby is a huge airfield, at Kurumoch, which is completely empty. This is where the special aircraft will land but it is also intended for use by additional fighter aircraft, to strengthen the defences in the event of war.

Close to Zhiguli is the city of Kuybishev. It, too, is closed to foreigners, and it is useful to remember that this was where the whole Soviet government was based during the last war.

PART FIVE

STRATEGY AND TACTICS

The Axe Theory

1

For decades, Western military theorists have unanimously asserted that any nuclear war would begin with a first stage during which only conventional weapons would be used. Then, after a certain period, each side would begin, uncertainly and irresolutely at first, to use nuclear weapons of the lowest calibre. Gradually, larger and larger nuclear weapons would be brought into action. These theorists hold varying views on the period which this escalation would take, ranging from a few weeks to several months.

Being unopposed, this theory was to be found in the pages of both serious studies and light novels—the latter being fantasies with happy endings, in which a nuclear war was brought to a halt in such a way that it could never recur.

The theory that a nuclear war would take a long time to build up originated in the West at the beginning of the nuclear age. It is incomprehensible and absurd, and it completely mystifies Soviet marshals. For a long time there was a secret debate at the highest levels of the Soviet government—have the Western politicians and generals gone off their heads or are they bluffing? It was concluded that, of course, no one really believed in the theory but that it had been thought up in order to hide what Western policy-makers really believed about the subject. But then the question arose: for whose benefit could such an unconvincing and, to put it mildly, such a silly idea have been dreamed up? Presumably not for that of the Soviet leadership. The theory is too naive for specialists to believe. That must mean that it was devised for the ignorant and for the popular masses in the West, to reassure the man in the street.

2

The first American film I ever saw was *The Magnificent Seven* with Yul Brynner in the main role. At that time all I knew about the Americans was what Communist propaganda said about them and I had not believed that since my earliest childhood. Thus it was from a cowboy film that I began to try to form my own independent opinions about the American people and about the principles by which they live.

American films are not often shown in the Soviet Union, but after *The Magnificent Seven* I did not miss a single one. The country as I saw it on the screen pleased me and the people even more so—good-looking, strong, masculine and decisive. It seemed that the Americans spent all their time in the saddle, riding on marvellous horses in blazing sunlight through deserts, shooting down villains without mercy. My heart belonged only to America. I worshipped the Americans—in particular for the decisiveness with which they kept down the number of crooks in their society. The heroes of American films would submit for long periods and with great patience to humiliation and insults and were cheated at every turn, but matters were always settled with a dramatically decisive gunfight. The two enemies gaze unflinchingly into each other's eyes. Each has his hands tensely over his holsters. No exchange of curses, no insults, not a superfluous movement. Dramatic silence. Both are calm and collected. Clearly death has spread its black wings above them. The gunfight itself almost represents death, for each of them. They look long and hard into each other's eyes. Suddenly and simultaneously both of them realise, not from what they see or hear, not with their minds or their hearts but from pure animal instinct, that the moment has come. Two shots ring out as one. It is impossible to detect the moment at which they draw their guns and pull the triggers. The dénouement is instantaneous, without preamble. A corpse rolls on the ground. Occasionally there are two corpses. Usually the villain is killed but the hero is only wounded. In the hand.

Many years passed and I became an officer serving with the General Staff. Suddenly, as I studied American theories of war, I came to an appalling realisation. It became clear to me that a modern American cowboy who is working up to a decisive fight will always expect to begin by spitting at and insulting his opponent and to continue by throwing whisky in his face and chucking custard pies at him before resorting to more serious weapons. He expects to hurl chairs and bottles at his enemy and to try to stick a fork or a tableknife into his behind and then to fight with his fists and only after all this to fight it out with his gun.

This is a very dangerous philosophy. You are going to end up by using pistols. Why not start with them? Why should the bandit you are fighting wait for you to remember your gun? He may shoot you before you do, just as you are going to slap his face. By using his most deadly weapon at the beginning of the fight, your enemy saves his strength. Why should he waste it throwing chairs at you? Moreover, this will enable him to save his own despicable life. After all, he does not know, either, when you, the noble hero, will decide to use your gun. Why should he wait for this moment? You might make a sudden decision to shoot him immediately after throwing custard pies at him, without waiting for the exchange of chairs. Of course he won't wait for you when it comes to staying alive. He will shoot first. At the very start of the fight.

I consoled myself for a long time with the hope that the theory of escalation in a nuclear war had been dreamed up by the American specialists to reassure nervous old-age pensioners. Clearly, the theory is too fatally dangerous to serve as a basis for secret military planning. Yet, suddenly, the American specialists demonstrated to the whole world that they really believed that this theory would apply to a world-wide nuclear war. They really did believe that the bandit they would be fighting would give them time to throw custard pies and chairs at him before he made use of his most deadly weapon.

The demonstration was as public as it possibly could be. At the end of the 1960s the Americans began to deploy their anti-missile defence system. They could not, of course, use it to defend more than one vitally important objective. The objective they chose to protect was their strategic rockets. They did not decide to safeguard the heart and mind of their country—the President, their government or their capital. Instead they would protect their pistol—in other words they were showing the whole world that, in the event of a fight, they did not intend to use it.

This revelation was greeted with the greatest delight in the Kremlin and by the General Staff.

3

The philosophy of the Soviet General Staff is no different from that of the horsemen whom I had watched riding the desert. "If you want to stay alive, kill your enemy. The quicker you finish him off, the less chance he will have to use his own gun." In essence, this is the whole theoretical basis on which their plans for a third world war have been drawn up. The theory is known unofficially in the General Staff as the "axe theory." It is stupid, say the Soviet generals, to start a fist-fight if your opponent may use a knife. It is just as stupid to attack him with a knife if he may use an axe. The more terrible the weapon which your opponent may use, the more decisively you must attack him, and the more quickly you must finish him off. Any delay or hesitation in doing this will just give him a fresh opportunity to use his axe on you. To put it briefly, you can only prevent your enemy from using his axe if you use your own first.

The "axe theory" was put forward in all Soviet manuals and handbooks to be read at regimental level and higher. In each of these one of the main sections was headed "Evading the blow." These handbooks advocated, most insistently, the delivery of a massive pre-emptive attack on the enemy, as the best method of self-protection. This recommendation was not confined to secret manuals—non-confidential military publications carried it as well.

But this was trivial by comparison to the demonstration which the Soviet Union gave the whole world at the beginning of the 1970s, with the official publication of data about the Soviet anti-missile defence system. This whole system was, in reality, totally inadequate, but the idea behind it provides an excellent illustration of the Soviet philosophy on nuclear war. By contrast to the United States, the Soviet Union had no thought of protecting its strategic rockets with an anti-missile system. The best protection for rockets in a war is to use them immediately. Could anyone devise a more effective way of defending them?

4

In addition to such elementary military logic, there are political and economic reasons which would quite simply compel the Soviet command to make use of the overwhelming proportion of its nuclear armoury within the first few minutes of a war.

From the political point of view, the turning point must be reached within the first few minutes. What alternative could there be? In peacetime Soviet soldiers desert to the West by the hundred, their sailors jump off ships in Western ports, their pilots try to break through the West's anti-aircraft defences in their aircraft. Even in peacetime, the problems involved in keeping the population in chains are almost insoluble. The problems are already as acute as this when no more than a few thousand of the most trusted Soviet citizens have even a theoretical chance of escaping. In wartime tens of millions of soldiers would have an opportunity to desert—and they would take it! In order to prevent this, every soldier must realise quite clearly that, from the very first moments of a war, there is no sanctuary for him at the other side of the nuclear desert. Otherwise the whole Communist house of cards will collapse.

From an economic point of view, too, the war must be as short as possible. Socialism is unable to feed itself from its own resources. The Soviet variety is no exception to this general rule. Before the revolution, Russia, Poland, Estonia, Lithuania, and Latvia all exported foodstuffs. Nowadays they have not enough reserves to hold out from one harvest to the next. Yet shortage of food leads very quickly to manifestations of discontent, to food-riots and to revolution. Remember what happened in Novocherkassk in 1962, throughout the Soviet Union in 1964 and in Poland in 1970 and 1980. If socialism is unable to feed itself in peacetime, when the whole army is used to bring in the harvest, what will happen when the whole army is thrown into battle and when all the men and vehicles at present used for agriculture are mobilised for war?

For these reasons, the Communists are forced to plan any adventures they have in mind for the second part of the year, for the period when the harvest has already been brought in, and to try to finish them as quickly as possible. Before the next season for work in the fields comes round.

The Strategic Offensive

1

Soviet generals believe, quite correctly, that the best kind of defensive operation is an offensive. Accordingly, no practical or theoretical work on purely defensive operations is carried out at Army level or higher. In order that they should take the offensive, Soviet generals are taught how to attack. In order that they should defend themselves successfully, they are also taught how to attack. Therefore, when we talk of a large-scale operation—one conducted by a Front or a Strategic Direction—we can talk only of an offensive.

The philosophy behind the offensive is simple. It is easy to tear up a pack of cards if you take them one by one. If you put a dozen cards together it is very difficult to tear them up. If you try to tear up the whole pack at once you will be unsuccessful: you will not be able to tear them all up, and, furthermore, not a single card in the pack will be torn. Similarly, Soviet generals attack only with enormous masses of troops, using their cards only as a whole pack. In this way, the pack protects the cards which make it up.

Observing this principle of concentration of resources, in any future war the Soviet Army will only carry out operations by single Fronts in certain isolated sectors. In most cases it will carry out strategic operations—that is to say operations by groups of Fronts working together in the same sector.

2

The scenario for a strategic offensive operation is a standard one, in all cases. Let us take the Western Strategic Direction as an example. We already know that this has a minimum of three Fronts in its first echelon, one more in its second echelon, and a Group of Tank Armies in its third. The Baltic Fleet operates on its flank. Each of its Fronts has one Tank Army, one Air Army and two All-Arms Armies. In addition, the Commander-in-Chief has at his disposal a Corps from the Strategic Rocket Forces, a Corps from the Long-Range Air Force, three airborne divisions and the entire forces of Military Transport Aviation. The rear areas of the Strategic Direction are protected by three Armies from the National Air Defence Forces.

A strategic offensive is divided into five stages:

The first stage, or initial nuclear strike, lasts for half an hour. Taking part in this strike are all the rocket formations which can be used at that stage, including the Corps from the Strategic Rocket Forces, the rocket brigades of the Fronts and Armies, the rocket battalions of the first division echelon and all the nuclear artillery which has reached the forward edge of the battle area. The initial nuclear strike has as its targets:

Command posts and command centres, administrative and political centres, lines of communication and communications centres—in other words, the brain and nerve-centres of a state and of its armies.

Rocket bases, stores for nuclear weapons, bases for nuclear submarines and for bomber aircraft. These targets must be knocked out in order to reduce Soviet losses at the hands of the enemy to the absolute minimum.

Airfields, anti-aircraft positions, radar stations, to ensure the success of the offensive breaks in the enemy's defenses, must be made for Soviet aircraft. The main groupings of the enemy's forces. Why fight them if they can be destroyed before a battle can begin?

In addition to the forces directly under the command of the C-in-C of the Strategic Direction, units of the Strategic Rocket Forces will also play a supporting role in the initial nuclear strike. These will concern themselves in particular with attacks on the enemy's principal ports, in order to prevent the enemy from bringing up reinforcements and in order to isolate the European continent.

Soviet generals consider, with good reason, that an initial

nuclear strike must be unexpected, of short duration and of the greatest possible intensity. If it is delayed by as much as an hour, the situation of the Soviet Union will deteriorate sharply. Many of the enemy's fighting units may move from their permanent locations, his aircraft may be dispersed on to motorways; divisions of his land forces may leave their barracks, his senior leaders may move, with their cabinets, to underground shelters or to airborne command posts and the task of annihilating them will become extremely difficult, if not impossible. This is why the maximum possible number of nuclear weapons will be used to deliver an initial nuclear strike.

The second stage follows immediately upon the first. It lasts between 90 and 120 minutes. It consists of a mass air attack by the Air Armies of all the Fronts and by all the Long-Range Air Force units at the disposal of the C-in-C of the Strategic Direction.

This attack is carried out as a series of waves. The first wave consists of all the available reconnaissance aircraft—not only those of the reconnaissance regiments but also the squadrons of fighters and fighter bombers which have been trained in reconnaissance. In all, more than a thousand reconnaissance aircraft from the Strategic Direction will join this wave; they will be assisted by several hundred pilotless reconnaissance aircraft. The primary tasks of the aircraft in this wave are to assess the effectiveness of the initial nuclear strike and to identify any objectives which have not been destroyed.

Immediately behind these aircraft comes the main wave, made up of all the Air Armies and Corps. Nuclear weapons are carried by those aircraft whose crews have been trained to deliver a nuclear strike. The targets of this wave are in the same categories as those of the rockets which delivered the initial nuclear attack. But, unlike the rockets, these aircraft attack mobile rather than stationary targets. They follow up after the rockets, finishing off whatever the latter were unable to destroy. Among the first of their mobile targets are: tank columns which have managed to leave their barracks, groups of aircraft which have succeeded in taking off from their permanent airfields and in reaching dispersal points on motorways, and mobile anti-aircraft weapons.

The Soviet commanders believe that this massive air activity can be carried out without heavy losses, since the enemy's radars will have been destroyed, many of his computer systems and lines of communication will have been disrupted and his aircrews and anti-aircraft forces will have been demoralised.

While these massive air operations are taking place all staff personnel will be working at top speed on evaluation of the information which is coming in about the results of the initial nuclear strike. Meanwhile, all the rocket launchers which took part in the initial nuclear strike will be reloading. At the same time, too, the rocket battalions of the divisions and the rocket brigades of the Armies and Fronts, which did not take part in the initial strike because they were too far behind the front line, will move up to the forward edge of the battle area at the maximum possible speed.

All aircraft will then return to their bases and the third stage will begin immediately.

The third stage, like the first, will last only half an hour. Taking part in it will be even more rocket launchers than those involved in the first stage, since many will have moved up from the rear areas. The thinking behind this plan is simple: in battle the enemy's prime concern will be to hunt out and destroy all Soviet rocket launchers; each of these should therefore inflict the maximum possible damage on the enemy before this happens. The aim is to destroy all those targets which survived the first and second stages, and to put the maximum possible number of the enemy's troops and equipment, especially his nuclear weapons, out of action.

The fourth stage lasts between 10 and 20 days. It can be broken down into offensive operations by individual Fronts. Each Front concentrates all its efforts on ensuring success for its Tank Army. To achieve this the All-Arms Army attacks the enemy's defences and the Front Commander directs the Tank Army to the point at which a breakthrough has been achieved. At the same time, the entire resources of the Front's artillery division are used to clear a path for the Tank Army. The rocket brigades lay down a nuclear carpet ahead of the Tank Army, and the Air Army covers its breakthrough operation. The Front's anti-tank brigades cover the Tank Army's flanks, the airborne assault brigade seizes bridges and crossing points for its use, and the diversionary brigade, operating ahead of and on the flanks of the Tank Army, does everything possible to provide it with favourable operating conditions.

The Tank Army is brought up to a breach in the enemy defences only when a real breakthrough has been achieved and once the Front's forces have room for manoeuvre. The Tank Army pushes forward at maximum possible speed to the greatest depth it can reach. It avoids prolonged engagements, it keeps clear of pockets of resistance and it often becomes separated by considerable distances from the other components of the Front. Its task, its aim, is to deliver a blow like that from a sword or an axe: the deeper it cuts, the better.

An All-Arms Army advances more slowly than a Tank Army, destroying all the pockets of resistance in its path and any groups of enemy troops which have been surrounded, clearing up the area as it moves forward.

A Tank Army is like a rushing flood, tearing its way through a gap in a dyke, smashing and destroying everything in its path. By contrast an All-Arms Army is a quiet, stagnant sheet of water, flooding a whole area, drowning enemy islands and slowly undermining buildings and other structures until they collapse.

During the first few hours or days of a war, one or all of the Fronts may suffer enormous losses. But it should not be assumed that the C-in-C of a Strategic Direction will use his second echelon Front to strengthen or take the place of the Front which has suffered most. The second echelon Front is brought into action at the point where the greatest success has been achieved, where the dyke has really been breached or where at least a very dangerous crack can be seen developing.

The fifth stage lasts 7–8 days. It may begin at any time during the fourth stage. As soon as the C-in-C is sure that one of his Fronts has really broken through, he moves up his second echelon Front and, if this manages to push through the opening, he brings his striking force, his Group of Tank Armies, into action. This operation by the Group against the enemy's rear defences represents the fifth stage of a strategic offensive.

This Group of Tank Armies consists of two Tank Armies. However, by this time the Tank Armies of the Fronts may already be in action against the enemy's rear defences. These Tank Armies may be taken away from the Front Commanders, at the decision of the C-in-C, and incorporated in the Group of Tank Armies. Towards the end of the action there may be five or even six Tank Armies in the Group, bringing its establishment up to as much as 10,000 tanks. If during a breakthrough half or even two thirds of these are lost, the Group still will be of impressive strength.

However, the Soviet General Staff hopes that losses will not be as large as this. Our pack of cards effect should manifest itself. Moreover, the operations of the Group of Tank Armies will be supported by all the resources available to the C-in-C of the Strategic Direction. All his rocket and air forces will be attacking the enemy with nuclear weapons, his airborne divisions will be dropped to help the Group to advance. Lastly, the whole Baltic Fleet will be supporting the Group. If the Group manages to advance, the whole of the forces available to the State, up to and including the Supreme Commander himself, can be massed to support it.

3

The strategic offensive has one alternative form. This is sometimes known as a "Friday evening" offensive. It differs from the normal version only in dispensing with the first three stages described above. The operation therefore begins at the fourth stage—with a surprise attack by a group of Fronts against one or more countries.

In practice, what happened in Czechoslovakia was an operation by a group of Fronts, carried out swiftly and without warning. Significantly this operation caught the Czechs off guard—profiting by the Friday evening relaxation of the State apparatus after a working week. Because of the small size of Czechoslovakia and the evident disinclination of the Czech army to defend its country, the C-in-C did not bring his Group of Tank Armies forward from Byelorussia and the Front commanders did not push their Tank Armies into Czechoslovakia. Only a very small number of tanks took part in the operation—some 9,000 in all, drawn from the tank battalions of the regiments involved, the tank regiments of the divisions and the tank divisions of the Armies.

The success of the Czech operation produced a new optimism in various other countries in Europe, which realised that they could hope to be similarly liberated in the course of a few hours.

The terrible epidemic of pacification which subsequently swept through Western Europe aroused new hopes of success through a bloodless revolution in the hearts of the Soviet General Staff.

"Operation Détente"

1

In the winter of 1940, the Red Army broke through the "Mannerheim Line." No one knows what price it paid for this victory, but, time and again, demographers have come up with the same figure—a total of 1,500,000 human lives. Whether this is accurate or not, the losses were so staggering, even by Soviet standards, that the advance was halted the very moment Finnish resistance was broken.

The following summer Soviet tanks were rumbling through the streets of three sovereign states—Estonia, Lithuania and Latvia. Since then, Soviet tanks have visited Warsaw, Berlin, Prague, Vienna, Bucharest, Budapest, Sofia, Belgrade, Pyongyang and even Peking. But they never dared to enter Helsinki.

Finland is the only country which has fought a war against Soviet aggression without ever having allowed Soviet tanks to enter its capital.

It is therefore surprising that it is Finland which has become the symbol of submission to Communist expansion. Halted by the valour with which this brave country defended itself, the Communists changed their tactics. If they could not bring the Finns to their knees by fighting, they decided they would do it by peaceful methods. Their new weapon turned out to be more powerful than tanks. Soviet tanks entered Yugoslavia and Romania but both countries are independent today. They never reached Helsinki, but Finland has submitted.

This result surprised even the Soviet Communists themselves and it took them a long time to appreciate the power of the weapon which had fallen so unexpectedly into their hands. When they finally realised its effectiveness, they put it to immediate use against the remaining countries of Western Europe.

Its effects are to be seen everywhere around us. The Communists knew that they could never seize Western Europe so long as it was capable of defending itself, and this is why they concentrated their attacks on Western European determination to stand up to them.

Pacifism is sweeping through the West. It is doing the same in the Soviet Union. In the West, though, it is uncontrolled while in the USSR it is encouraged from above. However, both movements have a common aim. Western pacifists are fighting to stop the installation of new rockets in *Western* Europe. Soviet pacifists speak out for the same cause—against the installation of rockets in *Western* Europe.

Tactics

1

When I lecture to Western officers on tactics in the Soviet Army, I often close my talk by putting a question to them—always the same one—in order to be sure that they have understood me correctly. The question is trivial and elementary. Three Soviet motor-rifle companies are on the move in the same sector. The first has come under murderous fire and its attack has crumbled, the second is advancing slowly, with heavy losses, the third has suffered an enemy counter-attack and, having lost all its command personnel, is retreating. The commander of the regiment to which these companies belong has three tank companies and three artillery batteries in reserve. Try and guess, I say, how this regimental commander uses his reserves to support his three companies. "You are to guess," I say, "what steps a Soviet regimental commander would take, not a Western one but a Soviet, a Soviet, a Soviet one."

I have never yet received the correct reply.

Yet in this situation there is only one possible answer. From the platoon level to that of the Supreme Commander all would agree that there is only one possible decision: all three tank companies and all three artillery batteries must be used to strengthen the company which is moving ahead, however slowly. The others, which are suffering losses, certainly do not qualify for help. If the regimental commander, in a state of drunkenness or from sheer stupidity, were to make any other decision he would, of course, be immediately relieved of his command, reduced to the ranks and sent to pay for his mistake with his own blood, in a penal battalion.

My audiences ask, with surprise, how it can be that two company commanders, whose men are suffering heavy casualties, can ask for help without receiving any? "That's the way it is," I reply, calmly. "How can there be any doubt about it?"

"What happens," ask the Western officers, "if a Soviet platoon or company commander asks for artillery support. Does he get it?"

"He has no right to ask for it," I say.

"And if a company commander asks for air support—does he get it?"

"He has no right to ask for support of any sort, let alone air support."

My audience smiles—they believe they have found the Achilles heel of Soviet tactics. But I am always irritated—for this is not weakness, but strength.

How is it possible not to be irritated? A situation in which every platoon commander can ask for artillery support is one in which the divisional commander is unable to concentrate the full strength of his artillery in the decisive sector—a platoon commander cannot know which this is. A situation in which every company commander can call for air support is one in which the Commander of a Group of Armies is unable to bring together all his aircraft as a single striking force. To a military man this represents something quite unthinkable—the dispersal of resources.

2

The tactics used by Jenghiz Khan were primitive, in the extreme. His Mongolian horsemen would never engage in a single combat in any of the countries which his hordes overran. The training for battle which they received consisted solely of instruction in maintaining formation and in the observance of a disciplinary code which was enforced in the most barbarous way.

During a battle Jenghiz Khan would keep a close watch on the situation from a nearby hill. As soon as the slightest sign of success was visible at any point, he would concentrate all his forces there, sometimes even throwing in his own personal guard. Having broken through the enemy's line at a single point he would push irresistibly ahead and the enemy army, split in two, would disintegrate. It is worth recording that he never lost a battle in his life.

Centuries passed and new weapons appeared. It seemed that this ancient principle of war was dead and buried. That at least was how it seemed to the French armies at Toulon. But then the young Bonaparte appeared, mustered all the artillery at the decisive spot and won his first brilliant victory with lightning speed. Subsequently he always concentrated his artillery and his cavalry in large numbers. In consequence, his junior commanders were deprived of both artillery and cavalry. Despite this, for decades his armies won every battle. At Waterloo he paid the penalty for abandoning the principle of concentrating his forces in the most important sector. His defeat there was the price he paid for dispersing his resources.

More time passed, tanks, aircraft and machine-guns made their appearance. The principles of Jenghiz Khan and Bonaparte were completely forgotten in France. In 1940 the Allies had more tanks than the Germans. They were evenly distributed among infantry sub-units, whose commanders were proud to have tanks directly under their command. Their German opposite numbers had no such grounds for pride, and this was the reason why Germany's victory was so rapid and so decisive. The German tanks were not dispersed but were concentrated in what, by the standards of 1940, were huge groups. The Allied tanks were scattered, like widely-spread fingers, which could not be clenched to make a fist. The German tanks struck, as a fist, unexpectedly and at the weakest point. The Germans' success has gone down in history as a victory which was won by their tanks.

3

Soviet tactics are of the utmost simplicity; they can be condensed into a single phrase—the maximum concentration of forces in the decisive sector. Anyone who was found responsible for dispersing forces of divisional strength or above during the war was shot without further ado. At lower levels the usual penalty for wasting resources in this way was reduction to the ranks and a posting to a penal battalion, which would also lead to death, though not always immediately, it is true.

Every Soviet operation, from Stalingrad onwards, developed in the way water breaks through a concrete dam: a single drop seeps through a microscopic crack, and is followed immediately by a dozen more drops, after which first hundreds and then thousands of litres pour through at ever increasing speed, becoming a cataract of hundreds of thousands of tonnes of raging water.

Here is one entirely typical example of such a breakthrough, carried out by the 16th Guards Rifle Corps of the 2nd Guards Army at Kursk in 1943. During an offensive by nine forward battalions only one managed to make any ground. Immediately, the commander of the regiment to which this battalion belonged concentrated all his resources at that point, on a front one kilometre wide. His divisional commander thereupon threw all his forces into this sector. The breach slowly became deeper and wider and within half an hour the corps commander's reserves began to arrive. Within three hours, 27 of the 36 battalions belonging to the corps had been brought in to fight in the narrow sector, which was by now 7 kilometres wide. 1,087 of the 1,176 guns belonging to the corps, and all its tanks, were assembled in the breakthrough sector. Naturally, the battalion commanders who had been unable to penetrate the enemy's defences not only received no reinforcements, but had everything under their command taken away from them. And this was entirely as it should have been!

As the breach was widened, more and more forces were concentrated there. As soon as he was informed of the breakthrough the Commander of the Central Front, General Rokossovskiy, rushed an entire Army to the spot, with an Air Army to cover the operations. A few days later the Supreme Commander added his own reserve army, the 4th Tank Army, to the forces breaking through. Such a massive concentration of forces could not, of course, be withstood by the German commanders. Several hundred kilometres of their front disintegrated simultaneously and a hasty withdrawal began. The last big offensive mounted by the German army in World War II had collapsed. After this, the Germans never again launched a single large-scale attack, confining themselves to smaller operations, such as those at Balaton or in the Ardennes.

The moral of this story is clear. If every platoon commander had had the right to call for fire support for his unit, the corps commander would have been unable to concentrate his reserves in the breach and the Front would never have broken through. Without this, there could have been no success.

4

Modern Soviet tactics, then, follow in the footprints of Jenghiz Khan, Bonaparte, the German generals who won the battle for France and the Soviet generals in the war against Germany.

Nuclear weapons have changed the face of war, as did artillery in the middle ages, the machine gun in the First World War and the tank in the Second. The principles of military science have not been affected by these changes, for they are immutable—disperse your forces and you will lose, concentrate them and you will win.

The only amendment which needs to be made to these ancient principles in the nuclear age is that a commander must concentrate his nuclear forces, too, in the main sector, together with the artillery, aircraft, and tanks which he assembles there. The threat of a nuclear response, too, plays a role in tactics. The concentration of forces can be completed very rapidly today, and they are then a target for the enemy's nuclear weapons, whereas earlier he was unable to use them during the comparatively long time they took to assemble. Otherwise everything remains as it was. If a single company breaks through the battalion commander supports it with his whole mortar battery, leaving the other companies to fend for themselves. Informed of the success of the company, the commander of the regiment orders his tank battalions to the sector and arranges for his artillery to provide concentrated fire support, then the divisional commander moves in his tank regiment and he too brings in his entire artillery reserves; in addition, he may arrange to have nuclear strikes carried out ahead of his troops. Then, flooding through like the torrent, rushing through the broken dam, come all the tanks and artillery of the Army, all the tanks, aircraft, artillery and rockets of the Front, of the Strategic Direction, of the Soviet Union and of its satellites!

5

One further misunderstanding needs clarification. Although a platoon or company commander is not entitled to summon up aircraft or the divisional artillery, this certainly does not mean that Soviet forces operate without fire support. The commander of a Soviet motor-rifle battalion (400 men) has 6 120mm mortars at his disposal. The commander of an American battalion (900 men) has only 4 106mm mortars. The commander of a Soviet regiment (2,100 men) has a battalion of 18 122mm howitzers and a battery of 6 Grad P multi-barrelled rocket launchers. The commander of an American brigade (4,000–5,000 men) has no fire weapons at all. Commanders of Soviet and American divisions have approximately the same quantity of fire weapons.

Commanders of Soviet battalions and regiments, not being entitled to call on their divisional commanders for help have enough fire weapons under their command to follow up successes achieved by any of their platoons, companies or battalions. Since they are equipped with these weapons, the divisional commander is free to make use of the full weight of his divisional artillery wherever he decides it is needed.

Rear Supplies

1

Many Western specialists believe that in order to carry out an operation of the sort described it would be necessary to assemble a massive concentration of material resources and that the Soviet command would encounter extreme difficulty in providing its enormous forces with the supplies they would need.

This delusion is based on typical Western concepts of the organisation of the supply and replenishment of military forces.

The Soviet Army has a completely different approach to the problems of supply from that adopted in the West—one which avoids many headaches. Let us start from the fact that a Soviet soldier is not issued with a sleeping bag, and does not need one. He can be left unfed for several days. All that he needs is ammunition and this solves many problems.

The problem of supplying Soviet troops in battle is thus confined to the provision of ammunition. We already know that each commander has transport sub-units at his disposal; every regiment has a company which can transport loads of 200 tons, every division a battalion with a capacity of 1,000 tons, every Army a transport regiment, and so forth. All this capacity is used solely to move up ammunition for advancing forces. Each commander allocates a large proportion of this ammunition to the sector which is achieving success—the remainder suffer accordingly.

No less important during a rapid advance is fuel—the lifeblood of war. A basic approach has been taken to the problem of fuel-supply. As a condition for its acceptance by the armed Services, every type of Soviet combat vehicle—tanks, armoured personnel carriers, artillery prime movers, etc.—must have sufficient fuel capacity to take it at least 600 kilometres.

Thus, Soviet Fronts would be able to make a dash across Western Germany without refuelling. Thereafter, the pipe-laying battalion of each Army would lay a line to the Front's main pipeline which would have been laid by the Front's pipe-laying regiment. The Front's pipelines would be linked with secret underground main lines which had been laid down in Eastern Europe in peacetime. In addition, the C-in-C of a Strategic Direction has under his command a pipe-laying brigade, which can be used to assist the Fronts. At the terminals of the pipelines the pipe-layers set up a number of refuelling centres, each of which can simultaneously refuel a battalion or even a regiment. In addition, the Soviet Army is at present evolving techniques for using helicopters for fuel resupply. Let us take a division which is advancing. One of its tank battalions has stopped, on orders from the divisional commander, and is left behind by the other battalions. In a field by the road, on which the battalion has halted, a V-12 helicopter lands, carrying 40 or more tons of fuel. Within ten minutes it has refuelled all the tanks and taken off again. The battalion sets off for the front again, replacing another which halts to refuel. A single V-12 helicopter flying at low altitude at a speed of 250 kilometres an hour, can refuel a whole division in one day. It is not particularly vulnerable, since it is flying over its own rear areas, which are protected by the Air Defence Troops of the Land Forces. If trucks were used to supply a division hundreds of them would be needed, travelling on damaged, overloaded roads and presenting an excellent target. The destruction of a single bridge could bring them all to a halt. While a single truck carrying ten tons would take twenty-four hours to make a particular journey, a helicopter could do the same job in one hour. Even if helicopters were more vulnerable than endless convoys of trucks, Soviet generals would still use them, for time is far more precious than money during a war.

Provisions, spare parts, etc. are, quite simply, not supplied.

2

Now let us see how this works in practice. A division which is up to full strength, fully equipped, fed and fuelled, with more than 2,000 tons of ammunition, is moving up into action from the second echelon. This division can spend from three to five days in action, without rest for either its soldiers or its officers. The wounded are evacuated to the rear by the medical battalion, after first aid has been given.

Its companies, battalions and regiments waste no time waiting for spare parts for equipment which has been damaged. They simply throw it aside. The repair and refitting battalion mends whatever it can, cannibalising one tank to repair two or three others, removing its engine, tracks, turret and anything else which is needed. Any piece of equipment which is seriously damaged is left for removal to the rear by the Army's or the Front's mobile tank repair workshop.

In action, the division fights with great determination, but its numbers dwindle. Some of its fighting equipment is returned after repair, but not a great deal. After three to five days of hard fighting, the survivors are sent back to the second echelon, their place being taken by a fresh division which has been well fed and fully rested. From the remnants of the old division, a new one is quickly put together. Combat equipment is provided by the tank repair workshops. The fact that it belonged to some other division only the day before is immaterial. Reinforcements reach the new division from the hospitals—whether these soldiers and officers formerly belonged to other divisions, Armies or Fronts is also immaterial. With them arrive equipment from the factories and reservists—some of whom are older, others still very young boys. The division shakes down, exercises and allows its soldiers to get all the sleep they need. Then, after five days, it moves up into action, fully fed and fuelled, with 2,000 tons of ammunition.

Often, while it is re-forming, a division receives entirely new equipment, straight from the factory, but it may also be issued with older material taken from store, while its own, or what remains of it, is taken from it for some other division which is also re-forming, not far away.

Frequently, after a particularly punishing series of battles, a division cannot be re-formed. In this event all its commanders from company level upwards are withdrawn and what is left of the division is administered by the deputies to the battalion and regimental commanders and by the deputy divisional commander. This remnant will continue to fight, to the last man, while the divisional commander and his subordinates are in the rear, receiving new equipment and new soldiers. Within a short period of time they return to the battle in which what was left of their former division perished so recently.

One most important element needed for the rebuilding of a new division is its old colours. A fresh division can be set up very quickly around the old colours. But if the colours are lost—that is the end of the division. If such a thing should happen, all its former commanders are sent to penal battalions, where they expiate their guilt with blood, while their division is disbanded and used to bring others up to strength.

Here is an example from the history of the 24th Samaro-Ulyanovsk Iron Division, with which I entered Czechoslovakia in 1968.

The division was established in 1918 and was one of the best in the Red Army. Lenin corresponded personally with some of its soldiers. It was active in the war against Germany from the very beginning of hostilities and distinguished itself in the fighting near Minsk until, as part of the 13th Army, it found itself encircled. Part of the division managed to break out but its colours were lost. Despite its past achievements, the division was disbanded and its various officers were tried by military tribunals. In 1944, when the Red Army once again reached and then crossed the Soviet frontiers, a special commission began questioning local inhabitants in an attempt to discover where Soviet officers and soldiers who had been killed in action during the first days of the war were buried. A peasant, D. N. Tyapin, told the commission how he had found the body of a Soviet officer, wrapped in a flag, and how he had buried the body, with the flag. The grave was immediately opened and the colours of the 24th Iron Division were found. The flag was immediately sent away for restoration and, just as quickly, a new division was formed and given the old colours, the battle honours and the title of the old division. Today the 24th Iron Division is one of the most famous in the Soviet Army. However, despite the fact that it distinguished itself in the battle which ended the war, it was never made a Guards division. It was not forgiven for the loss of its colours.

PART SIX

EQUIPMENT

What Sort of Weapons?

1

I adore weapons. Of every sort. I love military equipment and military uniforms. One day I shall open a small museum, and the first exhibit which I shall buy for my museum will be an American jeep. This is a real miracle weapon. It was designed before the Second World War and it served from the first day to the last, like a faithful soldier. It was dropped by parachute, it was soaked in salt water, it smashed its wheels on the stony deserts of Libya and sank into swamps on tropical islands. It served honourably in the mountains of Norway and of the Caucasus, in the Alps and the Ardennes. And, since the war, can any other military vehicle have seen so many battles— Korea, Vietnam, Sinai, Africa, the Arctic, South America, Indonesia, India, Pakistan? And is there any sort of weapon which has not been installed on a jeep? Recoilless guns, anti-tank rockets, machine guns. And it has worked on reconnaissance duties, as an ambulance, a patrol vehicle, a commander and an ordinary military workhorse.

And how many types of tanks, guns, aircraft, rockets have come and gone in the time of the jeep? They were important and impressive, the jeep was grey and undistinguished. But they have gone and the jeep is still there. And how many times have they tried to replace the jeep? But it is indispensable. In the desert, more reliable than a camel, in the grasslands faster than a leopard, in the Arctic hardier than a Polar bear.

Another exhibit in my museum will be a Kalashnikov automatic assault rifle. Not one of those the terrorists used to kill the Olympic athletes or the one I had with me in Czechoslovakia or one of those the Communists killed doctors with in Cambodia. No, it will be one of the thousands captured by the

American marines in Vietnam and used in their desperate attempt to halt Communism and to avert the calamity which threatened the Vietnamese people.

American soldiers in Vietnam often mistrusted their own weapons and preferred to use their Kalashnikov trophies. This was not so simple, for they could hardly expect to be supplied with the proper rounds for these weapons but they used them nevertheless, capturing more ammunition as they fought. What is the secret of the Kalashnikov? It is uncomplicated and reliable, like a comrade-in-arms, and these are the two qualities of greatest importance in a battle.

2

My museum will have weapons from everywhere—from Germany and Britain, France and Japan. But the greatest number will come from the Soviet Union. I hate the Communists, but I love Soviet weapons. The fact is that Soviet designers realised, decades ago, the simple truth that only uncomplicated and reliable equipment can be successful in war. This is as true as the fact that the only plans which will succeed are those which are simple and easily understood and that the best battledress is the simplest and most hard-wearing.

Soviet requirements from a weapon are that it must be easy to produce and simple in construction, which makes it easier to teach soldiers to use it and simpler to maintain and repair.

Although the Soviet Union produced the same amount of steel as Germany, it built a much greater number of tanks. Moreover, because of the simplicity of their construction, it proved possible to repair tens of thousands of these tanks and to return them to battle two or even three times.

General Guderian admired Soviet tanks and wrote about them, enthusiastically and at length. He was insistent in urging that Germany should copy the T-34. The design of this Soviet tank was taken as a basis for the "Panzer" and shortly afterwards for the "Tiger-König." But the German designers were unable to meet the most important requirement—simplicity of construction. As a result only 4,815 Panzer tanks were built in all, while no more than 484 "Tiger-König" tanks were ever produced. In the same period the Soviet Union built 102,000 tanks, 70,000 of which were T-34s.

In considering these figures it should be remembered that, while most German tank factories were subjected to bombing, many Soviet factories were lost altogether—the Kharkov plant was captured by the Germans in the first months of the war, and this was the largest Soviet factory and the birthplace of the T-34; the Stalingrad tank factory was the setting for the fiercest fighting it is possible to imagine. Leningrad was besieged, but, despite being without steel or coal, the tank factory there, which was subjected to constant artillery bombardment, continued to repair tanks for three years. On some occasions tanks which still were under repair had to be used to fire through gaps in the walls at advancing groups of German soldiers. The only factory that was left was in the Urals and it was to this that the machinery was taken and set up, virtually in the open air, to produce the world's simplest and most reliable tank.

It should not be thought that Soviet equipment suffers any harmful effects because of its simplicity of design. Quite the reverse. In its time, the T-34 was not only the simplest but also the most powerful tank in the world.

3

When a MIG-25 landed in Japan, the Western experts who examined it marvelled at the simplicity of its design. Naturally, for propaganda purposes, the fighting qualities of this excellent aircraft were disparaged. One not particularly perceptive specialist even commented, "We had thought it was made of titanium but it turns out to be nothing but steel." It is, in fact, impossible to reach the speeds of which the MIG-25 is capable using titanium: yet the Soviet designers had managed to build this, the fastest combat aircraft in the world, from ordinary steel.

This is a most significant fact. It means that this remarkable aircraft can be built without especially complicated machine tools or the help of highly skilled specialists, and that its mass-production in wartime would be unaffected by shortages of important materials. Furthermore, this aircraft is exceedingly cheap to produce and could therefore be built in very great numbers if this were necessary. This is its most important characteristic; the fact that for two decades it has been the fastest interceptor aircraft in the world, with the highest rate of climb, is of secondary significance.

4

Technology is developing and each year equipment becomes more and more complex. But this does not conflict with the overall philosophy of Soviet designers. Of course, decades ago, their predecessors used the latest equipment available in their combat vehicles and aircraft and this equipment must then have been considered very complex. But the iron, unbreakable principle observed by Soviet designers retains its force. Whenever a new piece of equipment is being developed, making the use of highly complex tools and techniques unavoidable, there is always a choice of hundreds, even thousands of possible technical procedures. The designers will always select the very simplest possible of all the choices open to them. It would, of course, be feasible to produce an automatic transmission system for a jeep, but it is possible to get by with an ordinary one. This being so, there can be only one Soviet choice—the ordinary transmission.

I once saw a film comparing a Soviet and an American tank. A driver was given both models to drive and he was then asked—"Which is the better?" "The American one, of course," said the driver. "It has automatic transmission, whereas in the Soviet tank you have to change gear, which is not easy in a heavy machine." He is quite right—if you see war as a pleasant outing. But Soviet designers realise that any future war will be anything but this. They consider, quite correctly, that, if there are mass bombing attacks, if whole industrial areas are destroyed, if long-distance communications break down, mass production of tanks with automatic transmission would be out of the question. Equally it would be impossible to repair or service tanks of this sort which had been produced before the war. Accordingly, there can be only one choice—the ordinary, non-automatic transmission. This may be hard on the tank driver—he will get tired. But it will be easier for industry and for the whole country, which will continue to produce tanks by the ten thousand on machines which have been set up virtually in the open air.

5

The simplicity of Soviet weapons surprises everyone. But each type of equipment which is produced is turned out in two variants—the normal one and the "monkey-model."

The "monkey-model" is a weapon which has been simplified in every conceivable way and which is intended for production in wartime only.

For instance, the T-62 tank is one of the simplest fighting vehicles in the world. But as it was being designed, a still simpler version was also being developed, for wartime use. The "monkey-model" of the T-62 does not have a stabilised gun, carries simplified radio and optical equipment, the night-vision equipment uses an infra-red light source to illuminate targets (a method which is twenty years old), the gun is raised and turned manually, steel rather than wolfram or uranium is used for the armour-plating piercing caps of its shells.

Soviet generals consider, justifiably, that it is better to have tanks like these in a war than none at all. It is intended that the "monkey-model" approach will be used not only for building tanks, but for all other sorts of equipment—rockets, guns, aircraft, radio sets, etc. In peacetime these variants are turned out in large quantities, but they are only issued to countries friendly to the Soviet Union. I have seen two variants of the BMP-1 infantry combat vehicle—one which is issued to the Soviet army and another which is intended for the Soviet Union's Arab friends. I counted sixty-three simplifications which made the second "monkey-model" different from the original version. Among the most important of these were: The 73mm gun has no loading or round-selection equipment. Whereas in the Soviet version the gunner just presses the appropriate buttons and the round which he requires slides into the barrel, in the simplified model all of this has to be done by hand, and furthermore, the gun is not stabilised. The turret is rotated and the gun is raised mechanically. In the Soviet version this is done electrically—the mechanical system is there only as a back-up. The "export" version is armed with the Malyutka rocket, the Soviet one with the "Malyutka-M," which differs from the other model in having an automatic target guidance system. The "monkey-model" is without the lead internal lining on the walls, which protects the crew against penetrating radiation and against flying fragments of armour in the event of a direct hit. The optical system is greatly simplified, as is the communications equipment, there is no automatic radiation or gas detector, there is neither an automatic hermetic sealing system nor an air filtration system, for use in conditions of very heavy contamination, no automatic topographical fixation system is fitted and many other systems are missing.

When one of these "monkey-models" fell into the hands of Western specialists, they naturally gained a completely false impression of the true combat capabilities of the BMP-1 and of Soviet tanks. For what they were looking at was no more than a casing, or a container, like an empty money box which is of no value without its contents.

The Soviet Union is currently making deliveries abroad of T-72 tanks, MIG-23 fighters and TU-22 bombers. But these are different from the models with which the Soviet Army has armed itself. When one of a man's pockets contains banknotes and the other simply holds pieces of paper, it is quite impossible to tell which is which from the outside.

The current Soviet policy concerning equipment is a wise one—to amass first-class but very simple equipment in quantities sufficient for the first few weeks of a war. If the war continues, equipment will be produced on an enormous scale, but in variants which have been simplified to the greatest possible extent. Experience of producing both standard and "monkey" models is being gained in peacetime; the simpler variants are being sold to the "brothers" and "friends" of the USSR as the very latest equipment available.

Learning from Mistakes

1

The winter of 1969 was an exceptionally bitter one in the Soviet Far East. When the first clashes with the Chinese took place on the river Ussuri, and before combat divisions reached the area, the pressure exerted by the enemy was borne by the KGB frontier troops. After the clash was over, the General Staff held a careful investigation into all the mistakes and oversights which had occurred. It was quickly discovered that several KGB soldiers had frozen to death in the snow, simply because they had never received elementary instruction in sleeping out in temperatures below zero.

This was alarming news. A commission from the General Staff immediately carried out experiments with three divisions, chosen at random, and came to a depressing conclusion. Wartime experience had been irrevocably lost and the modern Soviet soldier had not been taught how he could sleep in the snow. Naturally he was not allowed a sleeping bag and of course he was forbidden to light a fire. Normally a soldier would spend nights when the temperature was below freezing-point in his vehicle. But what was he to do if the vehicle was put out of action?

The chiefs of staff of all divisions were immediately summoned to Moscow. They were given a day's instruction in the technique of sleeping out in snow at freezing temperatures, using only a greatcoat. Then each of them was required to convince himself that this was possible, by sleeping in the snow for three nights. (It should be remembered that March in Solnechnogorsk, near Moscow, is a hard month, with snow on the ground and temperatures below zero.) Then the chiefs of staff returned to their divisions and immediately the entire Soviet Army was put to a very hard test—that of spending a night in the open in numbing cold and without any extra clothing. It seemed as if those who were stationed in deserts in the south were in luck. But no—they were sent by turns to either Siberia or the north to be put through the same tough training. Thereafter, spending a night in the snow became a part of all military training programmes.

Two years before this, following the shameful defeats in Sinai, when it had become clear how much Arab soldiers fear tanks and napalm, urgent orders had been issued, making it compulsory for all Soviet soldiers and officers, up to the rank of general, to jump through roaring flames, and to shelter in shallow pits as tanks clattered by just above their heads, or, if they could not find even this protection, to lie on the ground between the tracks of the roaring vehicles.

The Soviet Army re-learned its lessons within a single day. I have felt napalm on my own skin, I have crouched in a pit as a tank crashed by overhead, and I have spent terrible nights in the snow.

At the beginning of the war, the Red Army had no idea how to organise the defence of the country or, particularly, of the large towns. It had never been taught how to do this. It had only learned how to attack and how to "carry the war on to the enemy's territory." However, the war began in accordance with the plans of the German General Staff rather than of their Soviet opponents. One catastrophe followed another. Attempts to defend Minsk lasted for three days, to hold Kiev for two days. Everyone was at their wits' end to know how to organise things better. Kiev fell at the end of September and by October Guderian was approaching Moscow. Suddenly, something quite astonishing happened. Soviet defences became impenetrable, specifically those around Moscow, Tula and Tver'. For the first time in the course of the Second World War, the German military machine was brought to a standstill. It is said that freezing weather played its part in turning the tide. This was true enough in November and December, but in October the weather was sunny. Something had happened; a radical change had occurred. The next year, the battle for Stalingrad took place—the city was defended throughout the summer, and frosts played no part in the outcome. This campaign will go down in history as a model for the defence of a large city. A second such model is the defence of Leningrad which held out for almost three years, during which one and a half million of its citizens lost their lives. It was under attack for two winters and three summers. Freezing temperatures played no role here either—the city could have been taken during any season in these three years.

In the Soviet Army the dividing line between inability to perform a particular role and the capacity to carry it out with great professional skill is almost indiscernible. Transitions from one to the other occur almost instantaneously, not only in tactics, strategy and the training of personnel but also in equipment programmes.

2

At the beginning of the 1960s a discussion developed in the Western military journals about the need for a new infantry combat vehicle: this must be amphibious, well armoured, and highly manoeuvrable, and must have considerable fire-power. The Soviet military press responded only with a deathly silence. The discussion gathered strength, there was much argument for and against the proposition, intensive tests were carried out . . . the Soviet Union remained silent.

One night towards the end of 1966 heavy transporters arrived at our military academy carrying unusual vehicles of some sort, which were covered in tarpaulins. These were BMP-1s—amphibious, fiendishly manoeuvrable, well armoured and heavily armed. By 1967 this vehicle was being produced in great numbers: meanwhile the discussion in the West continued. Only West Germany took any positive steps, by building the "Marder"—which was an excellent vehicle, but was not amphibious and carried almost the same armament as previous German armoured personnel carriers. Sadly, it was also exceptionally complicated in design.

In the early 1980s, the discussion is still in progress in the West; the first tentative steps have been taken, but at present, as before, the United States has armoured personnel carriers which are armed only with machine-guns. Of course, Western specialists have found many faults in the construction of the BMP-1. But this is yesterday's product—and the "monkey model" of it at that. The Soviet Union has been producing a second generation of BMPs in massive quantities for a long time now while, in the West, discussion continues.

The same has happened with military helicopters, self-propelled artillery, automatic mortars and many other types of equipment.

When will we be able to dispense with the tank?

1

One day, in Paris, I bought a book, published in 1927, on the problems of a future war. The author was sober-minded and reasonable. His logic was sound, his analysis was shrewd and his arguments unassailable. After analysing the way military equipment had developed in his lifetime, the author concluded by declaring that the proper place for the tank was in the museum, next to the dinosaur skeletons. His argument was simple and logical: anti-tank guns had been developed to the point at which they would bring massive formations of tanks to a complete halt in any future war, just as machine guns had completely stopped the cavalry in the First World War.

I do not know whether the author lived until 1940, to see the German tanks sweeping along the Paris boulevards, past the spot at which, many decades later, I was to buy my dusty copy of his book, its leaves yellowing with age.

The belief that the tank is reaching the end of its life is itself surprisingly long-lived. At the beginning of the 1960s, France decided to stop production of tanks, because their era was over. It is fortunate that this delusion was shattered by the Israelis' old "Sherman" tanks in the Sinai peninsula. Israel's brilliant victory showed the whole world, once again, that no anti-tank weapon is able to stop tanks in a war, provided, of course, that they are used skilfully.

The argument used by the tank's detractors is simple—"Just look at the anti-tank rockets—at their accuracy and at their armour-piercing capability!" But this argument does not hold water. The anti-tank rocket is a defensive weapon—part of a passive system. The tank, on the other hand, is an offensive weapon. Any defensive system involves the dispersal of forces

221

over a wide territory, leaving them strong in some places and weak in others. And it is where they are weak that the tanks will appear, in enormous concentrations. Even if it were possible to distribute resources equally, this would mean that no one sector would have enough. Try deploying just ten anti-tank rockets along every kilometre of the front. The tanks will then choose one particular spot and will attack it in their hundreds, or perhaps thousands, simultaneously. If you concentrate your anti-tank resources, the tanks will simply by-pass them. They are an offensive weapon and they have the initiative in battle, being able to choose when and where to attack and how strong a force to use.

The hope that the perfection of anti-tank weapons would lead to the death of the tank has been shown to be completely unfounded. It is like hoping that the electronic defences of banks will become so perfect in the future that bank robbers will die out as a breed. I assure you that bank robbers will not become extinct. They will improve their tools, their tactics, their information about their targets and their methods of misleading their enemies and they will continue to carry out raids. Sometimes these will fail, sometimes they will succeed, but they will continue so long as banks continue to exist. The robbers have the same advantage as tanks—they are on the offensive. They decide where, when and how to attack and will do so only when they are confident of success, when they have secretly discovered a weak spot in the enemy's defences, whose existence is unknown even to the enemy himself.

2

Soviet generals have never been faced with problems of this sort. They have always known that victory in a war can only be achieved by advancing. To them defensive operations spell defeat and death. In the best case, such operations can only produce a deadlock, and not for long, at that. Victory can only be achieved by means of an offensive—by seizing the initiative and raining blows on the enemy's most vulnerable areas.

Thus, to win, you must attack, you must move forward unexpectedly and with determination, you must advance. For this you need a vehicle which can travel anywhere to destroy the enemy, preferably remaining unscathed itself. The one vehicle which combines movement, fire-power and armour is the tank. Perhaps, in the future, its armour will be perfected, perhaps it will not have tracks but will travel in some other way (there have been wheeled tanks), perhaps it will not have a gun but be armed with something else (there have been tanks armed solely with rockets), perhaps all sorts of things will be changed, but its most important characteristics—its ability to move, to shoot and to defend itself—will remain. As long as there are wars, as long as the desire for victory lasts, the tank will exist. Nuclear war has not only not written it off, but has given it a new lease of life—nothing is so suited to nuclear war as a tank. To survive a nuclear war you must put your money on these steel boxes.

The Flying Tank

1

Drive a tank on to an airfield and park it near a military aircraft. Next put a helicopter between the tank and the aircraft. Now, look at each of them and then answer the question—which does the helicopter resemble more—the tank or the aircraft?

I know what your opinion will be. You don't need to tell me. But the Soviet generals believe that to all intents and purposes the helicopter *is* a tank. In fact they find it difficult to distinguish between the two. Certainly there is very little in common between the helicopter and the aircraft. Small details, like the ability to fly, but nothing more.

Of course, they are right. The helicopter is related to the tank, not to the aircraft. The reasoning behind this is simple enough—in battle a tank can seize enemy territory and a helicopter can do the same. But an aircraft cannot. An aircraft can destroy everything on the surface and deep below it, but it can not seize and hold territory.

For this reason, the Soviet Army sees the helicopter as a tank—one which is capable of high speeds and unrestricted cross-country performance, but is only lightly armoured. It also has approximately the same fire-power as a tank.

The tactics employed in the use of helicopters and tanks are strikingly similar. An aircraft is vulnerable because in most cases it can only operate from an airfield. Both the helicopter and the tank operate in open ground. An aircraft is vulnerable because it flies above the enemy. A helicopter and a tank both see the enemy in front of them. To attack, a helicopter does not need to fly over the enemy or to get close to him.

The introduction of the helicopter was not greeted with any particular enthusiasm by the Air Forces, but the Land Forces were jubilant—here was a tank with a rotor instead of tracks, which need not fear minefields or rivers or mountains.

It is therefore not surprising that the airborne assault brigades (which are carried by helicopter) form part of the complement of Tank Armies or of Fronts, which use them for joint operations with Tank Armies.

At the present moment the Soviet MI-24 is the best combat helicopter in the world. This is not just my personal opinion, but one which is shared by Western military experts. Knowing the affection which Soviet Marshals have for their helicopters, I prophesy that even better variants of these flying tanks will appear in the next few years. Or are they, perhaps, already flying above Saratov or somewhere, even though we have not been shown them yet?

The Most Important Weapon

1

Before the Second World War each army had its own approach to questions of defence. Drawing on their experience of the First World War, the French considered that their main problem was to survive artillery bombardments, which might continue for several days or even several months. The German generals decided that they must make their forces capable of repelling attacks by all enemy arms of service. The Soviet generals concluded that they must avoid diluting their resources and that they must concentrate on the most important of the arms of service. Since for them this was the tank, they saw defence purely as defence against tanks. Their defence system could therefore only be considered complete when their forces were asked to repulse tank attacks. If we can only stop the enemy's tanks, the generals reasoned, everything else will be halted, too.

They were right, as many German generals, the first of whom was Guderian, have acknowledged. Many of the battles which took place on Soviet territory followed a standard scenario. The German forces would launch a very powerful tank attack, which, from the second half of 1942 onwards the Soviet troops always succeeded in halting. This was the course of events at Stalingrad, at Kursk and in Hungary, in the Balaton operations. From 1943 onwards, having exhausted their capacity for launching such attacks, the German forces were ordered by Hitler to adopt a strategy of defence in depth. But this was not the way to oppose tanks. This strategy did not enable the German army to halt a single breakthrough by Soviet tanks.

Remembering the war, Soviet generals insist that defence must mean, first and foremost, defence against tanks. The enemy can gain victories only by advancing and, in the nuclear age, as before, offensive operations will be carried out by tanks and infantry. Other forces can not carry out an offensive: their only role is to support the tanks and the infantry. Thus, defence is essentially a battle against tanks.

The most important weapon in achieving victory is the tank. The most important weapon in depriving the enemy of victory is the anti-tank weapon. The Soviet Union therefore devotes great attention to the development of anti-tank weapons. As a result, it is frequently the first in the world with really revolutionary technical and tactical innovations. For example, as early as 1955, the USSR began production of the "Rapira" smoothbore anti-tank gun, which has an astonishingly high muzzle velocity. In its introduction of this weapon it led the West by more than a quarter of a century. In the same year a start was also made with production of the APNB-70 infra-red night sight, for the "Rapira." Sights of this type were not issued to Western armies for another ten years.

The Soviet Army takes exceptionally strict measures to safeguard the secrets of its anti-tank weapons. Many of these are completely unknown in the West. The Chief Directorate of Strategic Camouflage insists that the only anti-tank weapons which may be displayed are those which can be exported—in other words the least effective ones. The systems which may not be exported are never demonstrated but remain unknown from their birth, throughout their secret life and often, even, after their death. We will say something about these later.

3

Because they consider anti-tank warfare to be so important, Soviet generals insist that every soldier and every weapon system should be capable of attacking tanks.

Every soldier is therefore armed with a single-shot "Mukha" anti-tank rocket launcher. These rocket launchers are issued to all motor transport drivers and to those belonging to staff, rear-support and all other auxiliary sub-units.

When the BMP-1 infantry combat vehicle was being developed, the designers suggested a 23mm gun as its armament—this would be effective against infantry, and is simple and easy to load. But the generals opposed this; as a first priority, the vehicle must be capable of opposing tanks; it must have anti-tank rockets and a gun which, even though small, could be used against tanks. The BMP-1 was therefore fitted with a 73mm automatic gun, capable of destroying any enemy tank at ranges of up to 1,300 metres, with anti-tank rockets which can be used over greater ranges. The fact that 20mm automatic guns are fitted to Western infantry combat vehicles is met with friendly incomprehension by Soviet military specialists: "If such a vehicle is not capable of taking on our tanks, why was it built?"

It is true that a light anti-aircraft gun has recently been mounted on the BMP. But this does not indicate any alteration in its main function. This gun is installed as an auxiliary weapon, to supplement the anti-tank rockets and also as an anti-helicopter weapon. In other words, it is intended for use against the flying tank. Incidentally, the decision to fit it was taken only after the designers had been able to demonstrate that it could also be used against conventional, earthbound tanks.

All other Soviet weapon systems, even if they are not primarily intended as anti-tank weapons, must also be able to function as such. Accordingly, all Soviet howitzers are supplied with anti-tank shells and anti-aircraft guns are much used against tanks—their teams are trained for this role and are issued with suitable ammunition.

But this is not all. The new AGS19 Plamya rocket-launcher and the Vasilek automatic mortar can also be used against tanks, as a secondary function. They each have a rate of fire of 120 rounds a minute and both are capable of flat trajectory fire against advancing tanks.

Finally, the BM-21, BM-27, Grad-P and other salvo-firing rocket launchers can fire over open sights and flood oncoming tanks with fire.

Why are Anti-tank Guns not Self-propelled?

1

Why does the Soviet Union not use self-propelled anti-tank guns? This is a question which many are unable to answer. After all, a self-propelled gun is far more mobile on the battle-field than one which is towed, and its crew is better protected. This question has already been partially answered in the last chapter. The Soviet Union has some excellent self-propelled anti-tank weapon systems—but it does not put them on display. Nevertheless, it is true that towed guns are in the majority. Why is this so? There are several reasons:

Firstly: A towed anti-tank gun is many times easier to man-ufacture and to use than one which is self-propelled. In wartime it might be feasible to reduce the production of tanks; the effect of this would simply be to reduce the intensity of offensive operations. But a drop in the production of anti-tank weapons would be catastrophic. Whatever happens, they must be pro-duced in sufficient quantities. Otherwise any tank breakthrough by the enemy could prove fatal for the whole military produc-tion programme, for the national economy, and for the Soviet Union itself. In order to ensure that these guns are turned out, whatever the situation, even in the midst of a nuclear war, it is essential that they should be as simple in construction as possible. It was no chance that the first Soviet smoothbore guns to be produced were anti-tank guns. Smoothbore guns for Soviet tanks were brought out considerably later. Although a smooth barrel reduces the accuracy of fire, it enables muzzle velocity to be raised considerably, and, most important of all, it simplifies the construction of the gun.

Secondly: A towed gun has a very low silhouette, at least half that of a tank. In single combat with a tank, especially at maximum range, this offers better protection than armour plate or manoeuvrability.

Thirdly: Anti-tank guns are used in two situations. In defence, when the enemy has broken through, is advancing fast and must be stopped at any price. And in an offensive when one's own troops have broken through and are advancing rapidly, and the enemy tries to cut through the spearhead at its base, with a flank attack, cutting off the advancing forces from their rear areas. In both these situations, anti-tank guns must stop the enemy's tanks at some predetermined line, which he must not be allowed to cross. Towed guns are compelled, by the weight of their construction, to fight to the death. They are unable to manoeuvre or to move to a better position. Certainly, their losses are always very high. That is why they are traditionally nicknamed "Farewell, Motherland!" But by stopping the enemy on the predetermined line, the anti-tank sub-units can save the whole division, Army and sometimes the whole Front. This is what happened at Kursk. If the anti-tank guns had been self-propelled, their commander would have been able to withdraw to a more advantageous position when he came under enemy pressure. This would have saved his small anti-tank sub-unit, but it might have brought catastrophe to the division, the Army, the Front and perhaps to several Fronts.

Lest seditious thoughts should enter the head of the anti-tank commander, and so that he should not think of pulling back in a critical situation, his anti-tank guns have no means of propulsion. In battle their armoured tractors are housed in shelters; they would scarcely be able to pull the guns away from the battle, under the deadly fire of the enemy. Only one option is available to the crews—to die on the spot, as they prevent the enemy from crossing the line which they are holding.

During the war, one of the main reasons for the unyielding stability of the Soviet formations was the presence among them of huge but virtually immobile units of anti-tank guns.

The Favourite Weapon

1

The Soviet commander's favourite weapon is the mortar. A mortar is simply a tube, one end of which rests on a base plate, while the other end points skywards, supported on two legs. It would be difficult to devise a simpler weapon, which is why it is such a favourite.

In 1942, a terrible year for the USSR, during which military production fell to a catastrophically low level, the mortar was the one weapon which remained available to every commander.

In three and a half years of war, the Soviet Union produced 348,000 mortars. In the same period, Germany produced 68,000. All the remaining countries put together produced considerably less than Germany. Furthermore, the Soviet mortars were the most powerful in the world and the number of bombs produced for each was the highest recorded anywhere.

Soviet commanders value the mortar so highly because of its reliability and its almost primitive simplicity, because it only takes a few minutes to teach a soldier how to use it, and because it needs almost no maintenance—its barrel is not even rifled! And they also like its immediate readiness, in any situation, to fire quite heavy bombs at the enemy, even though it lacks complete accuracy.

The pressure generated inside a mortar barrel when it fires is relatively low and therefore a mortar, unlike a gun or a howitzer, can fire cast-iron rather than steel bombs. This adds two further advantages—firstly, simplicity and cheapness of production, secondly the fact that when a cast iron bomb bursts it shatters into very small splinters, which form a dense fragment pattern. Steel gun and howitzer shells are not only more expensive but are more solidly constructed and therefore produce a smaller quantity of splinters, which do not cover the area so densely.

In France and the US, after the war, mortars were improved. They had rifled barrels which gave them greater accuracy. As early as 1944, a Soviet designer, B. L. Shavyrin, had suggested that Soviet mortars should be rifled, but he was firmly rebuffed—it was simpler to make ten smoothbore mortars than one with rifling. Even if a rifled mortar was twice as effective as a smoothbore one, the latter would therefore still be a far better proposition. If it was only twice as effective, but cost ten times as much to produce, it must rate as a very poor weapon. I entirely agree with this point of view.

But what about accuracy? you will ask. It is of no significance. Soviet commanders have chosen a different way of approaching the problem. If you have to pay for accuracy with complexity of design, you are following the wrong path. Quantity is the better way to exert pressure. Since two simple, smoothbore mortars can do the work of one rifled one we will use the two simple ones, which will have the additional advantage of producing a lot more noise, dust and fire than one. And this is by no means unimportant in war. The more noise you produce, the higher the morale of your troops and the lower that of the enemy. What is more, two mortars are harder to destroy than one.

Yet another approach to the problem was devised. The lack of accuracy of Soviet mortars is more than made up for by the explosive power of their bombs. To Soviet commanders, the best mortar is a large one—the bigger it is the better. At present the largest American mortar is their 106·7mm, while the smallest Soviet one is 120mm. The biggest American mortar tar bomb weighs 12·3 kilogrammes, the smallest Soviet one 16 kilogrammes. But besides this small mortar, the Soviet Army has a 160mm version, which fires a 40 kilogramme bomb and a 240mm version which fires a 100 kilogramme bomb.

Anyone who has seen 120mm mortars firing, especially if he was near them, will never forget the experience. I have actually seen 12 240mm mortars in action together. These fire not 16 kilogramme but 100 kilogramme bombs. With twenty minutes, each mortar fired 15 bombs. This represented, as I later calculated, a total of 18 tons of explosives and cast-iron splinters. I found the noise absolutely staggering. It was amazing that men could retain their sanity in the midst of it. While the firing was in progress, one had the impression that thousands of tons of explosive were going off each second and the whole process seemed to last an age. The astonishing destructive power of these mortars makes up for any inaccuracy in aiming or in dispersion. I believe that this is the correct approach. Only one country, Israel, has had a chance to test the value of this exceptionally cheap and effective policy. Her army has 160mm mortars. I sincerely hope that she will progress further—she is on the right path.

2

The outstanding simplicity, reliability and ease of maintenance of the 240mm mortar are vital qualities, and they played a decisive role when the moment came to decide which should be the first artillery weapon to fire nuclear projectiles. It was the obvious choice and it is now many years since it was selected for this role. It was also a good choice, being comparatively small, manoeuvrable and easier to conceal than a gun. At the same time, it has a huge calibre, which solves several technical problems. Its muzzle velocity is considerably lower than that of a gun or a howitzer. There is therefore no danger that the bomb will explode as it is fired or that it will detonate accidentally. What could be better?

In 1970, a self-propelled version of the 240mm mortar was introduced. It was installed on a tracked GMZ chassis. This greatly increased its mobility, its ability to move across rough country and the protection provided for the crew. This development further increased the affection which the Soviet generals reserve for the mortar. At this period only Fronts and General Headquarters reserves were equipped with these weapons. However, Army and divisional commanders, as one man, implored every meeting they attended at the Ministry of Defence to give each divisional commander a battalion of these mortars and they also asked that each Army commander should have at least a regiment of them. Their pleas were heard and soon they received the mortars. And why not? It is after all, the simplest and the most economical weapon imaginable.

3

It's all right for the generals, you will say, but what about the battalion commanders? Must they be content with what their predecessors had in the Second World War? The number of mortars in a battalion could hardly be increased, for that would mean that half the infantry would have to be reclassified as artillery. Nor is it possible to increase the calibre of battalion mortars. This would make them too heavy to follow the infantry wherever it goes.

A way out of this situation, too, has been found. In 1971 the "Vasilek" automatic mortar was issued to battalions. Its introduction did not mean that the insistence on simplicity had been dropped. This automatic weapon is as uncomplicated as a Kalashnikov. When necessary, it can fire single shots. As an automatic weapon it fires 120 bombs a minute. It differs from all earlier mortars in being capable of both high and flat trajectory fire. It can fire both normal and anti-tank bombs. If necessary, a battalion commander can move his whole mortar battery to a sector threatened by enemy tanks and can shower them with 720 anti-tank bombs every minute.

The Vasilek is being produced on a self-propelled, armoured chassis and also in a towed variant. Six of them give a battalion commander greatly increased capability to bring concentrated fire to bear on a decisive sector.

Why do Calibres Vary?

1

When the Soviet Union first displayed the BMP-1 infantry combat vehicle in a parade, its designation and the calibre of its guns were unknown. From careful examination of photographs, Western analysts concluded that the calibre of the gun must be between 70 and 80mm. In this range there was only one gun—the 76mm, which is still, as it has been for many years a standard weapon in both the Soviet Army and the Soviet Navy. This gun was the most widely distributed of all Soviet artillery weapons before, during and after the war and its calibre occurs again and again in designations of Soviet equipment (e.g. T-34-76, the SU-76, the PT-76). Since this seemed a safe deduction, Western handbooks listed the new Soviet vehicle as the BMP-76.

Then several BMP-1s were captured in the Middle East and carefully examined. To the amazement of the specialists, it was established that the calibre of the gun was 73mm. This was virtually the same as the 76mm, so why were the Soviet designers not using this trusted calibre? Why the variation?

Meanwhile, photographs of new Soviet tanks—the T-64 and T-72—had begun to appear in Western journals. Painstaking analysis showed that the calibre of the gun carried by both these tanks was 125mm. But this calibre did not exist, either in the USSR or elsewhere. Many of the experts refused to accept the analysts' conclusion, asserting that the new tanks must have 122mm guns. 122mm—like 76mm—is a standard calibre, which has been in continuous use since before the Revolution. The 122 howitzer is the largest in use in the Soviet Army. Most heavy armoured vehicles had and still have guns of this calibre—the IS-2, IS-3, T-10, T10-M, SU-122, ISU-122, IT-122 and most recently the new, self-propelled "Gvozdika" howitzer, even though this appeared considerably later than the T-64. But then the new Soviet tanks began to appear abroad and all doubt ended—they *did* have 125mm guns. What was all this about? Why were all previous standards being abandoned? What lay behind it all?

2

The switch from existing calibres was not the result of a whim; rather, it was a carefully thought out policy—one which has a long history. It was initiated by Stalin himself, a few hours before Germany's surprise attack on the USSR.

It was on the eve of the war that the Soviet naval and coastal artillery were first issued with the excellent 130mm gun. This was subsequently used as an anti-tank gun and as a field gun and finally, in a self-propelled variant. Also just before the war, in the spring of 1941, a highly successful rocket launcher was developed in the USSR. This was the BM-13, which could fire 16 130mm rockets simultaneously. It later became known to the Soviet Army as the "Katyusha" and to the Germans as the "Stalin Organ." Naturally, the existence of both the gun and the rocket launcher were kept entirely secret.

In the first days of June 1941 the new rocket launcher was shown to members of the Politburo, in Stalin's presence. However, it was not fired, because artillery shells instead of rockets had been delivered to the test range. The mistake was understandable, in view of the great zeal with which secrecy was being preserved—how could the ordnance officers possibly have known of the existence of the 130mm rockets, which bore no resemblance to artillery shells?

Knowing Stalin, those present assumed that everyone responsible for this mistake would be shot immediately. However, Stalin told the Chekists not to get involved and went back to Moscow.

The second demonstration took place on 21 June at Solnechnogorsk. This time everything went off very well. Stalin was delighted with the rocket launcher. Then and there, on the range, he signed an order authorising its issue to the Soviet

Army. However, he directed that henceforth, in order to avoid confusion, the rockets should be referred to as 132mm, not as 130mm.

Accordingly, while the rocket launcher continued to be known as the BM-13 (13cm being 130mm), the rockets were henceforth referred to, despite their true calibre, as 132mm. That very night the war began.

During the war, projectiles of all types were fired in enormous quantities, reaching astronomical totals. They were transported for thousands of kilometres, under constant enemy attack. While they were being moved they had to be trans-shipped again and again and this was done by schoolboys, by old peasants, by convicts from prisons and camps, by German prisoners and by Soviet soldiers who had only been in the army for two or three days. Orders and requisitions for the rockets were passed hastily by telephone from exchange to exchange and made all but inaudible by interference. But there were no mistakes. Everyone could understand that "We need 130s" was a reference to artillery shells and it was equally clear that "1-3-2" meant rockets.

In 1942 the design of the rockets was modernised and their grouping capability and destructive effect were improved. In the process, they became slightly thicker, and their calibre was increased to 132mm—thus coming to match their designation.

Stalin's decision had proved correct and, as a result, a series of artillery weapons with unusual calibres were developed during the war. They appeared, of course, only when an unusual shell or rocket was designed. For instance, in 1941 a start was made with the development of a huge mortar which was needed to fire a 40 kilogram bomb. The calibre of the mortar could have been, for instance, 152mm, like the great majority of Soviet guns and howitzers. Obviously, however, a howitzer shell would be unsuitable for a mortar and vice versa. A mortar fires a particular type of projectile, which must itself be of a certain calibre. This was the requirement which resulted in the development of the 160mm mortar. Immediately after the war, 40mm grenade launchers appeared. There had never before been a weapon of this particular calibre in the Soviet Army. There were 37mm and 45mm shells. But a grenade launcher uses its own type of projectile and a special calibre was therefore selected for it.

Soviet designers took steps to correct past mistakes, which

had been tolerated until Stalin's sensible decision. The calibre of the standard Soviet infantry weapon is 7·62mm. In 1930, a 7·62mm "TT" pistol was brought into service, in addition to the existing rifles and machine-guns of this calibre. Although their calibre is the same, the rounds for this pistol cannot, of course, be used in either rifles or machine-guns.

In wartime, when everything is collapsing, when whole Armies and Groups of Armies find themselves encircled, when Guderian and his tank Army are charging around behind your own lines, when one division is fighting to the death for a small patch of ground, and others are taking to their heels at the first shot, when deafened switchboard operators, who have not slept for several nights, have to shout someone else's incomprehensible orders into telephones—in this sort of situation absolutely anything can happen. Imagine that, at a moment such as this, a division receives ten truckloads of 7·62mm cartridges. Suddenly, to his horror, the commander realises that the consignment consists entirely of pistol ammunition. There is nothing for his division's thousands of rifles and machine-guns and a quite unbelievable amount of ammunition for the few hundred pistols with which his officers are armed.

I do not know whether such a situation actually arose during the war, but once it was over the "TT" pistol—though not at all a bad weapon—was quickly withdrawn from service. The designers were told to produce a pistol with a different calibre. Since then Soviet pistols have all been of 9mm calibre. Why standardise calibres if this could result in fatally dangerous misunderstanding?

Ever since then, each time an entirely new type of projectile has been introduced, it has been given a new calibre. Naturally, shells for the BMP-1 gun are not suitable for the PT-76 tank—that was already obvious when work on the design of the new vehicle and of its armament was begun. Therefore it should not have a 76mm gun but something different—for instance, a 73mm one. The shells for the new T-62 tank were of a completely new design and would obviously not be suitable for use in the old 100mm tank guns. In that case, the calibre here too, should be something quite different—for instance, 115mm. The same went for the T-64 and T-72. Their shells had to be quite different from those of the old heavy tanks. So that the old and the new types of ammunition should not be mixed up, it was decided that the new shells should be 125mm whereas the old ones were 122mm. There are dozens of similar examples.

There are exceptions. In some cases it is essential to use a particular calibre and no other. For example, the 122mm, 40-barrel multiple rocket launcher must be of precisely that calibre—no more and no less. Its rockets are therefore given a special designation; they are called "Grad" rockets. This is the only way in which they are ever referred to—they are never called "122mm" rockets. One makes this a habit from one's very first day. Then, if someone orders "1-2-2" he is referring to howitzer shells, but if he orders "Grad," he means rockets.

3

Western analysts find it hard to understand why the Soviet Union has turned away from its old, well-tried standard calibres. Soviet analysts, for their part, wonder why Western designers stick so stubbornly to old specifications. The British have an exceptionally powerful 120mm tank gun. An excellent weapon. They also have a useful 120mm recoilless gun. One of them was developed some time ago, the other more recently. Obviously, they use quite different shells. Why not use different calibres—one could be 120mm, the other 121mm? Or leave the calibres as they are; just change the designation of one to 121mm. Why not?

The same applies to West Germany and to France. Both countries have excellent 120mm mortars and both are working on the development of new 120mm tank guns. Of course this works well enough in peacetime. Everything is under control when the soldiers are professionals, who are quick to understand a command. But what happens if, tomorrow, middle-aged reservists and students from drama academies have to be mobilised to defend freedom? What then? Every time 120mm shells are needed, one will have to explain that you don't need the type which are used by recoilless guns or those which are fired by mortars, but shells for tank guns. But be careful— there are 120mm shells for rifled tank guns and different 120mm shells for smoothbore tank guns. The guns are different and their shells are different. What happens if a drama student makes a mistake?

The Soviet analysts sit and scratch their heads as they try to understand why it is that Western calibres never alter.

Secrets, Secrets, Secrets

1

The 41st Guards Tank Division was issued with T-64 tanks at the beginning of 1967. Of course, its soldiers knew nothing about this. They joined the division, served it honourably for two years and then went back to their homes; other soldiers came, learned something about tanks but went home having heard nothing about the T-64 and never having seen one. In 1972 the division was re-equipped with the new T-72s and the T-64s were sent to Germany. The soldiers, of course, knew nothing about this—neither that the division had received new tanks nor that the old ones had gone. The soldiers serve in a division, they are trained by it for war but they know nothing about its tanks.

To the Western reader this may seem rather strange. However, when I came to the West and took my first look at Western armies, I was astounded to discover that Western soldiers knew the names of their tanks, and that they drive and fire from them. This seemed absurd to me, but I was unable to obtain any explanation of this strange policy.

In the Soviet Army everything is secret. When the war began it was not only the German generals who knew nothing about the T-34 tank—even the Soviet generals knew no more than they did. It was being mass-produced, but this was kept secret. Not even the tank forces knew of its existence. The new tanks were moved from the factories to some divisions, but only to those which were a long way back from the frontiers. They were ferried by a factory team (totalling 30 drivers for the whole of the Soviet Union) in convoys, the like of which had never been seen before, escorted by NKVD officers, who were forbidden even to talk to the drivers. They travelled only at night and the tanks were always completely covered with tarpaulins. The routes they took were closed to all other traffic and heavily guarded. When the tanks reached their destination, they were off-loaded by the factory team, who then drove them into vehicle parks, surrounded by high walls, inside which they were put into storage.

The tank crews were quickly instructed on various features of the new tanks, but they were not told what the new tanks were called or shown them. The gunners were, however, introduced to the new gunsights and taught how to use them, firing from old tanks. The drivers were given intensive training in the old tanks after being told that there was a new tank in the offing, which had to be driven rather differently. The drivers did not, of course, know whether the division already had this new tank or not. The tank commanders, too, were told a certain amount and shown how to service the engine, but they were not told the name of the tank from which the unusual engine came or given its horse-power. In short, the division was simply retrained, but only used the old tanks.

Then came the war, unexpected and terrifying. The first echelon divisions, which had good, although not secret equipment, were torn to pieces in the first battles. While this was happening, the divisions in the rear areas received orders to go into the tank parks, to take the tanks out of storage and to familiarise themselves with them. It took them two weeks to do this and after a further two weeks they reached the front. Then in these completely unknown tanks, the divisions took on Guderian's armoured columns. It was soon clear that they could operate them very well. After all, a driver who can handle a Volkswagen like a champion would not take long to master a Mercedes. That is how it was done in the Soviet Army then and how it will be done in future—they learn on a Volkswagen, but keep the Mercedes secretly hidden away until it is really needed.

But, of course, the T-34 was not the only surprise awaiting the Germans. They discovered the existence of the "KV" heavy tank only when they met it in action; before that they had not even heard of it. Nor, for that matter, had its Soviet tank-crews had any idea of its existence—the KV had been secretly stored away. The German troops soon met the "Stalin Organ" for the first time, too, and panicked when they did so. In peacetime sub-units armed with these excellent weapons had masqueraded as pontoon-bridge battalions, whose uniforms they had worn, with the result that most of their own soldiers had not realised that they were in reality rocket troops. Their retraining started only when the war began, but even then only the battery commanders knew the correct designation of their rocket launchers. The remaining officers, NCOs and other ranks did not even know what the equipment which they were using in battle was called. The launchers were marked with the letter K (standing for the Komintern factory in Voronezh). Naturally, no one, even the battery commanders, knew what this stood for and the result was that the soldiers on every front almost simultaneously christened these splendid weapons "Katerina," "Katya" or "Katyusha." It was under this last name that they went down in history. Their correct designation—BM-13—was only allowed to be used in secret documents from the middle of 1942 onwards and it was not used in unclassified papers until after the end of the war.

2

The policy of observing the strictest rules of secrecy has completely justified itself. For this reason it is universally accepted and is applied with ever greater rigour. As a result, officers serving in a nuclear submarine may know, for instance, the output of the boat's reactor, if they are involved in its maintenance, but they will not know the maximum depth to which the boat can dive, since this does not concern them. Others may know this maximum depth, but will not know the range of the missiles which the submarine carries.

This policy of secrecy is applied to the production of heavy assault guns, mounted on tank chassis. A tank with a fixed turret is an excellent weapon. True, its arc of fire is reduced, but against this, a more powerful gun can be installed, the quantity of ammunition it carries can be increased, its armour can be strengthened without increasing its overall weight and, most important, it is much easier to manufacture. Guns of this sort are indispensable, when used in close conjunction with tanks with normal turrets. Both the Soviet and the German generals came to realise their value during the war, but since then only the former have continued to produce them. In order that other countries should not be tempted to introduce this simple but excellent weapon, all Soviet heavy assault guns are protected by strict security measures. Their production has continued, without a break, ever since the war. Every motor-rifle regiment (inside the USSR, but not abroad) has one battery of heavy assault guns. In the 1950s the powerful D-74 (122mm) was mounted on a T-54 tank chassis, then the M-46 gun (130mm) was installed on the T-62 tank chassis. All regiments, without exception, have heavy assault guns of this type. They are kept in mothballs for decades, never seeing the light of day. Their crews train on T-54 and T-62 tanks. Sometimes they are shown the gunsights of the assault guns. They know the tactics which will be used and they know how to service the engines. If war should break out their commander would disclose to them that instead of tanks they were about to be equipped with something which was similar but far more powerful and better armoured. In the middle of the 1970s all these guns were replaced by more powerful models but, naturally, they were not melted down. Instead they were either sent to the Chinese frontier to be installed in concrete emplacements or sent to holding depots, in case they should come in useful one day.

3

The same secrecy is maintained around the IT-1 and IT-2 anti-tank rocket launchers and the Rapira-2 and Rapira-3 anti-tank guns.

The IT-1 is built on a T-62 tank chassis but is armed with the "Drakon" anti-tank rocket instead of a gun. Each Army has one battalion of IT-1s, which are kept in mothballs, well concealed and never seen even by the battalion's own soldiers. If the Army to which it belongs is posted abroad, the battalion remains on Soviet territory, to all appearances an ordinary tank battalion. Its soldiers are given instruction in tactics and driving and maintenance of the vehicles but ordinary tanks or training simulators are used for this.

In this way it is possible to serve out your time in the Soviet Army, learning nothing—or very little—about its equipment.

How Much Does All This Cost?

1

Nothing at all. I will repeat that. All this costs nothing at all.

Let us imagine that you work at a full-time job, but that your wife does not. You give her an allowance and she has no other source of income. You start to give her driving lessons and decide to make yourself some money by doing so. After all, you are using up energy, time, labour, nerves and petrol. But now answer a question—is it more in your interest to make your wife pay through the nose for her lessons, or to keep the price low? Which will be more profitable for you?

If you were giving lessons to a neighbour, of course, you would ask as high a price as you felt you could. But what should you do when you are teaching your own wife? The more money you make her pay, in the hope of becoming rich, the more she will need from you, for where else could she get it?

If you lower your fee, you will need to give your wife less, and she will let you have less back. You soon realise that whatever you charge she will just be taking money from your pocket and then returning it to you.

Now, turn your thoughts to the 6th Guards Tank Army, with its thousands of tanks and tens of thousands of men. Imagine yourself to be the Communist Pharaoh, the General Secretary of the Communist Party of the Soviet Union. Something strange—goodness knows what—is going on in Czechoslovakia. To safeguard yourself you decide to move the 6th Guards Army up to your frontier with this fraternal state. It is only possible to move a thousand tanks over a distance of a thousand kilometres by rail, for tanks wear out roads very fast—and vice versa. How much is this going to cost you? You summon the Minister of Railways (being nationalised, the railways are fully controlled by the people—in other words by the government—that is, by you personally) and put this question to him. He tells you—"100 million rubles." This means that you will have to take 100 million rubles out of the State's pocket and give it to the Army; the Army pays the money to the railways, which, in turn, puts this, the profit they have made, back into the State's pocket. What on earth is the point of taking it out in the first place, if it was going to be put back almost immediately? So, in fact, it does not get taken out in the first place. The General Secretary just summons the Minister and tells him to move the 6th Guards Tank Army. The Minister says "Yes, Sir," clicks his heels and does as he has been told. That is all. No money is needed for the operation. The same system applies to any movement by individual soldiers. An officer comes to a railway station and shows papers which say that in the national interest he is to proceed to the Far East. What would be the point in giving the officer money, for him to pay a State organisation, which must then refund the same money to the State?

In the Soviet Union everything has been nationalised. Private deals are forbidden. Since everything is in the hands of the State, prices for goods produced for the State have no meaning. Tanks, guns, rockets—none has any price inside the State. It is like growing a strawberry in your garden, selling it to yourself and eating it, moving the money you pay for it from your right pocket to your left one. Your strawberry only acquires a price if you sell it to someone else and put the money he pays you into your pocket. In the same way, Soviet tanks acquire a price only when someone abroad buys them.

For the State, which owns all the safes in the land, to move billions of rubles from one safe to another is meaningless. So nothing is moved. A Ministry simply receives an order to produce a thousand tanks or rockets or bombers and to deliver them to the armed forces. That is all. If a minister does not carry out his orders he loses his place at the ministerial feeding-trough. Money of a sort is paid to the workers but it is really nothing but the equivalent of ration cards. Workers are given just enough to buy bread or potatoes, a poor quality suit every three years and vodka every day. This money is printed by the State but it is not recognised by anyone abroad, since it can not be exchanged for gold.

In the Soviet Union there are virtually no taxes, because

they are not needed. Everything is in the hands of the State, everything has been nationalised. A Soviet banknote is essentially a ration card, issued by the State for work done in its interests. Why hand out ten ration cards and then take five of them back again? The State does not grow any richer by re-acquiring these cards, which do not help to make more meat available in the shops. Accordingly, the State, which prints these cards, produces only enough to buy the amount of bread, potatoes, rotten meat and old fashioned clothes which it is prepared to distribute to its citizens. The latter eat the meat and give the ration cards back to the State, which hands them out again.

Sometimes the State becomes more concerned about producing tanks than food, but it must continue to hand out ration cards to the people. This creates inflation, since now the ration cards can not even purchase bread and this soon has a calamitous effect on the whole huge military machine.

It is a good thing that there are capitalists in the world, ready to come forward with help at times like these.

Copying Weapons

1

The Soviet Union has designed a large number of first-class weapons, among them the T-34 tank, the Kalashnikov automatic assault rifle and the IL-2 Shturmovik ground attack aircraft. Even today, in the early 1980s, no one has succeeded in improving on the performance of the Soviet 130mm gun, although it was developed as long ago as 1935. The Soviet Union was the first to use rockets fired from an aircraft—this was in August 1939 in Mongolia, in combat with Japanese aircraft. A Soviet motor torpedo boat (under Egyptian colours) was the first in history to use rockets to sink an enemy ship. The Soviet Union was the first to use the BM-13 salvo-firing rocket launcher. The Soviet Union was the first, many years ago, to realise the value of smoothbore guns, with their astonishingly high muzzle velocity, and it was the first to mass-produce automatic mortars and many other excellent types of weapon.

At the same time, the Soviet intelligence services, the largest in the world, search unceasingly for anything new in the field of military equipment. The enormous extent of Soviet activity in this sphere beggars description. Soviet intelligence succeeded in obtaining all the technical documentation needed to produce nuclear weapons, in winning over a number of distinguished scientists and in ideologically recruiting others as agents.

Since the war, the Soviet Union has succeeded in copying and in putting into mass production the American B-29 bomber, British Rolls-Royce aircraft engines, American lorries and German V-2 rockets. It has also completed the development of a number of German rocket designs which were still unfinished at the end of the war. It has stolen plans for the construction of French anti-tank rockets, American air-launched missiles, laser range-finders, stabilisers for tank guns, rocket fuel, special dye-stuffs and many, many other highly important products.

PART SEVEN

THE SOLDIER'S LOT

Building Up

1

For 35 years (between the ages of 17 and 50) all Soviet men—and all the Soviet women whose professions might make them useful to the Armed Forces—remain on the register of those liable for military service, forming the Armed Forces reserve. This register, listing all these individuals, is maintained by Rayon City, Oblast, and Republic Commissars, who come under the orders of the Organisational Directorate of the Military Districts and, thus, ultimately, of the Chief Organisational Directorate of the General Staff.

The tens of millions of people on the register may be called up without notice, if either partial or full mobilisation is announced.

As soon as a young man is 17, he appears before a medical board and is listed on the register. The next year, as soon as he is 18, he is called up for service in the Armed Forces. Depending on the date of his birthday, this may happen in the spring (in May or June), or in the winter (in November or December).

Conscripts spend two years in all Services and arms of service, except for the Navy, in which they serve for three years.

Every year, two intakes, each of approximately a million young men, join the Armed Forces and those who have completed their service are demobilized. Thus, every six months something like a quarter of the total number of other ranks changes over. New men join, the older ones leave, remaining on the reserve until they are 50.

2

Private Ivanov received instructions to report to the local assembly point on 29 May. In preparation he did three things:

— he got together with a gang of fellow spirits to beat up some of his enemies, in accordance with the principle—"Today you help me to knock the hell out of the people I don't like and then tomorrow I'll help you to do the same."

— he told his girl-friend that she was to wait two years for him, to go out with no one else and to write to him frequently—"Otherwise you'll see. I'll come back and kill you. You know me."

— on the night of 28 May he drank himself into complete insensibility. Parents realise that unless they hand over their drunken son to the assembly point by midday he will be punished under military law.

A convoy takes the crowd of drunk and half-drunk youths to the station, where they are put on a train and taken to their place of duty.

A soldier is not entitled to choose an arm of service, the area in which he will serve or the trade which he will follow in the army. Long before Ivanov received his call-up papers, the General Staff had sent all Military Commissariats details of the men they would be receiving and instructions on where they were to send them. Naturally, the General Staff does not go into details, saying no more than "150 men, of category 'O' are to be sent to Military unit 54678." This may be a unit of diversionary troops, it may be a nuclear submarine, or it may be something very secret indeed. The Military Commissar can only guess. (If the number has four figures the unit belongs to either the KGB or the Ministry of Internal Affairs. If it has five, it is a Ministry of Defence unit.) This is all he is told except that there is sometimes a minor additional requirement, such as "Category 'O,' but all are to be tall and physically well-developed."

The Military Commissar prepares groups of soldiers by categories—for instance, 5 men from Category 1, 100 from Category 2 and 5,000 from Category 3 to military unit 64192. The

Military Units receive their own instructions—"You will receive 100 men from Khabarovsk, 950 from Baku, 631 from Tbilisi."

Each Military District makes up several troop transports, provides escorts and officers, and sends them off to different corners of the huge country, while mixed columns move off to distant rocket batteries, fortified areas and motor-rifle divisions.

One requirement is sacrosanct when these selections are being made: whenever possible, Russians must not be stationed in the RSFSR, Ukrainians in the Ukraine or Latvians in Latvia. If there are disturbances among the Russian population of, for instance, Murom or Tolyatti or Omsk, these will be crushed, sometimes with considerable bloodshed, by non-Russian soldiers. If a strike breaks out in Donetsk (as one did in 1970) there will be no Ukrainian soldiers in the area. The soldiers stationed there are Tatars, Kirghiz, Georgians. It is all the same to them who they shoot at. What is important is that there is no one in the crowd confronting them whom they know and no one in it who speaks a language they can understand.

It is also essential to mix all the nationalities together in divisions, regiments and battalions. If one regiment contains too many Lithuanians and another too many Tatars, this must result from a slip-up by some military bureaucrat. The punishment for such mistakes is harsh.

The movement of such colossal numbers of men takes up two whole months. Surprisingly, the machine works extremely smoothly, rather like a sausage machine—all sorts of pieces of meat, some onions, some rusks, and some garlic are put in at one end and out of the other come solidly compressed rolls of well-mixed human material.

3

A column of new recruits is not a sight for anyone with weak nerves. Traditionally, anyone joining the army dresses in such rags that you wonder where on earth he found them. For recruits know that any more or less useable article—socks which are not in tatters, for instance—will immediately be seized from them by the soliders escorting the column. So they dress in the sort of rags which should be thrown on a bonfire—a mechanic's boiler suit, solid with grease, a painter's working clothes daubed with paint of all colours, even a sewage-collector's overalls. Many of them will have black eyes, acquired in farewell fights with their local enemies. All are unshaven, uncombed, shaggy, dirty—and drunk, into the bargain.

All the officers and soldiers escorting the column are armed. The roughest, toughest sergeants and other ranks are chosen for this job. They stop the fights which keep breaking out, giving the recruits new bruises as they do so. The young newcomers quickly feel the weight of a sergeant's fist and soon realise that it is best to do what he tells them—and that the same goes for a soldier, who may himself have spent a fortnight in the same sort of column, swapping punches with those around him, as recently as a year ago.

Anyone who has once seen for himself what a column of these new recruits looks like will understand why there are no volunteers in the Soviet Army, why there never could be and why there is no need for them. The whole system is too inflexible, too regulated, and too tightly controlled to concern itself with any individual's opinions or wishes. Everyone is simply grabbed, indiscriminately, as soon as he reaches 18, and that's that.

How to avoid being called up

1

At some juncture long ago, before Stalin, in Lenin's day, the wise decision was taken that the state apparatus should be manned, not by riff-raff, but by comrades of proven worth, who were responsible, experienced and dedicated to the popular cause. In order that the state should not be infiltrated by alien elements at some stage in the future, it was decided that successors to this ruling group should be prepared and that it was essential to ensure that these young people were appropriately educated. Educational establishments were therefore set up to prepare the future ruling class, and these were filled, for the most part, with the children of the comrades of proven worth, who were themselves dedicated to the revolutionary cause. The comrades were very pleased with this plan and have never since contemplated any deviation from the course approved by Lenin.

As an illustration—the Minister of Foreign Affairs of the USSR, Comrade A. A. Gromyko is, of course, a person of proven worth. It follows that his son, too, must be dedicated to the people's cause; this means that Comrade Gromyko's son can become a diplomat and, provided that it is possible to check that Comrade Gromyko's son has made a success of this career, the grandson of Comrade Gromyko, too, can enter the diplomatic service. Comrade Gromyko's deputy is Comrade Malik. He, too, is a trusted person, dedicated to the national cause and this means that the road to a diplomatic career is also open to both his son and his grandson.

The comrades of proven worth got together and agreed among themselves that, since their children were already dedicated to their Motherland and prepared to defend its interests throughout their entire lives, there was no need for them to enter the army.

257

Accordingly, when the sons of the comrades of proven worth reach 17 they are not required to register for military service; instead, wasting no time, they enter the Institute of International Relations. After qualifying there, they go off to spend not just two years but the whole of their lives defending the interests of their Motherland at the most exposed portion of the front line in the battle against capitalism—in Paris, Vienna, Geneva, Stockholm or Washington. This is why the children of the comrades of proven worth do not have to be ferried around in dirty railway trucks, are not punched in the mouth by sergeants, and do not have their gold teeth pulled out, and why, too, their girl-friends do not need to wait for them for two or three years.

Lest the absurd idea should enter anyone's head that the sons of the comrades of proven worth are not defending socialism, with weapons in their hands, they are given military awards for their service from time to time. The son of that most responsible and trusted of all comrades, Brezhnev, for instance, spent years defending the interests of socialism in the barricades of Stockholm; on his return from this most crucial operation he was given the military rank of Major-General even though he has never spent a day in the army, or indeed as much as an hour locked in a railway wagon with a lot of grubby recruits.

In the KGB, as in the Ministry of Foreign Affairs, they read the works of Lenin and therefore, following his precepts, they, too, admit to their training establishments the sons of comrades of proven worth, rather than just anyone. And because these boys, too, will have to spend their lives defending socialism, they are also given exemption from military service.

The Workers' and Peasants' State contains a mass of other important state organisations and undertakings for which future leaders must be prepared. To train them an enormous network of higher educational institutions has been set up. The comrades of proven worth have decreed that anyone entering one of these higher educational institutions is to be granted exemption from military service. The universities organise military training courses, of limited scope, and these are considered sufficient.

2

In every town there is at least one institute which is ultimately controlled, through a series of intermediate authorities, by the First Secretary of the Oblast Committee of the Party. Naturally, the First Secretary's own children do not attend this institute. They study somewhere in Moscow. But he has a Second Secretary and a Third; they have deputies, who themselves have assistants, who have consultants. All of these have children. Formerly all those concerned with the administration of the Oblast sent their children straight to the local institute where, since they were the children of trusted comrades, they were received with open arms. Nowadays, things have changed somewhat. The Third Secretary of the Oblast Committee will telephone his opposite number in a nearby town—"My son is due for call-up in the autumn and your boy next spring. If you'll look after my son, I'll do the same for yours." A mutually beneficial exchange is arranged. A couple of lotus-eaters are admitted to two higher educational institutions, without being required to pass any examinations. However, they find themselves in neighbouring towns, rather than at home, and they are also regarded as "workers and peasants" rather than as the sons of comrades of proven worth. But then, first in one town and then in the other, the two Third Secretaries are suddenly seized with the desire to improve the living conditions of students. Not everyone can be given a rent-free apartment, of course, so the Oblast Committee allocates just one. Thus only one student gets one—our own, dear "worker-peasant." With considerable effort he obtains his certificate of higher education. Everyone else is sent off to work in Siberia but he is found a place with the Oblast Committee, as an assistant. Time passes quickly, he climbs steadily upwards and before long his own son is growing up and will soon be eligible for army service. Meanwhile, however, the system has become more complicated. Mutually helpful exchanges between two neighbouring towns are too conspicuous. So our worker-peasant doesn't enrol his son in the nearest town. Instead, the son of someone who appears to be a true member of the working class enters an institute in a third town, without having to pass exams, while from this third town to ours comes an apparently straight-forward young man, the son of some official or other, whose name no one knows. A flat is quickly found for this young man, who then gets a post with the Oblast Committee. He finds a job there for someone else, who reciprocates by letting him have a car, without payment, and who in his turn does the same for yet another person. The wheel turns on and hundreds of thousands of parasites avoid having to endure the railway wagons or the brutish armed sergeants.

3

But what happens if your father is not among those at the helm of the Workers' and Peasants' State? In that case if he will just slip the Military Commissar a few thousand rubles, you can be found unfit for military service and your name removed from the register. The Military Commissar in Odessa was shot for doing this, the same happened in Kharkov, in Tbilisi, every year for five years in succession, they sent a Military Commissar to gaol but that did not solve the problem so they had to shoot the sixth one. They would hardly have shot a Military Commissar—a Colonel—for misdeeds involving a few thousand rubles. The sums concerned must have been very large indeed.

And if your father has not got a few thousand rubles to spare? Then you could cut off your trigger finger with an axe. Or you could stick a small piece of foil on your back when you go for your X-ray, so that they decide you have tuberculosis and turn you down for the army. You could go to prison. But if you haven't the courage for any of these, brother, you'll find yourself in that dirty railway wagon.

If you can't, we'll teach you;
if you don't want to, we'll make you

1

The column of recruits finally reaches the division to which it has been allocated. The thousands of hushed, rather frightened youths leave the train at a station surrounded by barbed wire, their heads are quickly shaven, they are driven through a cold bath, their filthy rags are burned on huge fires, they are issued with crumpled greatcoats, tunics and trousers that are too large or too small, squeaky boots and belts. With that the first grading process is completed. It does not occur to any of them that each of them has already been assessed, taking into account his political reliability, his family's criminal record (or absence of one), participation (or failure to participate) in Communist mass meetings, his height and his physical and mental development. All these factors have been taken into account in grading him as Category 0, 1, 2, and so forth and then allocating him to a sub-category of one of these groups. There will be no more than ten Category 0 soldiers in a whole motor-rifle division—they will go to the 8th department of the divisional staff. In each intake there will be two or three of them, who will replace others who are being demobilised, and who will themselves join the reserve. They have no idea that they are in this particular category or that files exist on them which have long ago been checked and passed by the KGB.

Category 1 soldiers are snapped up by the divisional rocket or reconnaissance battalions or by the regimental reconnaissance companies. Category 2 soldiers are those who are able to understand and to work with complicated mathematical formulae. They are grabbed by the fire-control batteries of the artillery regiment, of the anti-aircraft rocket regiment and of the self-propelled artillery battalions of the motor-rifle and tank regiments.

And then there are the soldiers of my own arm of service, the tank crews—Category 6, thanks to the swine who do the planning in the General Staff. But nothing can be done about that—the army is enormous and bright soldiers are in demand everywhere. Everyone is after the strong, brave, healthy ones. Not everyone can be lucky.

A detachment is set up in each battalion, to handle the new intake. The battalion commander's deputy heads this and he is assisted by some of the platoon commanders and sergeants. Their task is to turn the recruits into proper soldiers in the course of one month. This is called a "Young Soldier's Course." It is a very hard month in a soldier's life; during it he comes to realise that the sergeant above him is a king, a god and his military commander.

The recruits are subjected to a most elaborate and rigorous disciplinary programme; they clean out lavatories with their tooth-brushes, they are chased out of bed twenty or thirty times every night, under pressure to cut seconds off the time it takes them to dress, their days are taken up with training exercises which may last for sixteen hours at a stretch. They study their weapons, they are taught military regulations, they learn the significance of the different stars and insignia on their officers' shoulder boards. At the end of the month they fire their own weapons for the first time and then they are paraded to swear the oath of allegiance, knowing that any infringement of this will be heavily punished, even, perhaps, with the death-sentence. After this the recruit is considered to have become a real soldier. The training detachment is disbanded and the recruits are distributed among the companies and batteries.

2

Socialists make the lying claim that it is possible to create a classless society. In fact, if a number of people are thrown together, it is certain that a leading group, or perhaps several groups, will emerge—in other words different classes. This has nothing to do with race, religion or political beliefs. It will always happen, in every situation of this sort. If a group of survivors were to reach an uninhabited island after a shipwreck and you were able to take a look at them after they had been there only a week, you would undoubtedly find that a leader or leading group had already emerged. In the German concentration camps, no matter what sort of people were imprisoned together, they would always establish themselves in stratified societies, with higher and lower classes.

The division into leaders and followers occurs automatically. Take a group of children and ask them to put up a tent; do not put one of them in charge but stand aside and watch them. Within five minutes a leader will have emerged.

A group of short-haired recruits nervously enters an enormous barrack room, in which two, three or even five hundred soldiers live. They quickly come to realise that they have entered a class-dominated society. Communist theory has no place here. The sergeants split the young soldiers up by platoons, detachments and teams. At first everything goes normally—here is your bed, this is your bedside locker in which you can keep your washing-kit, your four manuals, brushes and your handbook of scientific communism and nothing else. Understand? Yes, sergeant.

But at night the barrack-room comes alive. The recruits need to understand that it contains four classes—the soldiers who will be leaving the army in six months, those who will go after a year, a third class who have eighteen months still to serve and, lastly, they themselves, who have a full two years to go. The higher castes guard their privileges jealously. The lower castes must acknowledge their seniors as their elders and betters, the seniors refer to inferiors as "scum." Those who still have eighteen months to serve are the superiors of the new recruits, but scum, naturally, to those who have only a year to go.

The night after the new intake has arrived is a terrible one in every barracks: the naked recruits are flogged with belts, and ridden, bareback, by their seniors, who use them as horses to fight cavalry battles and then they are driven out to sleep in the lavatories while their beds are fouled by their elders and betters.

Their commanders know what is going on, of course, but they do not interfere; it is in their interests that the other ranks should be divided among themselves by barriers of real hatred.

The lowest class have no rights whatsoever. They, the scum,

clean the shoes and make the beds of their seniors, clean their weapons for them, hand over their meat and sugar rations, sometimes even their bread to them. The soldiers who are soon to be released appropriate the recruits' new uniforms, leaving them with their own worn-out ones. If you are in command of a platoon or a company you are quite content with the situation. You order your sergeants to get something done—digging tank pits, for instance. The sergeants give the senior soldiers this job to do and they in turn hand it on to the scum. You can be confident that everything will be finished in good time. The senior soldiers will do nothing themselves but they will make each of the scum do enough for two or three men. You can take your sergeants off into the bushes and hand out your cigarettes; whatever you do, don't fuss. Wait until someone comes to report that the job has been done. This is your moment: appear like the sun from behind the clouds, and thank the senior soldiers for their hard work. I assure you—both the senior soldiers and the scum will love you for it. . . .

Six months pass and a new consignment of scum joins your sub-unit. Now those who suffered yesterday have a chance to vent their rage on someone. All the humiliations and insults which they have suffered for six months can now be heaped on the newcomers. Meanwhile those who still insult and beat them up continue to be regarded as scum by their own superiors.

These are the circumstances in which a soldier begins to master the rudiments of the science of war.

1,441 Minutes

1

"Roll on my demob!" "I wish you all a speedy demob—make sure you deserve it!" "They've taken everything else away, but they can't take my demob!" "Demobilization is as inevitable as the collapse of capitalism." These are sentences you will see scribbled on the wall of any soldiers' lavatory. They are cleaned off every day but they are soon back again, in paint which is still wet.

Demobilization comes after two years' service. It is the day-dream of every soldier and NCO. From the moment a recruit joins the army, he begins to cross off the days to his demob. He lists the days left on the inside of his belt or ticks them off on a board, a wall, or on the side of his tank's engine compartment. In any military camp, on the backs of the portraits of Marx, Lenin, Brezhnev, Andropov and Ustinov you will find scores of inscriptions such as "103 Sundays left to my demob," accompanied by the appropriate number of marks, carefully ticked off one by one in ink or pencil. Or "730 dinners to my demob" and more marks. Or, frequently "17,520 hours to my demob" or, even more often, "1,051,200 minutes to my demob."

A soldier's day is split up into a number of periods of so many minutes each and this makes it most convenient for him to calculate in minutes. The Soviet soldier reckons that his day lasts just a little bit longer than it does for any other inhabitant of the planet, so in his calculations he reckons that a day contains 1,441 minutes—a minute longer than it does for the rest of us.

A minute is the most convenient division of time for him, although he has to count in seconds, too.

265

2

The soldier's second day-dream, after his demobilization, is—
to be allowed to sleep for 600 minutes. Theoretically, he is
allowed 480 minutes for sleep. Of course, one of the scum gets
only half this: as he moves into a higher caste and becomes
more senior he sleeps longer and longer. A month before his
demobilization a senior soldier hangs a note above his bed "Do
Not Tilt! To be Carried Out First In Case Of Fire."

Reveille is at 0600 hours. Wake up, jump out of bed, trousers and boots on, run outside for a rapid visit to the lavatory,
sprint to the door, which is jammed with people, another sprint
and you are on the road outside, past the sergeants who are
lying in wait for the "last on parade." By 0605 the company
is already moving briskly along the roads of the military camp.
In rain and wind, in hail and snow—just boots and trousers,
chests bare. Running and PT until 0640—35 minutes of really
hard physical exercise.

Then the company goes back to the barrack-room with 20
minutes to wash and make beds. During this time the scum
have to make both their own beds and those of the senior
soldiers. At 0700 there is morning inspection; the sergeant-
major spends half an hour on a rigorous check of the company's
general tidiness, haircuts, contents of pockets, etc. After this,
the company falls in and moves off, bawling a song and march-
ing in time to it, to the dining hall. An attentive observer would
notice that the number of soldiers in the company is now greater
by a quarter than it was during the PT parade. Actually, when
the orderly first shouted, "Company. On your feet!" at reveille,
by no means everyone jumped hastily out of bed. The most
senior of the soldiers, those with only six months to go before
their demob, get up unwillingly and slowly, stretching, swear-
ing quietly to themselves, not joining in the rush to the lavatory
or tearing off to the parade. While the rest of the company
marches round the corner, they go quietly about their own
affairs. One may stretch out under his bed to sleep for another
half hour, others doze behind the long row of greatcoats, which
hang from pegs by the wall, and the rest may tuck themselves
away somewhere at the back of the barrack-room by a warm

pipe from the furnace-room. Whatever they choose to do, they don't turn out for PT with the rest of the company. They keep an eye out for the patrolling duty officers, quietly changing their hiding places if he approaches. Eventually they go and wash, leaving their beds to be made by the scum.

The Soviet Army serves a meagre breakfast. A soldier is allowed 20 grammes of butter a day, but since, theoretically, 10 of these are used for cooking, there are only 10 grammes on his plate. With this, for breakfast, he receives two slices of black bread, one of white, a bowl of kasha and a mug of tea, with one lump of sugar.

Butter and sugar are used as a sort of currency, with which to placate one's seniors for yesterday's mistakes or for some piece of disrespectful behaviour. They are also used as stakes for bets so that many of the soldiers have to hand over their breakfast butter or sugar—or both—to those who have been luckier than them at guessing the results of football or hockey matches.

There is not much bread, either, but if a soldier somehow manages to get hold of an extra slice, he will always try to make his tiny portion of butter cover it too, so that it is bread and butter rather than just bread that he is eating. Several soldiers from my company once spent a day working in the bakery and, of course, they helped themselves to a few loaves, which they shared with the other members of their platoon. Each of them had ten or fifteen slices of bread to spread his butter on and was able to eat as much as he wanted, for the first time for months. But there was very little butter indeed for each slice. I was not far away, and, seeing how they were enjoying themselves, I went over and asked how they could tell which of the slices had butter on them. They laughed and one held a piece of bread above his head and gently tilted it towards the sun. The answer became clear—a slice on which there was even the smallest scraping of butter reflected the sunlight.

3

At 0800 hours there is a regimental parade. The deputy regimental commander presents the regiment for inspection by the commander. Then the day's training, which lasts for seven hours, begins. The first hour is a review period, during which officers from the regimental or divisional staffs test the extent to which officers, NCOs and soldiers are ready to proceed with the forthcoming day's work. Soldiers are questioned on what they learned during the previous day, what training they received and what they have memorized. For me, as for any commander, this was a most uncomfortable hour. During this review period, too, orders by senior commanders from regimental level up to that of the Minister of Defence himself are read out, together with the sentences imposed on the previous day by Soviet Army military tribunals—outlines of cases involving five to ten years' imprisonment, and sometimes death sentences.

If the review period ends early, the rest of the hour is used for drill. After this come three periods, each of two hours. During these each platoon works in accordance with a training schedule which covers the following subjects:

Political training	Technical training
Tactics	Weapons of mass destruction and
Weapon training	Defence against these
Drill	Physical training

The number of hours spent on each subject varies considerably, depending on the arm of service and the Armed Service in which the soldiers are serving. However, the general plan of work is the same everywhere—a review period, drill and then six hours of work on the subjects listed above in accordance with individually arranged training schedules.

Ninety-five per cent of all work, except for political training, is done out of doors, rather than in classrooms—in the open country on ranges, in tank training areas, in tank depots, etc. All periods, except for political training, involve physical work, which is often very strenuous.

For instance, tactical training may involve six hours digging trenches in blazing sun or in a hard frost, high-speed crossings of rivers, ravines, ditches and barricades, rapid erection of camouflage—and everything is done at the double. Instruction in tactics is always given without equipment. Thus, a tank crew it told to imagine that they are in a tank, attacking the enemy "on the edge of the wood over there." Having run to the wood, the crew returns and the tank commander explains the mistakes they made—they should have attacked not on the crest of the hill but in the gully. Now, once again . . . Using this system of instruction, you can quickly teach a crew, who may be unable to understand complicated explanations, how an enemy should be attacked, and how to use every hollow in the ground to protect their own tank in battle. If they don't, well they just run off again, and again, and again for the whole six hours if necessary.

Weapon training involves study of weapons and of combat equipment. But you should not imagine that a platoon sits in a classroom, while the instructor describes the construction of tanks, guns and armoured personnel carriers.

The sergeant shows a young soldier an assault rifle. This is your personal weapon. You strip it like this. You are allowed 15 seconds to do this. I will show you and then we will practise it—do it again—and again—now do it with this blindfold. And again . . . This is our tank. It carries 40 shells, each of which weighs between 21 and 32 kilogrammes, according to type. All the shells are to be loaded from these containers through this hatch into the tank's ammunition store. You've got 23 minutes to do this. Go! Now do it again—and again—and again.

Any process, from changing a tank's tracks or its engine to running in rubber protective clothing during CW training, is always learned by practical experience and practised again and again until it becomes entirely automatic, every day, every night for two years. So many seconds are allowed for each part of the operation. Make sure you do it this time: if you don't you'll have to practise it again and again and again, at night, on Sundays, on Sunday nights.

Exceptional physical strain is put upon Soviet soldiers. During his first days in the army a young recruit loses weight; then, despite the revolting food, he begins to put it on, not as fat, but as muscle. He starts to walk differently, with his shoulders back, a mischievous twinkle appears in his eye and he begins to acquire self-confidence. After six months, he begins to develop considerable aggression, and to dominate the scum. In his battles with the latter, he wins not only because of tradition, or the support of his seniors, his NCOs and officers— he is also physically stronger than they are. He knows that recruits coming into the army are far weaker than he is—he has six months of service behind him. Within a year he has become a real fighting-man.

A Soviet soldier is forced to adapt to circumstances. His body needs rest and he will find a thousand ways to get it. He learns to sleep in any position and in the most unlikely places. Don't ever think of giving an audience of Soviet soldiers a lecture with any theory in it—they would fall asleep at your very first words.

At 1500 hours the platoon, exhausted and dripping with sweat, returns from training, and tidies itself up. Hastily, everyone cleans boots, washes, puts things right—at the double, all the time. Dinner parade—they march off, singing, to the dining hall and spend 30 minutes there over disgusting, thin soup, semi-rotten potatoes with over-salted fish and three slices of bread. Hurry, hurry. "Company, on your feet! Fall in!" Dinner is over. They march off, singing, to the barrack-room. From 1600 to 1800 they clean weapons, service equipment, clean the barracks and tidy the surrounding area. From 1800 to 2000 "self-tuition." This means training which is devised not by the divisional staff but by the sergeants. "50 press-ups. Now do it again . . . You didn't make much of a job of loading those shells. Try it again . . . Now once more . . . The time you took to run three kilometres in your respirator was poor. Go and do it again."

From 2000 to 2030—supper. Kasha or potatoes, two slices of bread, tea, a lump of sugar. "Butter?—you had that this morning." After supper a soldier has 30 minutes of free time. Write a letter home, read a paper, sew up a senior soldier's collar-lining for tomorrow's inspection, clean his boots until they gleam, iron his trousers.

At 2100 hours there is a formal battalion, regimental or divisional parade. Evening roll-call, a run-through of the time-table for tomorrow and of the results of today's training, more sentences imposed by military tribunals and then an evening stroll. This takes the form of 30 minutes of drill, with time kept by drum-beat, and training songs, yelled out by several thousand voices. At 2145 the soldier reaches the barracks again, washes, cleans his teeth, polishes and cleans everything for next morning. At 2200—lights out. For those, that is, who are not on night exercises. The timetable makes provision for 9 hours of night training each week. No allowance is made for loss of sleep. These night exercises can, of course, go on for any length of time. And those who are not on night exercises may be got out of bed at any moment by a practice alert.

4

Saturday is a working-day in the Soviet Army. What makes it different from other days of the week is that the soldiers have a film-show in the evening. No—not about James Bond, but about Lenin or Brezhnev.

Sunday is a rest-day. So reveille is at 0700 hours, instead of 0600. Then, as always, morning toilet, PT, breakfast. And then free time. This is what the political officer has been waiting for. There is one of these "Zampolits," as they are called, in each company, battalion, regiment and so on. The Zampolit can only work with the soldiers on Sundays, so his whole energy is devoted to that day. He arranges tug-of-war competitions and football matches—more running! He also gives lectures about how bad things were before the Revolution, how good life is nowadays, how the peoples of the world groan under the yoke of capitalism and how important it is to work hard to free them. In some regiments the soldiers are allowed to sleep after dinner. And how they sleep—all of them! On a bright sunny Sunday, sometimes, a division looks like a land of the dead. Only very occasionally is a single figure—the duty officer—to be seen walking around. The silence is astonishing and unimaginable at any other time. Even the birds stop singing.

The soldiers sleep on. They are tired. But the Zampolits are not tired. They have been resting all week and now they are bustling about, wondering what to organise next for the soldiers. How about a cross-country run?

Sunday does not belong to the Soviet soldier, and so he reckons, reasonably enough, that this day, too, lasts 1,441 minutes instead of 1,440.

Day After Day

1

Practice makes perfect. This is a wise saying, which the Soviet Army accepts. Accordingly, during his service every soldier goes through the same cycle of instruction four times.

Each of these lasts for five months, with one month as a break before the next one begins. During this interval, the soldiers who have completed their service are demobilized and the new intake arrives. In this month the recruits go through their Young Soldier's Course: the remainder overhaul and repair equipment and weapons, and do maintenance work at barracks, camps and firing-ranges. They are also used for various sorts of heavy work. This is not always for the Armed Forces; sometimes they become labourers on State projects. Then the five-month cycle of instruction begins. All the subjects in the training schedule are covered but during the first month the emphasis is on the individual training of each soldier. The youngest ones learn what they need to know and do, while the older ones repeat everything for the second, third or fourth time. As a soldier's service lengthens, the demands he must meet increase. A soldier who has only just joined may be required to do, for instance, 30 press-ups, one who has served for 6 months 40, after a year he will have to do 45 and after 18 months 50. The standards required increase similarly in every type of activity—shooting, running, driving military vehicles, resistance to CW materials, endurance without an air-supply in a tank under water, etc.

In the second month, while work continues on the improvement of individual skills, sections, crews and military teams are set up. In reality they exist already, since 75% of their members are soldiers who have already served in them for at least six months. The young recruits adapt quickly, for they are made to do the work for the whole team: the older members do not exert themselves but they squeeze enough sweat for ten out of the new arrivals so as to avoid being accused of idleness themselves and in order not to incur the wrath of their platoon or regimental commander.

From the second month, weapon training is no longer individual but to whole sections. Similarly, the sections, teams and other basic combat units receive all their tactical, technical and other instruction as groups. At the same time, members of these sections, teams and groups learn how to replace one another and how to stand in for their commanders. Sub-machine gunners practise firing machine-guns and grenade launchers, machine gunners learn to drive and service armoured personnel carriers, members of rocket launcher teams are taught how to carry out the duties of their section commander. Members of tank, gun, mortar and rocket-launcher crews receive similar instruction.

The third month is devoted to perfecting unit and in particular platoon cohesion. Exercises lasting for several days, field firing, river crossing, negotiation of obstacles, anti-gas and anti-radiation treatment of personnel and equipment—the soldiers carry all these out as platoons. During these exercises, section commanders receive practice in commanding a platoon in battle. Then come field firing and other practical exercises lasting for two weeks each, first at company, then at regimental and finally at divisional level. Two final weeks are taken up with large-scale manoeuvres, involving Armies, Fronts or even complete Strategic Directions.

After this an inspection of all the formations which make up the Soviet Army is carried out. Checks are carried out on individual soldiers, sergeants, officers, generals, sections, platoons, companies, batteries, battalions, regiments, brigades, divisions and Armies. With this the cycle of instruction is completed. A month is set aside for repair and refurbishing of equipment, firing-ranges, training grounds and training centres. In this month, again, the demobilization of time-expired soldiers and the reception of a new intake of recruits takes place. This is followed by a repetition of the entire training cycle—individual instruction and then the welding together of sections, platoons, companies, battalions, regiments, divisions, then the large-scale exercises and finally the inspection. So it goes on, over and over again.

Why does a soldier
need to read a map?

1

Most Soviet soldiers do not know how to read a map. This is
the absolute truth. They are just not taught to do so. What is
more, there is no intention that they should learn, since it is
not considered necessary.

In the West you can buy a map at any petrol station. In the
USSR any map with more than a certain amount of detail on
it is classified as a secret document. If you lose a single sheet
of a map you can be put in prison for a long time—not a
luxurious Western prison, but something quite different.

The fact that maps are regarded as secret gives the Soviet
command a number of important advantages. In the event of
a war on Soviet territory an enemy would have considerable
difficulty in directing his artillery fire, or his aircraft, or in
planning operations in general. Thus, in 1941, the German
command had to use pre-revolutionary maps, printed in 1897,
to plan its air raids on Moscow. From time to time single Soviet
maps fell into the hands of German troops, but this only occurred accidentally so the maps were unlikely to be consecutive
sheets. When the Germans entered Soviet territory, it was
noticeable that the accuracy of their artillery fire from covered
fire positions fell off sharply. They were unable to use their
V-1 and V-2 rockets.

By making the map a secret document the Communists
achieved something else—attempting to flee from the Soviet
paradise without a map is a fairly risky undertaking. On one
occasion a Soviet soldier swam across the Elbe near Winterberg
and asked for political asylum. When he was asked if he had
any secrets to disclose he revealed that he had spent the last
eighteen months painstakingly gathering every crumb of in-

formation he could lay his hands on. He was carefully questioned and was then sentenced to death and shot. He had swum the Elbe at the wrong point and had fallen into the hands of the East German frontier guards, who had questioned him, in broken Russian, at the request of their Soviet comrades. If he had swum across the Elbe a few kilometres further north he would have landed safely in West Germany—if, that is, he had avoided treading on mines or being torn to pieces by guard dogs.

2

In the Soviet Army there are, it is true, hundreds of thousands of soldiers who have been instructed in map-reading. But they are only those who would need to use a map in battle—reconnaissance and assault troops, SPETSNAZ diversionary troops, topographers, missile control operators, aircrew, artillerymen, etc.

An ordinary tank crew member or infantry soldier does not need a map. He does not take operational decisions, he obeys them. Remember Soviet tactical theory—no battalion, no regiment, division or Army advances independently. Even a Front can only operate independently in exceptional circumstances. A Soviet offensive is a massive avalanche of tanks, supported by a storm of artillery fire. All this is directed at a single, narrow sector of the enemy's front. Individual initiative could ruin the overall plan. In many cases, regimental and divisional commanders have no authority to deviate from the route they have been ordered to follow. In this situation an ordinary soldier does not need a map. His function is to keep his weapons and equipment in good order and to use them skilfully, to advance bravely and with determination in the direction indicated by his commander, and to push forward at all costs and whatever the losses. The Soviet soldier is not expected to pore over a map—there are any number of others who are doing that— but to refuel a tank quickly, to unload ammunition as fast as he can, to aim accurately and to fire cold-bloodedly. His task is to work as fast as he can, repairing damage to his personal weapons or changing rollers or tracks on tanks, putting out fires, driving his tank under water towards the enemy's shore.

He must go without sleep for three days and without food for five, he must sleep in the snow in his shabby greatcoat and carry out the orders of his commander unquestioningly. The Soviet Army teaches him to do all this. But it only teaches map reading to those who will command and direct this soldier.

Those who built the Great Pyramids were probably not particularly well-educated and often they probably did not even understand each other, since slaves had been driven together from distant areas to build the huge structures. But the pyramids turned out none the worse for that. The slaves were not expected to carry out intricate calculations or to make precise measurements: all that was required from them was obedience and diligence, submission to the lash and willingness to sacrifice themselves in order that some unknown but most desirable aim should be achieved. Soviet generals adopt a similar position— surely it is not necessary to involve every slave in plans of such enormous complexity. Soviet generals are not arrogant; they are completely satisfied with a soldier who, even if he cannot read a map, does not strike, does not set up trades unions, does not pass judgement on the actions of his commanders and only gets his hair cut when a sergeant tells him to.

The Training of Sergeants

1

Soldiers are glad when their column reaches their new division and they are told that they are joining, for instance, the 207th Motor-Rifle Division, the 34th Guards Artillery or the 23rd Guards Tank Division. They know and are ready for what awaits them. But they are seriously alarmed if they discover that they are joining the 92nd Motor-Rifle Training Division, the 213th Motor-Rifle Training Division or the 66th Guards Motor-Rifle Training Division. The word "Training" has an ominous sound to a recruit. True, it means that he will never be one of the scum, that he will never have senior soldiers above him, but, instead, he will become a sergeant in six months' time, standing above both scum and senior soldiers, as their lord and master. But he knows that for this he will have to pay a very heavy price—six months in a training division.

Formerly each regiment trained its own sergeants. In addition to its four or five battalions and its various companies, each regiment had a "regimental school." The regimental commander put his best company commander in charge of this school. If the last of an officer's postings contained the words "commanded the regimental school" this showed that at one stage he was regarded as the best young officer in his regiment. The regimental commander devoted equal attention to his choice of platoon commanders from this school and he also sent the most ferocious of his sergeants there. Then each company commander would pick out the most promising of his recruits and would send them to the school. Their training would turn them into real wolf-hounds; they would return to their company with their sergeant's shoulderboards and lead its soldiers to glory.

But the system of regimental schools had one shortcoming.

Different nationalities have differing temperaments and their own traditions. Any Soviet officer will confirm that a Tatar makes the best sergeant of all. Ukrainians are very good sergeants. The Lithuanians are not bad. But the Russian, while he makes a good soldier or a good officer, is not a good sergeant. The great Russian people must forgive me, but this is not just my opinion: it is that of the majority of Soviet officers.

It may, of course, be that all Soviet officers are mistaken but, anyway, the regimental schools certainly accepted all the Tatars they were offered, immediately. They took the Ukrainians and the Lithuanians, too, but Georgians, Russians, Uzbeks and Azerbaidzhanis were given no places. Now, consider what happens when mobilization is ordered. All divisions, wherever they are permanently garrisoned, will call up their reservists and fill all their vacancies. Next second formation divisions—"invisible divisions" are formed. In the process, it comes to light that in the Tatar Republic all the reservists are sergeants and that there are no other ranks. The situation in the Ukraine and in Lithuania is almost the same. In the other republics though, all the reservists are private soldiers and there are no sergeants at all. While it is true that for instance, Georgians make excellent officers, they are not accepted for training as sergeants, because they are too warm-hearted and this makes them ready to overlook trifling mistakes. Trifling mistakes are precisely what a sergeant is concerned with—he must never overlook them and he must punish those responsible without mercy. So, how could you ever build up a division in Georgia?

The General Staff racked its brains for a long time over this problem, but finally adopted the radical solution of disbanding all the regimental schools and of training sergeants centrally, in training divisions.

2

Naturally, the standard of sergeants and their authority dropped sharply as this decision was implemented. Whereas previously each company commander had picked out one of his recruits and told him, "You are going to be a sergeant," now there was no such personal selection. One column of recruits was sent to a normal division, another went to a training division: it was done quite haphazardly. Against that, the General Staff now knows that, under the mobilization plans, Georgia, for instance, needs to produce 105,000 sergeants from its reserve but that in fact it has only 73,000. The remedy is obvious—in the near future the requisite number of new intake columns from Georgia must be sent to training divisions. All the General Staff needs to do is to work out what sort of sergeants it needs—rocket troops, artillery or infantry—and to issue the necessary instructions to local Military Commissars about the numbers they are to send to each training division.

Of course, in formulating these instructions, the General Staff does not forget to ensure that a suitable mixture of nationalities is retained in each division.

3

A training division has the same establishment, organisation and equipment as a normal motor-rifle division. Three of the most important battalions—the reconnaissance, communications and rocket battalions—are combat sub-units which are identical with those in a normal division. All the other regiments and battalions of the division keep their weapons mothballed, holding additional weapons for training purposes. The training divisions have no fixed establishment of personnel: every six months each division receives ten thousand recruits to train. After five months of brutally tough training these trainees become sergeants and are sent to combat divisions, to replace those who have been demobilized. Then the training division receives another ten thousand and the cycle begins again. Thus each training division turns out twenty thousand sergeants a year.

Each trainee spends half of his first year at the training division, is promoted and then spends the remaining eighteen months of his service with a combat division.

Training divisions are located only on Soviet territory. If war should break out their current intake would be promoted ahead of time and they would call up their reserves, take their weapons out of storage and function as a combat division.

Each of the regiments of a training division trains sergeants in one particular field, following a specialised curriculum. The artillery regiment trains 1,500 artillery sergeants, the engineering battalion turns out 300 engineer sergeants with varying specialist qualifications, and so forth. A very large proportion of tank crew members pass through the training divisions, since the commander, gunner and driver of a tank are all NCOs: only the loader is a private soldier. Since the newest Soviet tanks carry no loaders, every member of a tank crew will henceforth pass through a training division. In the artillery the proportion of sergeants is much lower. In the infantry, units with armoured personnel carriers have one sergeant to each section, those with infantry combat vehicles have three sergeants to each section. The training of sergeants in the various different fields proceeds in accordance with the requirements of the combat divisions.

In the tank training regiments, the first battalion usually trains tank commanders, the second, the gunners and the third, the drivers.

At the conclusion of their training all trainees sit examinations. If they pass them the specialists (gunners, tank drivers, radio operators, etc.) become lance-corporals; those who pass with distinction become junior sergeants. Gun-, tank- and section-commanders become junior sergeants: those who pass with distinction receive immediate promotion to sergeant.

4

A training division has no scum or senior soldiers. All 10,000 recruits arrive and leave the division at the same time. The division does, however, have sergeants, and their influence is a hundred times greater than that of the sergeants in combat divisions. In a combat division, while a sergeant must not be over-familiar with his senior soldiers, he must at least respect them and take their opinions into account. In a training division, on the other hand, a sergeant simply dominates his trainees, totally ignoring any views they may have. In addition, each platoon commander in a training division, supervising thirty or forty young trainees, is allowed to retain the services of one or two of the toughest of them. A sergeant in a training division also knows that he would have nothing like the same authority in a combat division. While he is still a trainee, therefore, he picks noisy quarrels with his fellows, in the hope that his platoon commander will notice and decide that he is someone who should be kept on to join the staff after the end of the course. He cannot afford to reduce his aggressiveness if he succeeds in landing a job with the training division, or he may find himself sent off to join a combat division, having been replaced by some young terror who is only too ready to spend all his nights as well as his days enforcing order and discipline. (If, however, this should happen, he would soon realise that he is unlikely to be sent on anywhere else from a combat division and that he can therefore afford to let up a bit and to slacken the reins.)

Discipline in a training division is almost unbelievably strict. If you have not experienced life in one you could never imagine what it is like. For instance, you might have a section of non-smokers headed by a sergeant who does smoke. Every member of the section will carry cigarettes and matches in his pocket. If the sergeant, apparently without realising that he is doing so, lifts two fingers to his mouth, the section will assume that he is in need of a cigarette. As one, ten trainees will rush forward, pulling cigarette packets from their pockets. The sergeant hesitates, considering which of the ten stands highest in his favour at that moment, and finally selects one of the cigarettes he is offered. By doing so, he rewards a trainee for his recent performance. Ten packets of cigarettes disappear in a flash; in their place appear ten lighted matches, held out for the sergeant's use. Once again he pauses, looking thoughtfully from face to face—whom to reward this time? One match goes out, burning the fingers of a young trainee, who stoically endures the pain, even though it brings tears to his eyes. The sergeant accepts the light offered by the soldier next to him and puffs contentedly away.

Each day the sergeant picks one of the trainees and puts him in command of the others. The trainee must spend the day devising fresh torments for his fellows. If he really distinguishes himself by his inventiveness, he will receive the greatest honour of all—he will be allowed to polish the sergeant's boots that evening. The trainees fight a silent battle among themselves, every hour of every day, for this privilege.

Power depraves those who wield it and a sergeant in a

training division is as depraved as it is possible to be. He uses his power to manipulate his subordinates, gradually turning them into real man-eaters.

Service in a training division is the pipe-dream of many Soviet officers. It is generally believed that in a training division one does no work at all. But this is not true: I know because I have served in one. The work is sheer drudgery. It is true that you never need to teach the trainees anything—their sergeants do that. It is true that every square metre of asphalt is scrubbed with toothbrushes. It is true that the floors in the lavatories shine almost as brightly as the sergeant's boots. It is true that no sergeant will ever step out of line, for fear of being posted to a combat division.

Against all this, however, the number of suicides in the training divisions must exceed the figures for any similarly-sized group of people anywhere else in the world. If a trainee in your platoon or your company kills himself, your own record of service will carry a black mark. And this black mark will never be erased. Each officer must therefore keep a constant watch on each of his trainees. As soon as he spots the slightest indication that something is wrong he must take action. He must pick out and give power to the trainee who appears to have reached the end of his tether and to be about to turn on his platoon, to blaze away at them, at his officers and at anyone else nearby and then, calmly changing the magazine, to send another long burst ripping through his own young body.

But how can you watch them all? Can you get to the right one in time to make him so drunk with power that he will resist the temptation to kill himself?

The Corrective System

1

Some say that before the Revolution the Russians were slaves in chains. Many believed this and many others still do so. Napoleon was one of these and he decided that he would conquer the country by winning over its down-trodden serfs. As he entered Russia, therefore, he published a manifesto, freeing the peasantry from serfdom. However, for whatever reason, the Russian peasants did not view him as a liberator and they ignored his edict. More than that, they rose against him, everywhere he or his armies appeared. Eventually they drove him from Russian soil, ignominiously abandoning his armies as he did so.

The Communists claim that they liberated the Russian people. Yet, when the war began, these same Russians greeted their foreign invaders with tears, with flowers and with enthusiastic hospitality. What can have brought them to the point at which they would greet even Hitler as their saviour and liberator?

The Soviet forces surrendered to Hitler in regiments, divisions, corps and Armies. In September 1941 the 5th, 21st, 26th, and 37th Armies surrendered simultaneously and without resistance. In May 1942 the whole of the South-Western Front, the 6th, 9th and 57th Armies, the 2nd, 5th and 6th Cavalry Corps, the 21st and 23rd Tank Corps surrendered in the Kharkov area. They fought for four days and laid down their arms on the fifth. At the same moment, the 2nd Shock Army capitulated on the North-Western Front. What is more, they then turned their weapons against the Communists. Soldiers, officers, and generals of every nationality of the Soviet Union surrendered, although the Russians were the most numerous, both in numbers and as a percentage of the total Russian population of the country. The Russian Liberation Army was the largest of all the anti-Communist forces, drawn from the inhabitants of the pre-revolutionary Russian Empire, which were set up during the Second World War. By the end of the war it consisted of approximately one million Russian soldiers and officers, who had chosen to fight against the Soviet Army. It could have been still larger than this, but Hitler would not give his whole-hearted support to Lieutenant-General A. Vlasov, the leader of the Russian anti-Communist movement. With unbelievable short-sightedness, he embarked upon a bloodthirsty campaign of terror against the inhabitants of the territories occupied by his armies. Compared to the liberation and collectivisation campaigns carried out by the Communists, this terror was relatively mild, but it deprived Hitler of any hope of winning the laurels of a champion of freedom.

But the Communists were not idle. They did everything they could to retain power and to prevent the total collapse of the Soviet Army. On 13 May, 1942 the murderous "Smersh" organisation—a military counter-intelligence service, operating independently of the NKVD—was established. Its most important task was defined by Beriya on 15 May as "fighting attempts to revive a Russian Army." That same day a new law on hostages was enacted, decreeing that the relatives of Soviet citizens who joined the Russian Liberation Army could be imprisoned for twenty-five years or shot. A day later new guidance on penal battalions was issued.

Penal battalions existed already but not in the form now envisaged. Nor had there ever been as many of them as was now proposed. Their final shape was decided upon in May 1942. The original proposals were confirmed and they have not changed from that day to this. Let us look at them more closely.

2

The old Russian Army had a good tradition: if its soldiers considered a war to be a just one they would fight like lions. If they believed it to be unjust and unnecessary for the Russian people, they would simply stick their bayonets in the ground and go home. That is what they did in 1917 and they did it again in 1941. Millions of Russian soldiers could see no reason to defend the Communist regime. Proof that this was a widespread attitude was provided by the Armies who gave themselves up. The same opinion was shared by hundreds of thousands of Ukrainians, who established the Ukrainian Insurgent Army, by Cossacks, Georgians, Lithuanians, Latvians, Crimean Tatars and by many other peoples who, before the Revolution, had fought fearlessly for the interests of the Russian Empire against every foreign invasion.

The Communists are clever people. They saved their dictatorship in a most original way—by developing a new use for penal battalions, which proved to be a decisive force in the battles with the German army. The Germans choked on the blood of the Soviet penal battalions. Also, with the help of the penal battalions, the Communists destroyed millions of their potential and actual domestic enemies and put an end for several decades to the growth of disobedience and resistance to their regime.

Until May 1942, each Army fighting at the front had one penal battalion. These battalions were used in defence as well as during offensives. After this the situation altered—the battalions were only to be used, according to the new policy, in offensives. In defence they were to be employed only to counter-attack—and, after all, a counter-attack is itself an offensive action on a small scale. In addition to the battalions already serving with Armies, other battalions, subordinated to Fronts, were introduced. Each Front commander henceforth had between 10 and 15 penal battalions at his disposal.

Each battalion had an administrative group, a guard company and three penal companies. The permanent component of the battalion—the command staff and the guards—consisted of ordinary soldiers and officers who were selected for their obtuseness, their ferocity and their fanaticism. They were rewarded with unheard-of privileges. The officers received seven times the normal pay—for each year of service they were given seven years towards their pension.

The penal battalions contained individuals who had shown reluctance to fight and others who were suspected of cowardice. With them were officers and soldiers who had been sentenced for various crimes and offences. The officers who were sent to the battalions lost any decorations they had been awarded, together with their ranks, and joined the battalion as privates.

During periods of calm the penal battalions were kept in the rear. At the last moment before an offensive, they were brought up, under guard, and positioned at the forward edge of the battle area. As the artillery preparation began, the guard company, armed with machine guns, would take their place behind the penal companies, who were then issued with weapons. Then, on the command "Advance to attack!" the guard company's machine guns would force the reluctant penal companies to get to their feet and to advance. Being unable to move in any other direction, they attacked, frenziedly. The most brilliant victories achieved by the Soviet Army were bought with the blood of the penal battalions. They were given the hardest and most thankless tasks. They would break through the enemy's defences and then, sweeping through their midst, trampling on their corpses, would come the élite Guards divisions. Thereafter no one wanted the penal companies in the area. It was far better to let the Guards do the fighting.

During the assault on the German defences at Stalingrad, 16 penal battalions were concentrated in the 21st Army's breakthrough sector and 23 more in the 65th Army's sector on the Don Front. Soviet Fronts employed almost as many as this during the Kursk battles, to breach the German defences. At one point in the course of the fighting in Byelorussia, on the orders of Marshal Zhukov, 34 penal battalions were brought together and thrown into the attack, to cut a way through for the 5th Guards Tank Army. 34 battalions are the equivalent of almost 4 divisions. One should add that very few of them survived the engagement and that, of course, those who were fortunate enough to live through this battle were almost certainly killed in the next one.

Each penal battalion had an establishment of 360. This may seem a small number. Yet the capacity of these battalions was astonishing. Soviet generals loved to attack or counter-attack: anyone under the command who seemed to lack fighting spirit would quickly find himself serving as a private in a penal battalion. An unsuccessful attack brought certain death for the members of the penal companies—they were unable to escape and they were shot down by the guard company. If they succeeded in advancing, the process would be repeated, again and again. They would die, eventually, when they came up against an impregnable defence. The guard company would then return to the rear, and assemble a new battalion, which would resume the attack on the following day—or even the same day.

The official figures given for Soviet casualties during the Second World War is 20,000,000 officers and men. In reality, of course, the total was considerably higher. A large proportion of these millions reached their destiny through the sausage machine of the penal battalions. Much stupidity and idiocy was displayed in the war, there were many unnecessary and unjustifiable sacrifices. But this was an exception: a subtle and carefully thought-out policy of using the blood of potential internal enemies to destroy an external enemy—the German military machine. It was at once a shrewd and appalling scheme.

The German command understood the situation very well. But their outlook was too limited and too pedantic to allow them to adopt the correct riposte—retreating rapidly before the penal battalions, giving the latter a chance to find cover from the heavy machine guns, which threatened them from the rear, and to turn their weapons on the guard company. If Field Marshal von Paulus had done this at Stalingrad, the Soviet penal battalions would have cleared his path to the Volga. If von Manstein had done this at Kursk he would have won the greatest battle in tank history.

If...if...if only someone had realised how the Russians loathe Communism. If only someone had tried to tap this reserve of hatred.

3

In addition to the infantry penal battalions, which represented the majority, there were mine-clearing and air force penal units. The function of the mine-clearing units is self-explanatory but something more must be said about the air force penal companies. In addition to their bomb-loads and rockets the bombers and ground-attack aircraft carried cannon or machine guns in turrets for defence against enemy fighters. Why, reasoned our glorious Communist leaders, should honourable young Communists, devoted to the cause of liberating the working-class, die in our aircraft? Of course, our pilots must be trustworthy and dedicated (and there are hostages we can use to ensure that they remain so) but an air-gunner's duties could just as well be carried out by someone who is an enemy of socialism. And why shouldn't they be? He can't escape and he can't avoid fighting, since his own life depends on the outcome. By repelling enemy fighters he is first of all preserving his own worthless life, but he is also defending the aircraft, and with it the Communist cause.

From May 1942 onwards, penal companies of air-gunners were attached to all the bomber and ground-attack units of the Red Army. They were kept near the airfields, in stockades surrounded by barbed wire. Their training was rapidly completed. They were simply taught how to estimate the distance of an approaching enemy aircraft and how to fire their cannon or machine-guns. They were not given parachutes—they would not, in any case, have known how to use them. In order that no rash ideas should enter his head during a flight, the newly-fledged gunner was firmly strapped to his seat—as if for his own safety. The pilot in the IL-2 and IL-10 ground-attack aircraft was protected by armour-plating; behind him with his back to him, sat the gunner, who was protected only by his 12·7mm machine gun. Members of penal companies were also used as gunners on PE-2 and TU-2 dive-bombers and also on the PE-8 and other bombers.

In order to arouse the fighting spirit of these "flying convicts," an incentive was devised—their sentences were reduced by a year for each operational flight. At that time their standard sentence was ten years. Ten flights and you'll be free! This device worked, even though the gunners had not volunteered for the job. Nevertheless, the fighting spirit among these prisoners, who were really under sentence of death, was considerably higher than it was among their fellow-sufferers on the ground.

Whoever thought of this idea was certainly no fool. In the first place not many of the gunners survived nine flights. Anyone who did manage to do so was never sent on a tenth flight. His companions were told that he had been sent to another regiment, nearby, or released, whereas in fact the poor devil had been sent to serve for a year with a mine-clearing battalion. The pretext used was a standard one—"your nerves are in a bad state. The medical officer won't allow you to fly any more."

The average expectation of life in a mine-clearing battalion was, if anything, lower than that in the penal battalions which served with the infantry.

The death rate among the "flying convicts" remained exceptionally high. This did not greatly concern anyone—this was their inevitable fate. Unfortunately though, when an air-gunner was killed, his machine-gun would slip from his hands and its barrel would drop lifelessly downwards. This was a useful signal to the German fighters—the gunner in that aircraft has been killed, so the aircraft is defenceless. Let's get it!

The Soviet command finally realised, after questioning a number of German airmen who had been shot down, that, as he died, the air gunner was involuntarily signalling to the enemy that his aircraft was undefended. What could be done? You could not get two flying convicts into one cabin—and what would be the point, in any case, since the same burst of fire might kill both of them. Much thought was given to the problem. Then a brilliant idea occurred to Marshal of the Air Forces A. E. Golovanov, Stalin's former personal pilot and body-guard, whose job it had been to arrest marshals and generals for his master and to conduct them to Moscow. He thought of the idea of fixing a spring to the breech of an aircraft's machine gun. Whether the gunner was alive or not, the barrel of the gun would now keep pointing upwards. For this invention Stalin rewarded this favourite of his with the Order of Lenin.

4

In peacetime the penal battalions are known as Independent Disciplinary Battalions. Each commander of a Military District is responsible for two or three of them. Commanders of Groups of Forces stationed outside the USSR also have battalions of this sort under their command, but they are stationed on Soviet territory.

The disciplinary battalions have been organised in precisely the same way as the wartime penal battalions—administration, a guard company and three penal companies. In peacetime the officers serving with these battalions are paid at double rates—for each year of service they receive two years' pay and two years towards their pension.

The soldiers and sergeants on the permanent staff of these battalions have been sent to them by military tribunals which have sentenced them to work there for periods of between three months and two years. Time spent in a disciplinary battalion does not count as part of a soldier's military service. In my division, on one occasion, two sergeants got drunk the day before they were to be demobilized after two years' service. In their drunken state they were insufficiently respectful towards one of the staff officers. A tribunal sentenced each of them to lose his rank and to serve for two years with a disciplinary battalion. After two years they returned to the division, completed their remaining day's service and were demobilized.

Life in a Soviet disciplinary battalion today is a large subject, which should be discussed at length and separately. I will limit myself to saying that such a battalion will break the strongest of characters within three months. I have never, during my entire service, met a soldier who had spent time in one who showed the slightest traces of disobedience or indiscipline. It is a great day for any commanding officer in the Soviet Army when his unit is re-joined by someone whom everyone has forgotten and whom very few will recognise—a man sent to a disciplinary battalion some time ago for insubordination, or indiscipline or for some form of protest. The officers in the regiment and the division have mostly changed since his day, as have the overwhelming majority of sergeants and other ranks. Suddenly, he appears—quiet, downtrodden, submissive. He talks to no one and carries out all orders or instructions uncomplainingly. It is impossible to get him to say a single word about where he has been or what he has seen. His answers are monosyllabic and expressionless—"Yes" and "No" seem to be the only words left in his vocabulary. Then suddenly one of the longer-serving soldiers remembers—this was Kol'ka, the trouble-maker, the wit, a live-wire, forever suggesting risky escapades, who sang and played the guitar and was adored by all the local girls. Eighteen months ago he was sent to a disciplinary battalion for some trifling offence. The younger soldiers, gazing at this silent, gloomy new arrival, can only half-believe what they hear. The regiment quietens down, discipline improves, more respect is shown to its officers.

For minor offences a soldier does 3 to 15 days in the unit's guardroom. Any soldier who spends more than 45 days there in a year is automatically sent to a disciplinary battalion. There he is reformed: after he returns to his unit he will never again commit a disciplinary offence. He will never want to sit behind bars again.

Nevertheless, if war with the West should break out, Soviet

soldiers would surrender by the million. Disciplinary or penal battalions would not prevent this from happening. And the Politburo has no illusions about this.

PART EIGHT

THE OFFICER'S PATH

How to Control Them

1

I arrived at divisional headquarters early in the morning. The duty officer, a Lieutenant-Colonel, was welcoming. He had not slept all night and he might well have told me, peevishly, to go to hell. As it was, my brand-new lieutenant's shoulder-boards seemed to strike a chord in his memory, and he just smiled to himself and said, "Go out and take a walk for half an hour or so. It's still a bit early."

Half an hour later I returned to divisional HQ and was taken straight to the office of the head of the personnel department. He, too, was pleasantly welcoming. He had been sent my personal file a month earlier. After I had finished my training, I had taken my first leave as an officer, like all my companions from the military training college, but my file was already lying in front of this personnel officer, on that table, and at night it had been put in that safe over there. Probably he knew me better than I knew myself. He took a long look at me and then asked one question, which I had, of course, been expecting:

"How about changing to First Specialisation?"

Each military trade is referred to by a number. Before the war there were about 150 of them. Nowadays there are more than 1,000. But all-arms commanders are all First Specialisation men—and they are the ones who ensure that all the different arms of service and Armed Services work together properly. Those who command motor-rifle platoons, companies, battalions, regiments, divisions and all-arms Armies, Fronts and Strategic Directions are all First Specialisation officers. The Supreme Commander, too, has the same background. I am a tank officer and I love tanks, but now they are offering me an infantry job—one which is more difficult, but which has better prospects. The cushy jobs are always full, but there is a constant and acute shortage of officers in the infantry. Platoons are commanded by sergeants, because there are not enough lieutenants. In the infantry, one's chances of promotion are very good, but they are never able to find enough people who are prepared to put up with the hardships of infantry life. So they often ask officers with other specialisations—officers with tank, anti-tank and mortar training—this question.

"I am in no hurry. You've got time to think it over—and it is something you need to think about." Nevertheless, the personnel officer looks at me expectantly. I do not usually take long to make up my mind. I stand up and say, decisively, "I wish to transfer to First Specialisation."

He likes my reaction, perhaps not because he has succeeded so easily in getting me to volunteer for such a hellish job, but simply because he respects a positive attitude.

"Have you been able to have any breakfast yet?"—his tone alters.

"Not yet."

"There's quite a good café opposite Divisional HQ. Why don't you look in there? Meet me there at 10 o'clock and I'll take you to the divisional commander. I'll recommend you for a company straight away. I knew you would accept. In the divisional tank regiment you would only get a platoon and you'd have to do three years there before there was any prospect of promotion."

2

The order appointing me commander of the 4th motor-rifle company of the Guards motor-rifle regiment was signed at 10.03 hours. Already by 10.30 I was at regimental head-quarters. The regimental commander looked disapprovingly at my tank badges. I could see him thinking—a lot of you crooks wangle yourselves jobs in the infantry to see what you can get out of it. He asked me some standard questions and then told me I could take over the company.

The 4th Company had already been without a commander for three months. Instead of five officers it had only one, a lieutenant who was in command of the first platoon. He had graduated from his military training college the previous year, had commanded a platoon for six months and had been given command of the company. But then he had taken to drinking heavily and had been returned to his platoon. Equipment? The company had none. In the event of mobilization a regiment would receive agricultural lorries to do the job of armoured personnel carriers, but in peacetime the regimental commander has a number of APC's at his disposal, and these are used for the combat training of individual companies and battalions.

There were 58 NCOs and other ranks in the company, instead of the full complement of 101—the division was being kept below strength. Most of the company spoke Russian. Discipline was poor. Demobilization was approaching—an order would be coming from the Minister immediately after the inspection. In anticipation of this, the oldest soldiers had become slack, putting pressure on the scum, not to make them work hard but to get them to fetch vodka. There were 19 of these senior soldiers in the company. Their sergeants found them almost uncontrollable. The inspection was to begin in four days' time.

3

At a meeting that evening the regimental commander presented me to his hundred or so officers, who looked at me without particular interest. I clicked my heels and made a small bow.

The only subject discussed at the meeting was the forthcoming inspection. "And just in case the idea should occur to anyone—there is to be no cheating—better the truth, however unpleasant, than some elaborate cover-up. If I hear of any attempt to deceive the commission, to try to make things look better than they are, the officer concerned will lose his job and will be put under immediate arrest!" I liked this straightforward approach. That was the proper way to do things. It was quite wrong to sweep things under the carpet. The other officers nodded in agreement. The regimental commander finished his address and looked towards his chief of staff, who smiled jocularly. "Company commanders 20 rubles each, deputy battalion commanders 25, battalion commanders 30 and the rest know what they should give. Give your donation to the finance officer. I want to emphasise once again, that this is entirely voluntary. It's just a matter of hospitality." The pile of money in front of the finance officer grew steadily. I did not ask why we were handing over this money.

The Soviet Army has not only got more divisions and tanks, more soldiers and generals, than any other army in the world. It also has more pigs. Under the Socialist system of equitable distribution, more is collected from the industrious than from the idle and the peasants are given no incentive to work hard: any surplus they produce is just taken away from them. This means that the agricultural sector is unable to supply enough food for either the army or the defence industries. Because of this, each regiment has to keep pigs. No money is allocated for this purpose. The pigs are fed on left-overs from the kitchens. There are thousands of regiments in the Soviet Army: each of them has a hundred pigs. How could any army on earth have so many pigs?

In theory, the pigs are kept so that the diet of the soldiers can be improved. In practice they are all destined to feed the commissions which come to inspect the regiment. Some of their meat is made into excellent chops, gammon steaks and so forth. The remainder is sold, and the proceeds are used to buy caviare, fish, ham and other delicacies, all of which, with the meat, is for consumption by the commissions. And their vodka is bought with money from regimental funds, together with the "voluntary" donations provided by the officers.

4

Commissions are made up of staff officers from other military districts. For instance, this year, officers from the Baltic Military District may inspect the divisions in the Far Eastern and Turkestan Military Districts, while others from the Sub-Carpathian Military District will inspect those in the Moscow, Volga and Baltic Military Districts.

Staff officers are idealists, theoreticians who are remote from real life. They have forgotten, or perhaps have never known, the cost of human sweat. They expect soldiers to be able to answer questions about the principles of modern warfare, forgetting that some of them have never even heard the

Russian language until they entered the army. They expect soldiers to be able to do fifty press-ups, unconcerned that some of them come from families that have suffered for generations from undernourishment. It may have taken me two years to teach someone from this sort of background to do ten press-ups and both he and I may be proud of what we have achieved. But this would not satisfy a staff officer. Staff officers are used to moving armies across maps, like pawns on a chessboard, forgetting that a soldier may disobey an order, he may suddenly go mad, he may rebel against authority, oppose his superiors, or perhaps, driven to desperation, he may kill his unit commander. Do staff officers realise this? Like hell they do. And this is why they have to be entertained over and over again. A glass of vodka and another and another? A little pork? Some caviare? A helping of mushrooms and a little more vodka?

However, as I handed over my money for the vodka, it did not occur to me that a regimental commander needs to create a general atmosphere of friendliness and hospitality for the commission, I forgot about the bitter competition between company and battalion commanders, I completely overlooked the fact that the commission is not allowed to give everyone good marks and that, if one company succeeds by its welcome and hospitality in achieving an "Excellent" rating, another will have to suffer, because the commission is compelled to mark someone "Unsatisfactory."

I assumed that the regimental commander's warning against fraudulence was sincere. It did not occur to me that, if what was really going on became known, the commander himself would be dismissed immediately. At the same time, he could hardly advocate the use of deceit—he could be thrown into gaol for that. So what else could he have said?

Anyway the inspection began. I presented the company exactly as it was. But, all around us, miracles were being performed. The results achieved by the other companies were quite astonishing. In the 5th Company, for instance, they tested the drivers of armoured personnel carriers. The latter's knowledge of their vehicles was entirely theoretical. Yet all ten drivers were given "excellent" gradings for their performance in driving an APC over rough ground. It was only several months later that I discovered that the company commander had used up all the petrol allocated to him in training just two, not ten, of his drivers. During the test, the drivers took their places one after another in the APC and each one, as he got in, would close the hatch. Then one of the two experts who was already in the vehicle, would take the wheel and race the vehicle round the course.

All the soldiers in the 1st Company were graded "excellent" for their shooting. Their performance seemed too good to be true, but the members of the commission, who were quite sober at the time, had examined the target after each soldier had fired his rounds and had marked every bullet-hole with paint. Quite by chance, I discovered that the best shot in the company had been lying in some nearby bushes with a sniper's rifle, fitted with a silencer. He had helped his comrades out. Everyone was doing much the same sort of thing. Then there was the boozing. First the commission was entertained at regimental level and then came the turns of individual battalions and companies. No preparation at all had been made in my company. As a result, the marks which we were awarded turned out to be catastrophic. Each time I paraded the men after the inspection I would hear someone behind me mutter angrily, through his clenched teeth, "Scum!" He was, of course, addressing me.

Each officer is responsible for the unit under his command from the very moment he takes it over. He is answerable for everything, even if he has only arrived four days—or three hours—earlier.

My company got the worst marks in the whole regiment. It did not matter that the next worst did not get many more—a wide rift appeared between us and all the other companies. The officers laughed at me, openly, and on the doors of the company's barrack-room there appeared the inscription "SUC = Suvorov's Uncontrolled Company."

I reacted to all this mockery with a cheerful smile. Meanwhile, the companies which had taken between third and eighth places in the inspection were being put through "training" sessions by their officers. Ostensibly in order to correct the mistakes for which they had been marked down, they were taken off into open country and punished in the most brutal fashion, being made to run in gas masks and rubber protective clothing until they collapsed, unconscious. My company waited, mutely, for me to do the same. I did not delay. I drew up a training programme and had it approved by the regimental staff. I asked for the use of five armoured personnel carriers and for the help of a tank platoon, since my company had told me that they had had no instruction in working with tanks in action. Besides the tanks I applied for three blank rounds for the tanks' guns.

I took my company out to a training area and carried out ordinary training exercises with them. I explained anything they did not understand and then put them through their paces, but did not punish them in any way. Next I paraded them and called the oldest group of soldiers forward.

"You have done your duty honourably," I said to them, "and you have followed a hard road. Today you have come to its end. Your last day of training in the Soviet Army is over. I thank you for all you have done. I cannot reward you in any way. Instead, allow me to shake you by the hand."

I went up to each man and shook him firmly by the hand. Next I went back to the centre of the parade and bowed stiffly to them—something which, according to the regulations, should only be done in front of a group of officers. Then, at my signal, the three tanks suddenly shattered the quiet of the autumn woods by firing the blank rounds, one after the other. This was so unexpected that it made the young soldiers flinch.

"The Army salutes you. Thank you." I turned to the sergeant-major and told him to march the company back to the barracks.

Some days after this, late one evening, dozens of rockets suddenly soared skywards over the camp, thunderflashes and practice grenades exploded and bonfires were lit. The demobilization order, signed by the Minister of Defence, had arrived. It had been expected for some days but it always arrives without warning. As soon as they hear about it, those who are to be demobilized treat themselves to a firework display. For several days before the order every regiment has a team searching for illegally held rockets, training grenades and anything which could be used for a bonfire. They find and confiscate a lot but they cannot discover everything, for each soldier has been carefully gathering and hiding materials which he can use for the "ceremonial salute."

At the moment when the sky was suddenly lit up by blazing bonfires we, the officers, were in the middle of a Party meeting.

"Go and stop that!" the regimental commander snapped. The company commanders leapt to their feet and ran off to stop the row which their unruly charges were making.

The only people left in the room were the regimental doctor, the finance officer, some technical and staff officers who had no soldiers under their direct command, and me. I stood quietly watching what was going on outside the window. The regimental commander looked at me in astonishment.

"The 4th Company are not involved," I said, in answer to his unspoken question.

"Is that so?" he said, with some surprise and sent one of the other officers to check my claim.

It was indeed true that nothing was happening in the 4th Company. My tank salute had been a great deal more impressive than a few rockets and thunderflashes. The appreciation which I had shown had flattered the senior soldiers and had given them prestige and self-respect. While the barrack-rooms of all the other companies were being searched for anything which could be detonated or burned, they came to me to hand over a kit-bag full of odds and ends which they had collected and promised that they would not take part in the celebrations.

When the meeting was resumed, the regimental commander rebuked the other company commanders for their failure to prevent the outburst. Then he asked me to stand up and he commmended me for the way I controlled my men and made them behave as I wanted. It was never his way to ask officers how they achieved results. However, his chief of staff could not restrain himself and he asked me to tell them how I had handled the senior soldiers in my company, so that everyone could learn from my example.

"Comrade Lieutenant-Colonel—I gave my orders and they were obeyed." From the outburst of good-natured laughter with which this was greeted, I knew that I had been accepted as an equal by the regiment's officers.

5

A Soviet officer is someone who has no rights whatsoever.

In theory, he knows, he must encourage those who are diligent and careful; he must punish the idle and the undisciplined. But the dictatorship of the proletariat has produced a state in which authority is too centralised to permit him to use either a stick or a carrot. He is allowed neither. He is not entitled either to punish or to reward.

On Sundays, the commander of a sub-unit is allowed to

send 10% of his NCOs and soldiers into town during daylight hours. This might seem to be a way of encouraging those who deserve it. In fact, however, although he may make a soldier a present of eight hours in this way, he cannot be sure that his battalion or regimental commander will not overrule him by stopping all leave. Besides, platoon and company commanders themselves are not enthusiastic about letting soldiers out of camp. If a soldier is checked by a patrol in the town and they find the slightest thing wrong, the officer who allowed the soldier to leave his barracks is held responsible. A commander, therefore, prefers to send soldiers off for the day in a group, under the eye of the political officer. This is the only way in which Soviet soldiers are allowed to go into a town in Eastern Europe and it is very frequently used in the Soviet Union, too. Since a Soviet soldier does not like being part of a convoy, he just does not bother to leave camp.

A company commander may hold a soldier under arrest for three days, but a platoon commander is not allowed to do so. However, by giving the company commander this right, the Soviet authorities have him by the throat; when the state of discipline in a unit is being assessed, the number of punishments is taken into account. For instance, arrests might average 15 in one company each month, but 45 in another. Clearly, say the powers that be, the first company must be the better one. Three soldiers might be punished in the first company and ten in the second. Again, this is a clear indication that the first company is in better shape. This attitude on the part of the authorities forces unit commanders to hush up or ignore disciplinary offences and even crimes, in order not to drop behind their competitors. As a soldier comes to understand the system, he begins to break the rules more and more frequently and ingeniously, confident that he will not be punished. Many attempts have been made to establish different criteria for assessing the state of discipline, but nothing has come of them. So long as the present system lasts, a commander will avoid handing out punishments, even when they are really called for.

Deprived of the right to punish or reward, an officer devises and imposes his own system. Thus, in one company, the soldiers will know that, if anything goes wrong, their night exercises will always be held when it is raining and will drag on for a long time. In another, they will know that they will have to spend a lot of time digging trenches in rocky ground.

Every commander gradually refines his system and he may eventually manage to avoid arrests and officially recognised punishments completely: he comes to be obeyed, without having to resort to them.

6

As well as denying the officer any legal method of controlling his charges, the system also forces him to develop his own methods of instructing them. Nor is he given any proper guidance in ways of ensuring the obedience of the men for whom he is responsible. Those who understand how to exercise power in the USSR guard their knowledge jealously: they certainly do not write textbooks on the subject. This is done for them by professors, who have never set eyes on a soldier in their lives. These professors have no power themselves—they may understand how it is acquired and retained, but their knowledge is entirely theoretical.

Nor will a young officer's colleagues pass on their experience on to him, for it has cost them too much to be handed out free. Anything which he learns at his military training college about relationships with his subordinates is the product of a professor's imagination and is of no practical value.

Once he graduates from his training college, the young officer suddenly finds himself in the position of a lion-tamer in a cage of lions, except that he knows no more about lions than that they belong to the cat family. Thereafter, the system of natural selection comes into operation—if you understand how to control your troops you will be accepted by the system; if not you will be relegated to the humblest of roles.

You learn the techniques of control from your own mistakes—and, unless you are a fool, from the mistakes of others. For there will be mistakes in plenty to be seen everywhere around you.

As an example, for several years the commander of the guard company of the 5th Army Staff punished any form of disobedience without mercy. His company was considered one of the best in the whole, huge Far Eastern Military District. His excellent record was noted and he was nominated for a place at an Academy, which would enable him to develop and to get ahead. With only a month left in command of the company, he found it impossible to retain his tight hold—his thoughts were centring more and more on the Academy. He changed his way of exercising command. One evening he invited all his sergeants to his office and gave them a tremendous party. The night turned out to be an unpleasant one for him—the sergeants, having had a lot to drink, nailed him to his office floor. The unfortunate man obviously had a poor knowledge of history; he had not grasped the simple fact that a revolution does not occur during a period of terror, but at the moment when that terror is suddenly relaxed. Historically, the examples of the French Revolution and of the Hungarian uprising in 1956 illustrate this principle; it will continue to operate.

A tough commander may take a disobedient soldier into the company office and beat him unmercifully. The soldier writhes on the floor for a while but then he gets to his feet, seizes a lamp from the table and hurls it in the officer's face. The soldier will be court-martialled but the officer will never again be able to control his company; the soldiers will laugh at him behind his back.

A young officer in front of his soldiers says to them, "If you get good marks at the inspection I promise you I'll..." As an outside observer, you will see scepticism on the faces of the soldiers. You realise that the young Lieutenant is revealing one of his weaknesses, his desire to succeed. You can't always be kind to everyone, Lieutenant, and henceforth anyone whom you treat roughly will use this weakness against you. Everyone has a failing of some sort, but why let others realise it? They may prove to be anything but sympathetic.

Just look at this scene and always try to remember the golden rule of controlling others—NEVER PROMISE ANYONE ANYTHING!

If you are able to do something for another person—do it, without having made any promises. From this first rule there follows a second—NEVER THREATEN ANYONE!

You can punish someone and, if you consider it necessary, you should do so. But promises and threats simply weaken your authority as a commander.

After some time you will come to understand the most important rule of all, one which you have never been taught—RESPECT YOUR SOLDIERS.

If a commander is invited by his soldiers to sit at their table,

and if he accepts with the gratitude with which he would accept
an invitation from his colonel, he is never likely to suffer at
their hands. He can be sure that these soldiers will defend him
in battle, even if it should cost them their lives. If a commander
has learned to respect his soldiers (which means more than just
showing them respect), he will suddenly realise, with some
surprise, that he no longer needs informers in their ranks. His
men will come forward of their own accord, tell him what is
going on and ask for his help or protection.

A commander who respects a soldier can ask anything of
him and can be confident that the soldier will carry out all his
requests without pressure of any sort.

How Much Do You Drink
In Your Spare Time?

1

The regimental parade takes place every day at 0800 hours. All the officers of the regiment must attend. Some of them will already have supervised reveille and morning PT, so they will have had to have arrived at the barracks before 0600. If it takes them an hour to get to the unit, they will have had to get up very early indeed. From 0800 to 1500 hours all officers take part in the training programmes. If you are a platoon commander you work with your platoon. If you are a company commander, you may work with your company sergeants or with one of the platoons—perhaps one of the platoon commanders is on leave, or perhaps you have no platoon commanders in your company. Battalion commanders, their deputies and battalion chiefs of staff, either work with platoons which have no commanders or check the training being carried out by platoon or company commanders. Checking training is a good deal easier than being checked yourself.

Officers have lunch between 1500 and 1600 hours. From 1600 until the late evening they are involved in officers' meetings or Party meetings, or they attend Komsomol meetings held in platoons, companies or battalions. During this period, after their lunch, officers also receive their own training—they pore over secret orders, they are shown classified films, and so forth. Meanwhile, the cleaning of weapons and combat equipment is being carried out in sub-units and, although this is supervised by sergeants, the officers are responsible for the condition of the equipment, and they therefore need to take a few minutes to keep an eye on what is going on. Finally, the officer will have to give seven hours of instruction next day and he must prepare for this. The colonel comes over from divisional headquarters to see what preparations we are making. He states that the preparation for a two-hour training period must include a trip out to the training area, the selection of a good spot for the work which is to be done there and briefing for the sergeants on the way the training is to be carried out. Thereafter, sub-unit commanders are to return to the camp and to work with their sergeants, studying manuals, regulations and recommendations. Next, they are to draw up plans listing the exercises which are to be carried out, to have these approved by their immediate superiors and to prepare everything which will be needed—targets, simulators, combat equipment, etc.

From what the colonel says, it appears that the preparations for a two-hour exercise should take at least five hours. We express agreement, of course, but to ourselves we think, "You can get stuffed, Colonel. I give seven hours' instruction a day. If I prepare for it in the way you are suggesting, I shan't even have time to go to the lavatory. No, my dear Colonel, I'm not going to spend five hours preparing this exercise. I'll spend five minutes." As quickly as I can, I write out the plan for the exercise and explain to my deputy how he must prepare for it. Everything will sort itself out tomorrow. If time is really pressing, during the Party meeting I get hold of the plans I prepared for last year's exercise and carefully alter the date. That means we can use last year's plan over again.

In the late evening comes the second regimental parade and by 2200 hours the officers who are not involved in night exercises have finished for the day.

What shall I do now? I am unmarried, of course. Anyone idiotic enough to get married while he is a lieutenant soon regrets it bitterly. He and his wife never see each other. The regiment has no married accommodation for junior officers and the relationship is doomed to failure. Any sort of private life is severely discouraged under Socialism, as a potential source of discontent and disunity. The resources available to the Armed Services are used to build tanks, not to put up married quarters for lieutenants. I realised this a long time ago and this was why I have not got married.

So, what shall I do with my spare time? The library is already closed, of course, and so is the cinema. I have no interest in going to the gymnasium—I have been rushing about so much today that I feel utterly exhausted. I'll just go back to the officers' quarters, where all the young bachelors live. There is a television set there but I already know that the whole of today's programme is about Lenin. Yesterday it was about the dangers of abortion and the excellence of the harvest, tomorrow it will be about Brezhnev and the harvest or Ustinov and abortion.

As I enter the living room, I am greeted with delighted cries. Around the table sit fifteen or so officers. They have just begun a game of cards and thick clouds of cigarette smoke hang over them already. I got no sleep last night so I decide to play just one round and then go to bed. A place is made for me at the table and a large glass of vodka put down beside me. I drink it, smiling at my companions, and push a large sum of money over to the bank. Here we go.

Some time after one o'clock, officers returning from night exercises burst noisily into the room, dirty, wet and worn out. They are found places at the table and someone brings them glasses of vodka. They got no sleep last night and decide to go to bed after just one round.

I lose money fast. This is a good sign—unlucky at cards, lucky in love. I assure the sceptics around me that losing is really a sign of good fortune.

Three hours later, the commander of a neighbouring company appears, having just inspected the night guard. He is greeted with delighted cries. Someone produces a full glass of vodka for him. We have already got through a good deal and we have begun to drink only half a glass at a time. The new arrival got no sleep last night, so he decides to leave after one round. The money flows quickly from his pockets—this is not a bad sign. At least anyone who loses money is not hiding it in his pockets. By tradition the loser buys drinks for everyone else. He does so. We decide to play one more round. A good sign . . . we've drunk all that . . . someone is coming . . . they're pouring out more drinks . . . another round . . . a good sign . . .

At six o'clock the clear notes of a bugle float out over the regiment—reveille for the soldiers. When we hear it we all get up, throw our cards on the table and go off to bed.

At 0700 hours a soldier, designated by me as the best in my company, has to wake me up. This is no easy task, but he manages it. I sit on my bed and gaze at the portrait of Lenin which hangs on the wall. What would our great Teacher and Leader say if he could see me in this state, my face puffy with drink and lack of sleep? My boots have been carefully cleaned, my trousers pressed. This is not part of the soldier's duties, but evidently the senior soldiers have given him orders of their own. They must like me, after all!

The doors and windows swim before my eyes. Here comes the door floating past. It is essential not to miss this and to choose the right moment to run through it, as it passes. Someone helpfully pushes me in the right direction. Along the corridor there are ten doors and they are all swimming past me. I must find the right one. Somehow I manage it and I step under the freezing, searingly cold shower. Then comes breakfast and by 0800 hours, glowing and rejuvenated, I am present at the regimental parade, in front of my Guards company. Hell, I've forgotten my map case, which has got the day's programme in it! But someone helpfully hangs it over my shoulder and the working day begins.

2

The Communist Party hopes that an unconquerable soldier can be produced—one who is more dedicated to Leninism than Lenin himself, who is an athlete of Olympic standards, who knows his tank, his gun or his armoured personnel carrier at least as well as its designer. But, for whatever reason this is not how things work out, so the Party comrades call for a detailed training programme for soldiers and NCOs to be prepared. This is presented to the Central Committee, but it does not produce better soldiers. Clearly, the junior commanders are not fulfilling their norms. Check up on them!

And check on us they do, each day and every day. Everything is checked and tested—by the staffs of the battalions, regiments, Armies and Military Districts, by the General Staff and by a whole mass of committees which it has set up, by the Inspectorate of the Soviet Army, by the Directorate of Combat Training of the Soviet Army, by similar directorates within Military Districts, Armies and divisions and by the Strategic Camouflage Directorate. In addition, tank crews are checked and tested by their own commanders, artillery personnel by theirs and so on. The first question any commanding officer is asked is—have you had experience of working with the infantry? If he has, he is sent off to test them, and then they come back to test his sub-unit.

Hardly a day passes without two or three checks. Every commission which arrives to carry out a check has its own pet subject. Can your men get into an APC in ten seconds and out again in the same time? Of course they can't, I reply.

That's bad, Lieutenant. Haven't you studied the plan? We'll make a note of that. Cursing, I take the one APC I have been allocated off to a clearing in the woods and make my first platoon climb in and out of it again and again as the plan requires. But soon another commission appears and wants to know whether my men can reach the standards laid down for high-speed cross-country driving across broken terrain. No, I say, they can't. Well, Lieutenant, that's very bad. The assessors record this unsatisfactory finding and order me to begin training my drivers immediately, using the APC. I salute and recall the platoon which has been practising getting in and out of the APC, but I don't send the vehicle for driver-training. I'll keep the damned thing here with me, I decide. A new commission appears and asks their pet questions. How is your platoon getting on with firing automatic weapons from an APC? Not too well, I reply, but we are practising day and night. Here is the APC, there is the platoon and those are the machine-gun crews. The members of the commission smile and move on.

Two failures in one day. But no one is interested in the fact that I haven't got enough APCs. Even if I had, fuel would be short or there wouldn't be enough grenades or grenade launchers.

Two failures in one day—two failures to reach the norms prescribed in the programme for the training of NCOs and other ranks which has been approved by the Central Committee of the Communist Party!

I get back to my quarters late that evening, wet, dirty, tired and angry. I have had to do two night exercises, with two different platoons, straight off—two more teams have checked our performance and we've been awarded two more bad marks.

People make a place for me. Someone gives me a tumbler of vodka and tries to cheer me up—don't take it too seriously! I drink the vodka, but it is some time before it takes effect. So I have another. Now I'll play just one round of cards. But my anger does not evaporate. They pour me another drink.

Another round of cards. A sure sign . . . Someone bursts through the door . . . they pour him a drink . . . they pour me a drink . . . another round . . . a good sign . . .

At 0600 hours the bugle rouses us from the table. On it there are piles of cigarette ends, underneath it is a heap of bottles.

3

Gradually one gets used to checks and tests. One finds ways of dealing with the searching questions. I come gradually to the conclusion that it is quite impossible for me to meet the requirements of the training plan—for me or for anyone else. Its demands are too high and the training facilities are quite inadequate. Besides, the plan robs an officer of any initiative. I'm not allowed to give the company physical training if the plan shows that this is the period for technical training. During technical training I cannot show them how to replace the engine of a vehicle if, according to the plan, I should be teaching them its working principles. But I can't explain an engine's working principles because the soldiers don't understand Russian sufficiently well, so I am unable to do either one thing or the other. Meanwhile, the commissions keep arriving. In the evenings my friends tell me not to get upset. I do the same whenever I see signs that one of them is approaching breaking point. I hurry over and pour him a drink. I sit him next to me at table and thrust cards into his hand. Here, have a cigarette. Don't take it so hard . . .

After a few more months, I realise that it is essential for me to go through the motions of meeting the plan's requirements. However, I do not give all the drivers a chance at the wheel: instead I allow two or three of the best of them to use all the driving time which we are allocated. All the anti-tank rockets which we receive go to the three who perform best with the launchers; the other six will have to get by with theoretical training.

When a commission arrives, I tell them confidently that we are making progress in the right direction. Look at those drivers—they are my record-breakers—the champions of the company! The rest are coming along quite well, but they are still young and inexperienced. Still, we know how to bring them on. The commission is happy with this. And those are the rocket launchers. They could hit an apple with their anti-tank rockets (if you'd care to stand your son over there with an apple on his head). They are crack shots, the stars of our team! We'll soon have the others up to their standard, too. And these are our machine-gunners—three of them are quite superb! And this man is a marksman! And that section can get into an APC in seven seconds flat—which is faster than the official record for the Military District! How can the commission know that jumping into an APC is all that the section ever does, and that they have never been taught to do anything else?

People begin to notice me. They praise me. Then I am promoted to the staff. Now I walk about with a notebook, drawling comments—*NOT* very good. Have you not studied the Plan which the Party has approved? Occasionally I say— Not *TOO* bad. I know perfectly well that what I am seeing has been faked, that this is a handpicked team—and I also know the cost at which such results are achieved. But still I say Not *TOO* bad. Then I move off to the officers' mess so that they can ply me with food and drink.

The difference between the work of a staff officer and that of a sub-unit commander is that on the staff you have no responsibility. You also get a chance to drink but don't have to drink too much. All you do is walk about giving some people good marks and others bad ones. And you eat better as a staff officer. Those pigs are meant for visiting commissions, after all—in other words for us staff officers.

Drop in,
And We'll Have a Chat

1

The triangle of power represented by the Party, Army and KGB brings pressure to bear on every officer and, what is more, it does so with each of its corners simultaneously. I am conscious of three separate weights pressing down on me at the same time; the forces they exert are different and push in different directions. To accept the pressure of all three at once is impossible and if you are not careful you can find yourself caught and crushed between two of them.

To me, as a platoon or company commander, the power of the Army is personified by my battalion commander, by the commander of my regiment or division, by the Commander of the Army or Military District in which I find myself, by the Minister of Defence and by the Supreme Commander. As I advance in my career as an officer, there will always be enough gradations of authority above me for me to feel the weight of some superior's boots on my shoulders.

The Party, too, keeps an eye on each officer, NCO and other rank. Every company commander has a deputy who heads the political section. This deputy has equivalents at battalion and regimental level and each successive higher level. A political officer is not really an officer at all. He wears a uniform and has stars on his shoulders, but the extent of his success or failure is not dependent upon the judgements of military commanders. He is a man of the Party. The Party appointed him to his post and can promote and dismiss him: he is accountable only to it. The company "politrabochiy," as he is known, is subordinated to the battalion "politrabochiy" who is himself answerable to his regimental equivalent and so forth, right up to the Chief Political Directorate itself. This Directorate is in some senses a part of the Armed Services; at the same time, however, it is a full Department of the Central Committee of the Party.

The KGB, too, is active in every regiment. That inconspicuous senior lieutenant over there, the one whom our colonel has just acknowledged with a bow, represents a special department, and he controls a secret KGB network, which is at work in our regiment and also in its immediate surroundings.

2

The three forces push me in different directions, threatening to tear me apart. To manoeuvre between them is very difficult. Each of the three tries incessantly to control my very thoughts and to exclude the influence of its rivals.

The army is glad that I am a bachelor. It would be ideal if all officers were a species of crusading monks, content to live in a citadel which we would never leave, unless the State required us to do so. The divisional commander calls one of my platoon commanders forward and addresses him clearly and distinctly, so that everyone can hear. "I made a vow that I would defend our Motherland. Therefore I will defend you and I expect you to do the same for me. But I made no such vow to your wife, and so I cannot allow you to spend the night at home. You are an officer and you must be operationally available at any moment. Telephone your wife and tell her that, although she has not seen you for two months, she should not expect to do so for as long again. You can add that the situation in the Navy is even worse than in the Army!"

However, my situation does not please the Party at all. The olitical officer summons me and we have a long talk. "The country's birth-rate is catastrophically low. Even under the Mongols our population remained stable, but that is notthe case today, under Communism. Viktor, you are a Communist. You should fulfil your duty to the Party." I nod in agreement and ask, naively, "But will you find me accommodation? Will I be allowed leave overnight, even once a month?" The political officer bangs his fist on the table. He explains that a true Communist must do his duty to the Party, whether he has accommodation and free time or not.

"All right, I'll think about it," I say. "Yes, think about it—and soon," he calls after me. This puts me in a tricky situation. If some local prostitute now goes to the political officer and reports that I have spent the night with her, they'll make me marry her straight away. That is the policy of the Party. And I am a member of the Party. If I had not joined the Party, it would not have allowed me to become a company commander. On the other hand, having joined the Party, I must be guided by its wise policies.

The KGB, too, keeps a close eye on me. In every company there are sure to be half a dozen informers. And who is the first person on whom they report? The company commander, of course, although they also report on the man who is trying to penetrate my very soul, the political officer. So the Chekist runs into me, apparently by chance. "Drop in and we'll have a chat." When I do so, he, too, encourages me to marry. The KGB, too, is keen to get every officer married. They won't give me accommodation or time off either but they will put pressure on me.

The KGB likes to have a spy in each officer's home. If I do something wrong and my wife falls out with me, she will keep the Chekist informed of my interests and my contacts.

3

The Army would prefer me not to drink at all. The Party does not express itself clearly on the subject. From one point of view alcohol is obviously highly undesirable, but against this, they reason, what am I likely to begin thinking about if my head is not spinning with the accursed stuff? The KGB simply avoids expressing any opinion, but whenever I meet the Chekist he always offers me something to drink. If I don't drink anything at all, I am unlikely to unburden myself to him. And, if I don't drink myself into a stupor each evening, how can he hope to hear about my innermost thoughts?

The Army totally disapproves of alcohol. And yet the regimental shop sells shoe-polish, toothpaste, vodka—a great deal of vodka—and nothing else at all. Evidently, the Army's position is dictated by pressure exerted by the Party and the KGB, neither of which ever clearly states its own points of view.

4

There has been more fighting—a new war in the Middle East. Once again, our "brothers" have somehow suffered defeat. The Army requires me to explain to my soldiers the tactical errors which have led to this. I do so. I describe to them how a small, determined country wages war. No propaganda—heaven forbid! I simply describe the operations conducted by the two sides calmly and dispassionately, as if the war had been a game of chess.

Soon I find myself summoned to the political officer and then by the special department, too. So, no, this year I shan't be going to the Academy. If either the Party or the KGB are displeased with me, it is not worth the Army's while to stick up for me. My superiors are only human and they don't want to pick a fight with two such powerful forces just about me. There are plenty of other young officers in the Army this year who are eligible for the Academy in every respect.

Who Becomes
a Soviet Officer and Why?

1

The great ideals of Socialism are simple and can be understood by anyone.

Society is built upon reasonable principles. Unemployment is a thing of the past. Medical services are free. Food, in reasonable quantities, is free, too. Every person has a separate room, with light and ventilation. Water, drainage and heating are free. Everyone has the right to some free time. There are no rich or poor. Everyone has comfortable, durable clothing, appropriate to the time of year—and this is, of course, provided free. Everyone is equal before the law.

You may say that this is nothing but a beautiful dream, that no one has ever succeeded in building pure socialism. Nonsense. In every country there are already islands of pure, untainted Socialism, in which each one of these requirements is met.

Is there a prison in your town? If so, go and take a look at it—you will find yourself in a society in which everyone is fed, and everyone has work, in which clothing, accommodation and heating are all provided free.

Soviet Communists are frequently reproached for having attempted to build a socialist society but having produced something which closely resembles a prison. Such a charge is entirely unjustified. In the Soviet Union some of the inmates have larger cells than others, some eat well, others badly. There is complete confusion—a lot remains to be done to tidy up the situation. True socialism, in which everyone is truly equal, does not just resemble a prison—it is a prison. It can not exist unless it is surrounded by high walls, by watchtowers and by guard-dogs, for people always want to escape from any socialist regime, just as they do from a prison. If you try to nationalise medicine and, from the best possible motives, to guarantee work for all the doctors, you will find that they pack their bags and leave the country. Try to bring a little order into the situation and your engineers (the best ones), your designers, your ballerinas (again, the best ones) and many, many others will also flee abroad. If you continue your attempts to establish a model society you will need to build walls around it. You will be forced to do this sooner or later by the flood of refugees.

2

The Politburo is the governing body of the prison. You should not abuse them for the privileges they possess. Those in charge of a prison must be better off in some ways than the convicts. The KGB are the warders, the Party is the administrative and educational organisation, the Army guards the walls.

When I am asked why I chose to become a Soviet officer, I say that those who serve as guards are better fed and have a pleasanter and more varied life than those in the cells. It was only some time after I joined the Army that I realised that it is far easier to escape from a prison if you are one of the guards. Trying to escape from a cell is a hopeless business.

In most states, life in the armed services is far more strictly regulated than it is for most of the inhabitants.

In the USSR, however, the reverse is true. The whole society finds itself in prison and, even though the Armed Services are kept under the tightest possible control (although even guards must be relieved), the life of an officer is far better than the drudgery which is the lot of the ordinary Soviet citizen.

While I was still one of those guarding our beloved prison, I carried out a sociological investigation among my brother officers, in an attempt to discover what had led them to tie themselves, hand and foot, to the Soviet Army, without expecting any guarantees or any form of contract. Naturally, I approached my colleagues with the greatest care and discretion.

"You remember," I would ask, "how, when Khrushchev came to power he had 1,200,000 men thrown out of the Army with a stroke of his pen? Your father was one of them; after another three months he would have completed 25 years' service. He was kicked out like a dog, without any sort of pension, in spite of his medals and despite the blood which he had shed for the country during his four years of war service. How did you, Kolya/Valentin/Konstantin Ivanovich, come to choose an officer's career in spite of that?"

I collected several hundred replies to my question. They all amounted to the same thing—everyone wanted to escape the drabness of life in our prison cells.

Higher Military Training Colleges

1

If you decide to become a Soviet officer, you would be well advised to lose no time and to submit your application as soon as you leave school.

The training of officers is carried out by Higher Military Colleges. The authorities consider, reasonably enough, that if you are to become a good officer you must first be a good soldier. Training at a college lasts for between four and five years and during this time a future officer leads a tough existence, which combines the hardships of a soldier's life in barracks with the penury of a Soviet student's existence. Instruction begins at the very beginning, with a ferocious course of square-bashing. The sergeants who put you through this have completely arbitrary powers over you, whether or not you have already put in two years of military service. Once you have decided to become an officer, therefore, it is better not to wait until you get swept up as a conscript but to try to get into a College immediately you leave school. Unless you succeed, you will simply lose two years, and you will find yourself spending longer in a private's uniform, which, as you may have realised already, is not a pleasant experience.

Until some years ago, officers were trained at military schools. The courses lasted between two and three years, depending on the arm of service concerned. These schools gave a medium-level military education and the students became lieutenants upon the completion of their studies. At the beginning of the 1960s, Khrushchev, who was going through a peace-loving phase, threw 1,200,000 officers and NCOs out of the Army. A Soviet officer has no contract or other guarantee of tenure and so, if someone still had a couple of months to go to complete 25 years of service, he was simply dismissed, with the tiniest of pensions if he was lucky. If he still had some days to serve before completing 20 years of service no matter how unblemished he was kicked out without anything. Most of these unfortunates were officers who had served at the front and had undergone the worst horrors of the Second World War.

The Party was delighted, because they were able to reduce expenditure considerably. However, these short-term gains eventually led to colossal expense. For many years, no one had the slightest desire to become an officer—you give the Army 24 years of your life and then they drive you out like a dog: what happens to you then?

Immediately after the fall of Khrushchev, steps were taken to restore the prestige of officers. Their uniforms were improved, their salaries were increased, and they were given a number of additional privileges. But this did not cause young men to rush to join the colours. They wanted permanent guarantees for the future. A current joke ran: "If you can go to a tank training school—and they throw you out, you can become a tractor driver. If you go to a flying school, you can get straight into Aeroflot if you are sacked, but what will happen to political officers, if they make more cuts in the Army?" The answer was: "Political officers can easily get jobs with the post office, sticking stamps on envelopes, because they have such long tongues."

The solution which was found eventually was a good one for individuals as well as for the State. All military training schools were to be up-graded from medium to higher educational establishments and every student was to receive a university education and to be trained for a civilian profession, as well as for an army career.

First, the course of instruction given at the infantry training schools was reorganised, since it was the infantry which was feeling the shortage of junior commanders most acutely. The length of the course was increased from two years to four. Graduates from the school continued to emerge with a medium-level military education and the rank of lieutenant, but from now on they also received a higher general education, a normal university diploma and civilian professional training. The civilian professions for which those attending Higher Military Training Colleges are prepared normally include automobile engineering and the teaching of mathematics, physics, history, geography and foreign languages. Once the infantry training schools had been reorganised in this way, Colleges for tank, airborne and artillery officers were set up, and then, finally, others to serve the remaining arms of service.

2

At present there are 154 Higher Military Training Colleges in the Soviet Union. Their courses last for between four and five years. Each College has about 1,000 students and each therefore turns out between 200 and 250 lieutenants a year. Each has a Major-General, a Lieutenant-General or even a Colonel-General as Commandant.

In selecting a College one is, of course, completely ignorant of the choices which are available. Once a year the Army newspaper *Krasnaya Zvezda* publishes a long list of Colleges, together with their addresses and very brief explanatory notes on each.

You study this, scratch your head and plump for one of the Colleges which seems to cater for your interests. However, there are usually several which specialise in each field of study— thus, for instance, there are seven tank colleges. Some people choose the one closest to their homes but others may select one which is far away, in Central Asia or the Far Eastern Military District, because it is easier to get into.

However, there is so little information in the newspaper that you cannot even form the vaguest idea of what lies ahead of you. For instance, in the Tashkent Tank Officers Training College, in addition to the normal faculties, there is another faculty which trains tank officer cadets for service with the Airborne Forces. When you pass your examinations, you receive your officer's shoulder-boards and swear your oath of allegiance and then you suddenly find, to your great surprise, that you are to begin parachute training very shortly and that you are going to spend all your life jumping out of aircraft, until you break your neck.

The Moscow Officers Training College has no faculties at all, the one in Kiev, although it is in exactly the same category, has both general and reconnaissance faculties, and in Baku there is a marine infantry faculty. In Blagoveshchensk there is a specialist faculty which trains officers for work in Fortified Areas, and in Ryazan, besides a normal faculty, the Airborne Officers Training College contains a faculty which trains officers for diversionary units.

The young entrant, of course, knows none of this, so he may therefore end up, quite unintentionally, in a diversionary unit, in the marine infantry—or, indeed, anywhere else at all.

The situation is the same in the Air Force Officers Training Colleges—one trains fighter pilots, another pilots for transport aircraft and a third those who will fly long-range bombers for the Navy. But, of course, no one will explain this to you before you enter that particular college.

This is, perhaps, not so bad, but there are many Colleges about which nothing at all is said. For instance, the Serpukhov Engineer Officers Training College. If you look at the papers set for its entrance examinations, you will realise that they are unusually difficult. Some people are put off by this but it attracts others. If you succeed in gaining a place there, you will discover, during your second year, that you are being trained for service with the Strategic Rocket Forces.

3

Having chosen a College which appears to cater for your interests, even though you have no real idea what it offers, you should immediately apply to its commandant, saying that you want to become an officer and explaining what you want to do, attach your school-leaving certificate, references from your school and from the Komsomol and send everything off as quickly as possible to the College. In due course you will be summoned to sit the entrance examination.

My own choice was straightforward—the Kharkov Guards Tank Officers Training College. I scribbled my way through four exams, without particular difficulty. They tested me to find out what level I had reached at school, but it was clear that the standard of my knowledge was not particularly important and that they were more interested in my speed of reaction, in my general level of development and in the range of my interests. More important than the written tests were the medical examinations and the tests of physical development.

Secretly, before candidates were summoned to the examinations, of course, enquiries about them had been made with the local KGB offices; nothing was done until these were completed. The decisive part of the selection process, however, was a discussion which lasted for several hours, during which one's suitability—or lack of it—for commissioned rank in the Soviet Army was explored.

The assembly line moves fast. Three or four applications are usually received for each vacancy. Every evening there is a parade, at which one of the officers reads out the names of those who have been given a place and of those who have been rejected. Every morning, a new batch of hopefuls arrives and every evening, after a week spent at the College, groups of disappointed would-be entrants leave. If they have not done their military service they will be called up before long.

I was successful and joined a battalion—300 strong of young, shaven-headed new cadets. We were divided into three companies, each of three platoons. We were commanded by a lieutenant-colonel, who had a major as his deputy and political officer. The companies were commanded by majors, the platoons by captains and senior lieutenants. At that point we had no sergeants. In my own platoon of 33, only one had done his military service. All the rest had come straight from school. Evidently, not many of those who had already had the opportunity to see how an officer lived wished to take up the army as a career.

The first night after the battalion had been formed we found ourselves on a troop train, in goods wagons. No one knew where we were going. We travelled for three whole days and then we arrived at a training division. Most of us had only the vaguest idea what this meant, but one cadet, who had already served in the army for two years, became quite agitated. He had certainly not expected this. During his army service with a tank unit, he had been a loader and he had therefore escaped service with a training division, but he had heard a lot about such units. And now he found himself in one, with a contingent of scum.

The battalion now acquired sergeants—of the type who run training divisions—and life began to gather speed. Reveille, PT, training exercises, disgusting food, cold, night alerts. And together with this, came orders such as "Take a matchstick, measure the corridor with it, and then come and tell me how long the corridor is." Or, "Take your toothbrush and clean out the latrine. Report to me on the progress you've made by dawn."

No higher education for you for the present, my friends; first we must make good soldiers out of you!

A training division knocks all the independence and insubordination out of you. You learn a lot while you are there. You are taught to understand others and to represent them. You learn how to recognise scoundrels and how to find friends.

The first lesson which you learn is that soldiers and future officers must not be afraid of tanks. During each of the first few days you spend several hours getting used to them. At first it is easy—you lie at the bottom of a concrete-lined trench while a tank roars round and round above your head, crushing the concrete with its tracks as it does so. Then things get a bit more complicated—you are told that you are to take shelter in an unlined slit trench, which you are to dig. You are told that, provided you make the trench narrow enough, you will be safe. However, you are also told to cover your head with your tunic, so that if the trench should cave in, you will have a few lungfuls of air, which should be enough to enable you to dig yourself out. Next, you are told that you will be given one and a half minutes to dig your trench—and to jump into it, curled up like a hedgehog. You can see the tank, waiting not far away. Both of you are given the signal to start at the same moment. You start digging like a mole, as the tank bears down on you . . .

And so you carry on, day after day, sweating your guts out, until you have spots in front of your eyes, until you vomit from fatigue, until you collapse with exhaustion.

There is a lot more fun to be had during the training, besides your introduction to tanks—napalm, gas, rubber protective clothing worn in the blazing sun, barbed-wire obstacles

> "Accursed barbed wire obstacle
> Creation of the 20th century
> By the time a man has climbed across you
> He is no more than half a man"

—and the eternal pressure to save seconds. And the constant uncertainty . . .

After six months we finish the training course and the time

for assessment arrives. Hitherto, we have worn ordinary soldiers' shoulder-boards, but now, after the course, we are given black velvet ones with the gold stitching and the red piping of the cadets of a Tank Officers Training College. But not all of us get these. Forty out of our 300 received the shoulder-boards of junior sergeants and were sent off to become tank commanders and tank gunners. Our College did not ever want to see them darken its doors again.

The battalion was re-formed. Now it had only two companies, each of 130 cadets. We were sent back to the College for the next three and a half years.

4

The life of a cadet at a College is very little different from the one he led in the training division. The shoulder-boards are different, it is true, and he receives 10 rubles a month instead of 3. (In his third year he receives 15 and in his fourth 20.) And the food is better. But every College has a training centre. A cadet spends one or two weeks at the College studying theory—both military and civil. Then he goes to the training centre for the next one or two weeks. There he spends his time driving, shooting, doing night exercises, platoon engagements, encounter battles with tank companies, more driving, more familiarisation exercises with tanks and with napalm. More pressure to save seconds. More uncertainty.

You are constantly driven out of the College. The time you spend there only counts towards your army service if you are there for medical reasons. But since everyone is robustly healthy, this really does not apply.

One night, my friend Pashka Kovalev, who was already in his fourth year, with three months to go before he graduated, broke out of barracks. He had a girl-friend in Kharkov. He was away for three hours. He managed to get through the barbed-wire and other obstacles on his way back in without being spotted and he slipped quietly into bed. Before leaving, he had put his rolled greatcoat into the bed, and had laid out his dress uniform and boots beside it, in accordance with regulations. As a rule, anyone carrying out a kit inspection during the night would be sure to check that all footwear was properly displayed. But Pashka was clever—he made his unauthorised trip in running shoes.

Reveille, PT, and breakfast went by without incident. Then came the review period. There were about a thousand of us on parade. We stood, freezing, and listened to a string of orders issued by different authorities. These were read out in order of seniority: first came those from the Minister of Defence, then others from the Commander of the Military District, more from his director of training and, finally, those issued by the College Commandant. Suddenly, and without warning, Pashka was called out of the ranks and an order for his expulsion was read. His velvet shoulder-boards were ripped off and replaced with those worn by a private soldier. His absence had been detected by a surprise check during the night. The cadets who had been on guard duty that night were immediately arrested and thrown in the cells for ten days. Others were being woken up to take their place, as the commission which had made the check departed. They were told nothing of what had occurred. Pashka returned towards morning, crept in through a window in the latrines and got back into his bed. He did not realise that the guard had been changed and assumed he had got away with it. But, while he was breaking in, the order for his expulsion was being already drafted by the staff. It took no account of the four years he had spent at the College—four years which had made him feel that he was already almost an officer. He was sent to the training division at which we began our service.

Long afterwards, I heard that he had not been able to endure life in the training division, that he had finally refused to obey orders and had hit a sergeant. For this he was sent to a penal battalion for two years—which did not, of course, count as part of his military service. After this he would have been returned to the unit which had sent him to the penal battalion— the training division. Whether he ever did go back I do not know—I never heard anything more about him.

Duties and Military Ranks

1

I knocked on the door, waited for permission to enter and went in. The regimental commander, Colonel Dontsov, was standing. Despite this, a major, whom I did not recognise, was sitting by his side. I saluted smartly, clicking my heels as I did so.

"Comrade Colonel, may I have permission to make my report?"

"Ask the Major for permission."

I turned quickly to the Major.

"Excuse me, Comrade Major, I am Senior Lieutenant Suvorov. May I report to Colonel Dontsov?"

The major nodded, expressionlessly. I reported to the colonel on a duty trip I had just finished. He asked a few questions and then nodded, showing that he had no more to say. I again turned to the major.

"Comrade Major, may I have permission to leave?"

He said that I might go. I turned and went out.

The situation had been clear to me from the moment I entered. While I had been away from the unit, an officer of greater importance than our regimental commander had arrived, as his superior (and therefore also mine). If this major was more important than the commander of a regiment, he must be the equivalent of at least a deputy divisional commander.

In the corridor I met one of the orderly room clerks and I asked him, "Who's this new major, who is lording it over the boss?"

"He's an important man," said the clerk, with some awe. "He is the new divisional chief of staff. Major Oganskiy."

I whistled: from now on I knew whom to salute, whom to click my heels to.

The system of awarding military ranks in the Soviet Army is a fairly simple one, but it is different from those used elsewhere and therefore needs to be explained.

The system came into use during the war—effectively at the time of the battle for Stalingrad. In other words, it dates from the time when the Soviet Union first began to aspire to become a super-power. It is designed to take maximum advantage of the rivalry between the officers on each rung of the promotion ladder and to ensure that advancement comes as quickly as possible to the staunchest supporters of the regime— the hardest, most callous, most masterful and most competent.

To achieve this, the Soviet system applies the following simple rules:

1. Seniority depends, not on rank but on appointment. Only when two officers have no professional connection with one another, is seniority determined by rank.
2. An officer's eligibility for a higher appointment depends, not on his rank or length of service, but on his ability to command.
3. The time spent in a particular appointment is not limited in any way. Thus, an officer may command a platoon for the whole of his service or he may be given greater responsibility within a few months.
4. The appointment held by an officer makes him eligible for a particular rank. However, he is not given this rank unless he occupies an adequately responsible place on the ladder of service and has served for a given number of years.

The system for the advancement and promotion of officers in peacetime works in exactly the same way as it did during the war. We will therefore illustrate it with wartime examples.

Imagine that the deputy commander of a battalion is killed in action. A replacement is needed without delay. The battalion commander has only a limited choice. There are three companies in his battalion and the commander of one of these companies must take his deputy's place. In making his choice, the battalion commander will ignore an individual's expectations, his length of service and the number of stars on his shoulder-boards. What he needs, quickly, is the man who, in his opinion, will measure up best to new responsibilities. Of the three candidates one is, let us say, a captain, the second a senior lieutenant and the third a lieutenant who arrived recently from his military training school and who has been in command of his company for two weeks. The battalion commander knows that the captain is a heavy drinker, the senior lieutenant is a coward but that the lieutenant is neither of these. He therefore appoints the lieutenant as his deputy. The lieutenant will be promoted to a higher rank later, but the two other officers, with whom he was on equal terms until this moment, are now his subordinates. Shortly afterwards, the battalion commander is killed, at which point our lieutenant automatically takes his place, leaving the post of deputy battalion commander vacant once again. The new battalion commander must now decide— very quickly—who should fill the vacancy. He could select the alcoholic captain, although almost anyone else would be better, or he might choose a lieutenant who is even younger than him, who finished his training even more recently than he did, but who received better marks at the training school than he did himself.

Here are some examples from real-life. The first is from 1944, when the 29th Guards Rifle Division found itself in urgent need of a commanding officer for one of its regiments. Captain I. M. Tretyak was chosen. He was only twenty-one, but he had three and a half years of continuous service in action behind him. During these years he had worked his way steadily up the promotion ladder, having held every rank, one after the other. Understandably, he tended to be chosen whenever an officer was needed for a more responsible post. He was promoted later on but for the time being he commanded the regiment while still a captain. Under his command were eight lieutenant-colonels, and dozens of majors and captains. Subsequently he continued up the ladder with the same speed. Today he is a Marshal.

In 1942 the 51st Army was left without a commanding officer. The senior command decided that the best candidate for this post was Colonel A. M. Kuznetsov. The brigades and divisions in the army were commanded by generals, a general commanded each of the corps and, in four cases, had another general as deputy, the Army's administrative and staff departments bulged with still more generals, but Colonel Kuznetsov suddenly ascended, through their midst, to lead them all. He became the commander—he was the one you had to click your heels to.

The 58th Army, too, was commanded by a Colonel— N. A. Moskvin—in spite of the fact that there were generals galore on the Army's strength. But it was Colonel Moskvin to whom they and all their men became answerable, for he was the man whom the higher command selected as the best officer available.

The situation in peacetime remains exactly as it was during the war. The time an officer spends doing a particular job is not limited by any rules or regulations. Young officers arrive from their colleges and are given platoons. The regimental commander has the right to take one of them and put him in command of a company—and he can do this after the officer has been in charge of a platoon for only one day. In his own interests, a regimental commander will always select the harshest, the most demanding, and the most dependable of the officers at his disposal for the post.

A divisional commander appoints his deputy battalion commanders and all officers holding equivalent appointments under him. However, he may only make his choice from officers who have reached the immediately preceding grade—that is from among his company commanders but not from the latter's platoon commanders. In order to rise to the post of deputy battalion commander, a young officer must first please his regimental commander sufficiently to be put in charge of a company and then he must find favour with the divisional commander— without, however, falling out with his regimental commander, who has enough power to ruin the career of any officer who is under his command.

An Army Commander can choose his battalion commanders, but these must come from those who have done the job of deputy battalion commander. The Commander of a Military District can select and appoint deputies for his regimental commanders from any of his battalion commanders. Regimental commanders are appointed by the Minister of Defence.

The same procedure is followed at other levels. The chief

of staff of a Military District appoints battalion chiefs of staff, the Chief of the General Staff chooses the chiefs of staff for regiments.

All officers higher than regimental commander are appointed by the Administrative Department of the Central Committee. Appointments senior to that of divisional commander must also be ratified by the Politburo. However, the Politburo follows the principle used throughout—seniority is determined not by rank but by the appointment held—for it was the Politburo itself which devised this principle.

Each appointment in the Soviet Army is open only to officers of not more than a certain rank. Thus, a platoon commander may not be more than a senior lieutenant. Similarly, as regards command appointments:

A company commander may not be more than a captain.

A deputy battalion commander may not be more than a major.

A battalion commander/deputy regimental commander may not be more than a lieutenant-colonel.

A regimental commander/deputy divisional commander may not be more than a colonel.

A divisional commander/deputy Army commander may not be more than a major-general.

An Army Commander may not be more than a lieutenant-general.

A Front or Military District Commander may not be more than a general of the Army.

Minister of Defence, Chief of the General Staff, Chief of a Strategic Direction, Chief of an Armed Service may not be more than a Marshal of the Soviet Union.

The Supreme Commander during wartime ranks as Generalissimo of the Soviet Union.

The same applies to non-command appointments. Thus:

The chief of staff of a battalion must not be more than a major.

The chief of staff of a regiment must not be more than a lieutenant-colonel.

The chief of staff of a division must not be more than a colonel.

The chief of staff of an Army must not be more than a major-general.

The chief of staff of a Front must not be more than a lieutenant-general.

The chief of staff of a Strategic Direction must not be more than a colonel-general.

The chief of the General Staff is a Marshal of the Soviet Union.

In the financial branch, to take a further example, the financial section of a regiment will be headed by a captain, of a division by a major, of an Army by a lieutenant-colonel, of a Front or Military District by a major-general. The senior officer of the entire branch is a colonel-general.

An officer is given an appointment without reference to his rank: he will receive any promotion due to him subsequently. The following are the minimum times for which an officer must remain at each rank:

*Junior lieutenant	2 years
Lieutenant	3 years
Senior lieutenant	3 years
Captain	4 years
Major	4 years
Lieutenant-colonel	5 years

Above this rank there are no fixed terms.

Normally, the graduate of a Higher Military Training College (at which he has spent 4 years) becomes a lieutenant at 21. In theory, he will reach the rank of lieutenant-colonel in 19 years. However, in order to receive each promotion, he must not only serve for the requisite number of years but he must also be acceptable for an appointment which carries this rank.

If you are a platoon commander, provided that your platoon's performance is satisfactory, you will automatically become a senior lieutenant after three years. After three more

*This rank is given only to those who have undergone a shorter course of training.

years you become eligible for the next rank, that of captain. However, if you are still with your platoon, not having succeeded in being chosen to command a company, you will not be promoted. If you are already in charge of a company, or have progressed still further up the ladder, you will receive your captain's star immediately. Four years later, the time comes when you can be promoted to major; provided that you are by now deputy commander of a battalion your progress will not be held up. If you are still a company commander, you will have to wait for promotion. If you are never able to show that you are better than the other company commanders and that you should be promoted before them, you will never become a major.

In principle, therefore, an officer's appointment opens the way for his promotion, but promotion only follows after the completion of a certain number of years' service spent in the preceding rank. If you have ever been held back, and have lost some years in one particular rank, you will never catch up. When you are eventually promoted, you will still have to serve for the prescribed number of years in your new rank before you become eligible for the next one.

3

Here is another example from life. In August 1941, General Major A. M. Vasilyevskiy was appointed to head the Operational Directorate of the General Staff. At the same time he also became deputy to the Chief of the General Staff. The Operational (or First) Directorate of the General Staff is responsible for producing war plans.

This post is one of enormous importance by any standards, not only those of the Red Army. It is enough to say that it is in this Directorate that the Soviet Union's 5-year economic plans originate; thereafter, the Council of Ministers and the State Planning Commission decide how the requirements of the General Staffs are to be met, before proceeding, with the highly secret military plan as a basis, to draw up the All-Union Plan, in both its secret and open variants.

The German intelligence services concluded that the appointment of a mere colonel to such an august position was an indication that the role of the General Staff was being reduced in importance. The reason that they made this mistake was that the Germans did not understand the Red Army's simple principle—seniority is not determined by rank, but by appointment. Rank follows appointment, slowly but surely, just as infantry follows tanks which have suddenly and forcefully broken through into the rear of the enemy.

In fact there was nothing particularly astonishing about the appointment of the General Major to such a high post: the explanation was, quite simply, that the Supreme Commander decided that this particular officer would meet the demands of the job better than anyone else. This Vasilyevskiy did—within eight months he had become Chief of the General Staff.

Since he had risen to so high an appointment, the way to considerable further promotion was open to him. Stars rained down on his shoulder-boards. He passed quickly through the hierarchy of generals, wearing the four stars of a General of the Army for a mere twenty-nine days before being promoted to the rank of Marshal. After the end of the war with Germany he carried out a brilliant operation in Manchuria, becoming Commander-in-Chief of the Far Eastern Strategic Direction.

But we must not be misled. The Red Army is an enormous organisation and not everyone can succeed as Vasilyevskiy did. I have met hundreds of senior lieutenants who will stay at this rank for the rest of their lives.

Military Academies

1

In order to achieve high rank you need an appropriately senior appointment: in order to be considered for such an appointment you must have completed a course of studies at a Military Academy.

It will be recalled that Higher Military Training Colleges provide a higher general education but only a medium-level military one. Higher military education is the province of the Military Academies, of which there are 13 at present. Among these are the Frunze All-Arms, Armoured, Artillery, Engineering, Military-Political, Naval, two Air Force, two Rocket, Air Defence, and Chemical Warfare Academies. Officers spend three years at an Academy, which may be headed by a Colonel-General, a General of the Army, a Marshal of one of the arms of service or even the Chief Marshal of a particular service.

The road to an Academy is a hard one. First, one must have commanded at least a company. Secondly, the sub-units under your command must achieve excellent ratings for two years (which means that you must lay in enough vodka and proceed to pour it into the commissions which come to check you until they are afloat with it—assuming, of course, that they consent to drink with you at all). Thirdly, approval for your application for entry is required from all your superior officers up to and including your divisional commander. Any of these officers has the right to stop your application from going on to his immediate superior. If one of them does so you will have to wait until the following year and your battalion or company will have to maintain its excellent record. Finally, you will have to pass examinations, a medical commission, and interviews and, thereafter, succeed against the competition within the Academy itself.

Unless an officer manages to secure a place at an Academy, he will never command more than a battalion. If he is successful, he has three years of intensive work on a very wide-ranging and detailed curriculum. After graduation, wide horizons stretch before him. Quite young majors are frequently made regimental commanders, or, failing that, deputy regimental commanders, as soon as they have completed the course. Whatever happens the path upwards is now open.

2

Towering above all the Academies is the General Staff Academy. Entry to this is free of all the competition, examinations, applications and other problems involved in admission to the others. Everything is done for you by the Administrative Department of the Central Committee of the CPSU. The Central Committee selects those who will head the Red Army in the immediate future from among all the colonels who show promise and who are truly dedicated to the regime.

Of course, all the entrants to the General Staff Academy have already studied at a Higher Military Training College and then at the Frunze, Armoured or Air Academies, or at one of the others.

The lowest rank held by entrants is colonel and there are often several colonel-generals on the current list of those attending. Commanders of Armies, Military Districts, Groups of Tank Armies, Flotillas and Fleets are often invited to visit the Academy by the Central Committee.

Having completed his studies at this Academy, a general will rise higher and higher, leaving his former rivals far behind.

Generals

1

"How fine to be a General" runs a line from a popular song. And, indeed, seen from below, the life led by a general does seem to be a quite sublime existence.

A Soviet general enjoys a great many privileges. If he wishes, he can acquire his own harem. Soviet ideology will not stand in his way. Every divisional commander, every Army, Front and Military District commander has signal units, communications centres and telephone switchboards under his command, staffed by attractive girls who have been security-vetted. The general is their absolute master. He guards them jealously against the attentions of others.

While I was with the 24th Division, a senior lieutenant who was a friend of mine, became friendly with an attractive girl from the divisional communications battalion. He was hauled before an Officer's Court of Honour which sentenced him to revert to the rank of lieutenant. The girl was dismissed from the army, immediately. He had to face a charge of having attempted to penetrate the divisional communications centre, in which there were secret command channels and she was accused of complicity. Both were enormously relieved when these accusations were dropped and delighted to have escaped as lightly as they did. This episode served as a lesson to the whole division. During the same period, the divisional commander, in order to ensure that he kept in touch with the girls under his command, organised a number of them into a shooting team. On their days off, he would pack his "markswomen" into his car, take them off to the divisional firing range and train them, personally, there. Imagine the scene—a vast, empty stretch of country in the Carpathian mountains, a huge area, carefully guarded and completely shut off from the world. Thickly wooded mountains, rocky slopes intersected by streams rushing downhill over rapids—without a living soul for miles around. On Sundays, our general was joined at the range by the local Party bosses, who used to bring their own girls from Lvov. He trained them, too. He was quite a man. . . .

On a rather higher level, the entertainment of generals in the Soviet Army is catered for by professionals. Every Military District, Group of Forces and Fleet has its own troupe of singers and dancers. These are made up of professional performers, who are under contract to the Armed Services. They are subject to military discipline, for they are employees of the Armed Services just like the Army's doctors, nurses, typists and so forth. The Army is a more generous employer than any others. The girls in these ensembles—singers and dancers—are kept continuously and intensively at work entertaining the command staff. Generals' dachas have long since been transformed into temples dedicated to the worship not of Marx and Lenin but of Bacchus and Venus.

Athletically inclined young girls, especially gymnasts, are in special demand among our military leaders. The Army's Central Sports Club is one of the largest and richest in the USSR. Girls who have no connection whatsoever with the Armed Services can join this organisation and have all their living expenses paid. Sport in the USSR is an entirely professional affair. Sportsmen or sportswomen are paid, fed, clothed, and given decorations, accommodation and cars for their services—and the better they are the more they are paid. But their free and easy life must still be paid for by the athletes themselves. The girls pay in kind, becoming involved in prostitution while they are still very young. Those who are most amenable, as well as those who are most talented, are led by their coaches to the highest realms of professional sport.

2

What more can the generals want from life? Their dachas are huge and luxurious. Marshal Chuykov's dacha, for example, was built for him by two brigades of engineers, each of four battalions. More than 2,500 men were involved and they had the use of the best military engineering equipment.

Our military leaders fly off on hunting trips in helicopters, which they then use to drive game through nature reserves. They are given everything they need—quarters, cars, and all the cognac and caviare they want. Surely theirs must be a perfect existence? And yet the number of senior military leaders who commit suicide is exceptionally high. Of course, they do not shoot themselves when they become too fat or sated to go on but when rivals seize them by the throat and wrest their power from them.

During the Great Purge, 33,000 officers with the rank of brigade commander or above were executed in a single year. "But that was in Stalin's day" I shall be told—as if the very name of Stalin explains everything. But even since Stalin's day, generals have not been able to sleep peacefully at night. They are constantly plagued by uncertainty. Although Stalin is dead and gone, generals are still being offered up as sacrifices. The first victim was Lieutenant-General Vasiliy Stalin. He was thrown into a mental asylum immediately after Stalin's death and there he died, quietly and quickly. While his father was still alive, no one had diagnosed any abnormality. He was as strong as a bull; he was the only general of his rank in the whole Soviet Army who flew jet-planes.

After Stalin's death, Marshal of the Soviet Union Konev shot Marshal of the Soviet Union Beriya during a session of the Politburo itself. Next, Marshal of the Soviet Union Bulganin lost his rank and was driven in disgrace from his position at the head of the Soviet government. There was also the case of Marshal of the Soviet Union Kulik, demoted to major-general by Stalin, who had then sent him to prison and announced that he was dead. After Stalin, Kulik was released from prison and restored to his rank of lieutenant-general. He was promised promotion to Marshal if he could organise the design and production of the first Soviet intercontinental ballistic missile. He succeeded and in 1957 he again became a Marshal of the Soviet Union, although no explanation of his return from the dead was ever made public. When he received a telegram from the government announcing this and congratulating him, Kulik collapsed and died, from a heart attack, at the rocket range at Kapustin Yar. According to one story, when he received the telegram he shot himself.

Such has been the fate of various Marshals. The generals

fare worse. They are plagued, endlessly, by uncertainty. In one day, in February 1960, Khrushchev sacked 500 generals from the Soviet Army.

No Soviet general, and for that matter no Soviet officer or soldier—no single member of this enormous organisation— has any guarantee that he will be allowed to retain his privileges, his rank or even his life. They may drive him out, like an old dog, at any moment: they may stand him against a wall and shoot him.

Conclusion

Why don't they protest? Why don't they rebel? Can they really enjoy living like this? Why are they silent?

An excursion guide once showed me an area in a large Western city which he said was entirely controlled by the Mafia. Prostitutes, drug-peddlers, shoe-blacks, shopkeepers, owners of restaurants, cafés and hotels—all of them controlled, and protected by the Mafia.

Once we had emerged, unscathed, from this unhappy district, in our large tourist bus, and felt that we were back in safety, I put these same questions to our apprehensive guide. Why the hell didn't they protest? Everyone living there had grown up in freedom and democracy; behind them lay centuries of freedom of speech, of the press and of assembly. Yet, despite these centuries-old traditions, the inhabitants were silent. They had a free press on their side, the population of the entire country, running into many millions, the police, political parties, parliament, the government itself. And yet they said nothing. They made no protest.

The society from which I fled is not simply a spacious well-lit prison, providing free medical care and full employment. It, too, is under the control of a Mafia. The difference between Soviet society and the Western city which I visited, is that those who live where I used to live are unable to turn to the police for help, because the police themselves represent the mailed fist of our Mafia. The army is another section—the most aggressive one—of the Soviet Mafia. The government is the ruling body of the Mafia: parliament is the old people's home in which the aged leaders of the Mafia are cared for. Press, television, the judges, the prosecutors—these are not influenced by the Mafia—they are the Mafia.

343

Smart tourist buses pass through our unhappy capital. The drivers and guides belong to the Mafia. "Intourist" works for the KGB. "Aeroflot" is controlled by the military intelligence service, the GRU. Foreign tourists sit listening to the patter of the guides and wondering with amazement—why don't they protest? Can they really enjoy living like this? In their place, they think, I would write to the papers, or organise a demonstration. But clearly the KGB has stifled inhabitants so that they are unable to protest. The KGB has driven them to their knees and made them slaves.

My friend, you are right. We are slaves: we are on our knees: we are silent: we do not protest.

According to the estimates of demographers, based on official Soviet statistics, the population of my country should have reached 315 million in 1959. Instead, the census showed only 209 million. Only our own government knows what happened to the missing hundred million. Hitler is said to have executed 20 million. But where are the others? You must agree that no criminal organisation in your own country has shown such activity as our Soviet Mafia.

Having brought my countrymen to their knees, the Mafia triumvirate of the KGB, Party and Army moved on to conquer neighbouring countries. Today they are busy in your country, in your home town. They have stated openly that it is their dearest wish to do to the world what they have done to my country. They make no secret of it.

I spent thirty years of my life on my knees. Then I got up and ran. This was the only way I could protest against the system. Are you surprised, my dear Western friend, that I did not demonstrate against the KGB while I was living there? Well, there is something which surprises me, too. In your own beautiful country, the KGB, that monstrous organisation, is hard at work at this very moment, the Soviet Communist Party is subsidising a horde of paid hacks and crackpots, Soviet Military Intelligence is sending members of its diversionary units to visit your country, so that they can practise parachuting on to your native soil. The aim of all this activity is, quite simply, to bring you to your knees. Why don't you protest?

Protest today. Tomorrow it will be too late.

Index

THE NEW YORK TIMES BESTSELLER
PULITZER-PRIZE WINNING AUTHOR OF
<u>ADOLF HITLER</u> AND <u>THE RISING SUN</u>

JOHN TOLAND

INFAMY

PEARL HARBOR
AND ITS
AFTERMATH

A Selection of The Literary Guild and
The Military Book Club With 16 pages of photos

0-425-05995-X • $3.95   Price may be slightly higher in Canada.